Entrepreneurship in the Creative Industries

Phillip McIntyre • Janet Fulton
Susan Kerrigan • Michael Meany

Entrepreneurship in the Creative Industries

How Innovative Agents, Skills and Networks Interact

palgrave
macmillan

Phillip McIntyre
University of Newcastle Australia
Callaghan, NSW, Australia

Janet Fulton
University of Newcastle Australia
Callaghan, NSW, Australia

Susan Kerrigan
University of Newcastle Australia
Callaghan, NSW, Australia

Michael Meany
University of Newcastle Australia
Callaghan, NSW, Australia

ISBN 978-3-031-19454-2 ISBN 978-3-031-19455-9 (eBook)
https://doi.org/10.1007/978-3-031-19455-9

Cover illustration: Zoonar GmbH / Alamy Stock Photo

This Palgrave Macmillan imprint is published by the registered company Springer Nature Switzerland AG.
The registered company address is: Gewerbestrasse 11, 6330 Cham, Switzerland

In honor of Mihaly Csikszentmihalyi.
He lived life as it should be lived, he made a positive difference to so many people's lives, and he left his mark on our thinking.

Preface

This book attempts to uncover and explain many things. It comes in three connected sections. The first section asks the contextual question; why, at this point in time, did we arrive at such a heavy concentration on entrepreneurship in the creative industries? The second part of the book very pragmatically asks: if there is such an emphasis on entrepreneurship in the creative industries, which the evidence suggests there is, what do those who work, or want to work in the creative industries, need to do to pragmatically gain an income under these circumstances? The third and final section of the book gives empirical examples from the lives of those who have indeed found a way to successfully gain an income in the creative industries, and it highlights their entrepreneurial approach to that endeavor. Put very simply, the book answers three primary questions: How and why did we get here? Given that we are here at this point in time, how do we go about being entrepreneurial? Who has managed to do this in the creative industries, and how did they do it?

In answering these questions, this book examines both the creative industries and entrepreneurship as a creative system in action. It will help those who wish to work in the creative industries develop practical skills and a deep understanding of how creative and innovative agents, operating within and dependent on the structures of the world, attempt to bring novel and valued products, processes and ideas into being. That is what creative entrepreneurs do. At the same time, given the precarity of employment in the creative industries, we believe it is crucial that creative practitioners understand the value of gaining an income rather than getting a job, that is, they now need to develop an entrepreneurial mindset.

Understanding those ideas is an absolute necessity in understanding how the creative industries work.

This book not only exposes the workings of creativity and innovation within the creative industries, and the central role entrepreneurialism now plays in this industry, it also examines the historical, social, cultural, economic and political contexts the creative industries have come to exist in, detailing how individual agents take care of business inside these industries and contexts. The book applies these complex frames of reference to successful creative entrepreneurs in a series of case studies to demonstrate real-world applications of the theories and concepts we use to explain the necessity for entrepreneurship in the creative industries.

Acknowledgments

There are so many people to thank and acknowledge. We will live dangerously, selecting only a few and trusting that the others will eventually forgive us. The people at Palgrave Macmillan have been, as always, a pleasure to work with. Sarah Coffee is the very best of colleagues—and one hell of a copyeditor. Without the dedicated help of our research assistants and co-researchers across a number of projects much of this material would not have seen the light of day. In particular, we need to thank Alysson Watson, Lee-Anne Marsh, Claire Williams, and Evelyn King for their willingness to go the extra mile—and they did it all with a smile. The Australian Research Council has been very generous in its funding for our research in the field, and the various universities we are affiliated with have been very helpful in providing the institutional homes for us as we slaved over our hot laptops. It is worth noting that we have drawn on the following references to complete this book.

ARC LP130100348, McIntyre, P., Balnaves, M., Kerrigan, S., King, E. & Williams. C. *Creativity and Cultural Production in the Hunter: An Applied Ethnographic Study of New Entrepreneurial Systems in the Creative Industries*, 2013–2017.

ARC LP160101724, Cunningham, S., Hearn, G., McIntyre, P., Wikstrom, P. & Kerrigan, S. *Australian Cultural & Creative Activity: A Population & Hotspot Analysis*, 2016–2020.

McIntyre, P. (2016). What is the Fifth Estate and Why Does it Matter?: Digitisation, Globalisation, and Neoliberalism and Their Part in the

Creation of a Rapidly Changing World. *Communication Research and Practice, 2*, 437–450.
McIntyre, P. (2021). Songwriting Practice and Production: The Past Present and Future. *The Songwriting Studies Journal, 1*, 5–26.

Phillip

Working with the A Team has been, once again, a deep pleasure. Susan, Janet, Michael, and I have certainly done some stuff together. We've negotiated the shoals and privileges of academia, stood our ground as critical thinkers, played with the very best on the planet, and still managed a smile through it all. To have them as colleagues has been enough indeed but to have them as close friends constitutes another level of wonder for me. I am also deeply grateful to all of the students who have passed my way, undergraduate and postgraduate. There are far too many to mention but rest assured you have all bought me one of the greatest gifts, that is, to remind me there are truly outstanding human beings on this planet and that it will be safe in your hands. My family has, as ever, been so supportive of the things I do—they might rib me for it, but their love is palpable. Julie, a writer herself, stays my one true love. She creates the place I come home to.

Janet

Once again it has been a joy to work with these collaborative and intelligent scholars. Many, many thanks to Phillip, Susan, and Michael for your ongoing support and friendship. I hope we can continue to play together in this research space we love so much. And we joke about the Newcastle School of Creativity Research, but we have developed a core of creativity research in media and communication that is strong and internationally recognized.

It was during the writing of this book that our academic rock god Mihaly Csikszentmihalyi passed away. This giant in creativity research has guided my research over many years. We have dedicated the book to his memory, but I would like to pay personal tribute to him and acknowledge the impact he has had on my academic life. Vale Mike.

I would like to dedicate this book to my babies Jade and Peter who continue to be my rocks.

Susan

Co-writing this book with my colleagues and friends has been a delight, and I thank you for giving me the confidence to become a writer, something I never thought I could be. I am deeply grateful. Phillip, Janet, and Michael, I am in awe of your thirst for knowledge and I revel in our shared belief that theory and practice are not separate concepts. As co-authors we have consciously drawn on the unification of theory and practice to simplify the ideas of creativity, industries, and incomes, and I hope future readers will find it as fascinating as we have.

To my family, David, Alice, and Rose, thank you from the bottom of my heart for providing a much-needed balance for my creative obsessions.

Michael

To my co-authors, who are both friends and colleagues, I wish to express sincerest gratitude for their generosity, candor, rigor, and enthusiasm. My co-authors are leading international experts in the study of creative systems and creative industries. I have been blessed with the opportunity to work with them. This book is a function of a system at work—multiple domains, multiple fields, and multiple agents have contributed to its production. However, the raw drive and tenacity of my co-authors provided the energy to motivate the system. For this too I am grateful.

Most importantly I would like to dedicate this book to my wife, Elspeth Robertson, thank you for your love, support, patience, and 'food in adversity'.

Contents

About the Authors

Phillip McIntyre Professor Phillip McIntyre is a communication and media scholar who researches creativity and the creative industries using a systems-based approach. He has been a chief investigator on a number of Australian Research Council grants and published a number of books including *Creativity and Cultural Production: Issues for Media Practice* (2012). With his colleagues, he published *The Creative System in Action: Understanding Cultural Production and Practice* (2016), *Creating Space in the Fifth Estate* (2017), *Educating for Creativity in Higher Education; Integration of Research with Media Practice* (2018), and *Paul McCartney and His Creative Practice: The Beatles and Beyond* (2021). He was instrumental in establishing the Creativity in Higher Education Network (CHEN) and is a senior editor of the *Journal of Undergraduate Ethnography*. He is a long-term member of the Association for the Study of the Art of Record Production (ASARP) and was president of the Australian and New Zealand Communication Association (ANZCA) from 2016 to 2017. He delivered the inaugural keynote address for the AHRC-funded Songwriting Studies Research Network (SSRN) in Birmingham, UK, in 2019. It was entitled *Songwriting Practice and Production: The Past Present and Future*. For a complete overview, please see: https://www.newcastle.edu.au/profile/phillip-mcintyre#career.

Janet Fulton Dr Janet Fulton is an adjunct associate professor affiliated with RMIT University and a research associate with the News and Media Research Centre at the University of Canberra. Her research interests include creativity and cultural production, journalism, journalism education, and media entrepreneurship. This research has been published in books and journals and presented at national and international conferences. She is a co-editor of *The Creative System in Action: Understanding Cultural Practice and Production*, published in 2016 by Palgrave Macmillan, UK, and *Creating Space in the Fifth Estate* (2017), and a co-author of *Educating for Creativity Within Higher Education* (2018).

Janet is also active on social media with accounts on Academia.edu, LinkedIn, Instagram, Pinterest, and Twitter and has a WordPress site, which she uses for both personal and professional purposes. For a full bio, please see janetfulton.com.

Susan Kerrigan Professor Susan Kerrigan is a qualitative researcher investigating creative industries and a filmmaker who researches creative practice. She is Department Chair of Film, Games and Animation at Swinburne University of Technology, Australia. Susan has been chief investigator on two Australian Research Council Linkage Grants examining regional creative industries that have applied the creative systems in action approach. She is also an expert in creative practice, particularly for filmmaking. Susan has co-edited *Screen Production Research: Creative Practice as a Mode of Enquiry* (2018) and *The Palgrave Handbook of Screen Production* (2020) and has co-authored *Educating for Creativity Within Higher Education: Integration of Research into Media Practice* (2018).

Susan is on the editorial board for *The Journal of Media Practice and Education* and has co-edited ten special issues of journals on the topics of filmmaking, practice-led research, and screen production research. For a full bio, please see susankerrigan.wordpress.com.

Michael Meany Dr Meany's background includes work as a freelance writer, photographer, a typesetter and publication designer, and as a playwright. This diverse media background allows him to bring an eclectic mix of skills to his research. He was initially employed at the University of Newcastle as a lecturer in professional writing. However, as media technologies changed and converged so too did his teaching role and research interests. Desktop publishing evolved into web-design; film-based photography gave way to digital photography; audio and video on the web became multimedia; and web coding became interactive interface design.

His PhD, *The Performance of Comedy by Artificial Intelligence Agents* (2014), was an interdisciplinary study that amalgamated scripted artificial intelligence dialogue and computer interface scripting with the theory and practice of comedy and of creativity. His work since that time has continued to integrate the study of creativity with a range of disciplinary perspectives.

List of Figures

PART I

The Context for Creative Industries Entrepreneurship

CHAPTER 1

Introduction to Entrepreneurship in the Creative Industries

Working in the creative industries is certainly glamorous, and it is a lot of fun, but it's not easy. The path to making a secure, ongoing living in the creative industries is becoming increasingly arduous. Outsourcing, casualization, and the growth in precarious work, the blurring of amateur and professional roles, convergence across multiple platforms, incessant digital disruption in a globalized world, and the ongoing dominance of the political ideology of neoliberalism have all brought us to a space and time where secure employment in the creative industries is more difficult to obtain than ever before. The full-time ongoing jobs that are still available today are becoming increasingly rare. Many are simply disappearing. Multiple reports (e.g. Deloittes Australia, 2012; Dunlop, 2016; Frey & Osborne, 2013) indicate the reality of this situation, as does the scholarly research into creative labor (e.g. Curtin & Sanson, 2016; Hesmondhalgh & Baker, 2011; O'Donnell & Zion, 2019; Ross, 2009).

In the light of these changes, it is increasingly the case that the path to making a living in the creative industries is to learn how to generate a regular income rather than to continue to search for full-time ongoing employment. Despite the promotion of the success of the creative industries and the value of their economic contribution (e.g. CIIC, 2013; EC, 2017; Lhermitte et al., 2015; Trembath & Fielding, 2020; UNCTAD, 2008), at the production end of things, being an employee looked after by a large corporation who shoulders the burden of ongoing risk taking, if ever that was really the case, is fast disappearing. Despite the continuing

P. McIntyre et al., *Entrepreneurship in the Creative Industries*,
https://doi.org/10.1007/978-3-031-19455-9_1

existence of the whales (Davies & Sigthorsson, 2013, pp. 49–50), the big corporate players, it is increasingly the case that those lucky enough to work within the creative industries need to take on the pragmatics of being entrepreneurial more than ever before as they continue to practice their creative art and craft.

To practice entrepreneurially, however, requires risks—often large risks. More often than not, those risks lead to failure (McGrath, 2011; McRobbie, 2005, 2016; Rogers, 2003; Standing, 2011; Tahirsylaj, 2012) and sometimes the risks appear to be too great for the diminishing rewards that are available to the very large collection of plankton (Davies & Sigthorsson, 2013, pp. 49–50), the many SMEs, sole traders, contract workers, and freelancers who now constitute the bulk of those working in the creative industries. Nevertheless, those songs, films, books, ads, documentaries, podcasts, TV shows, theatre productions, radio broadcasts, features and news articles, and computer games, to name just a few of the outputs from the creative industries, still get made. Despite the rise of pro-ams and prod-users, the commitment required to produce high-quality creative work still remains the same. The expectations of the audience have not changed in that regard. There are many who still want, and indeed demand, to consume these things. But on the supply side, the fundamental shift that has taken place in how those producing these cultural items are remunerated has undergone a massive change. In an industry that values creativity above all else, creative practitioners are becoming increasingly aware of the need to prepare themselves, to use a term from Rosenbaum (2020), to become part of the often-uncertain gig economy. Within this context, the necessity of being entrepreneurial has become an overriding concern for those attempting to cope with the changes digitization, globalization, and the increasing dominance of neoliberal ideology have wrought.

These broad contextual changes also present possibilities and opportunities that can be taken advantage of. In this new world order of fluctuating social and economic fortunes, creative practitioners need to approach work quite differently. It is increasingly imperative that they understand the value of making a living rather than getting a job. To do this they must not only become adept in making things, through acquiring the relevant knowledge pertinent to their profession and the means to make those things, but also acquire practical entrepreneurial skills.

They must understand how to leverage their own personal attributes and also become very skilled at networking. They must become aware of all the interconnected activity that goes on around them at all scales of activity. This means not only keeping abreast of the skill and techniques one needs to know in order to make creative products, how to call up ideas, what is best practice in content creation, and so on, but to also actively gain an astute understanding of the way these practices are embedded in business settings, and the networked 'interactions between creative practitioners in designing products and processes' (Comunian, 2019, p. 41). Each creative practitioner must develop the ability to use local infrastructure and access finance in a cost-effective way, learn where grants and subsidies reside, as well as keep an eye on the changes in these. At the same time, they need to know how the dynamic global market for their creative products is actually performing week in, week out. They need to be well aware of the effect policy settings and legal requirements have on what they do. They also need contextual information at their disposal such as 'the impact of larger phenomena of convergence and globalisation' (Comunian, 2019, p. 41). This last means being able to read global trends as complex interconnected phenomena in a perpetual state of flux that, interacting across macro, meso, and micro levels of the creative industries system, deeply affect the daily practice of each creative individual.

This book attempts to uncover and explain many of these things. It comes in three connected sections. The first section asks the contextual question; why, at this point in time, did we arrive at such a heavy concentration on entrepreneurship in the creative industries? The second part of the book very pragmatically asks, if there is such an emphasis on entrepreneurship in the creative industries, which the evidence suggests there is, what do those who work or want to work in the creative industries need to do to pragmatically gain an income under these circumstances? The third and final section of the book gives empirical examples from the lives of those who have indeed found a way to successfully gain an income in the creative industries and it highlights their entrepreneurial approach to that endeavor. Put very simply the book answers three primary questions: How and why did we get here? Given that we are here at this point in time, how do we go about being entrepreneurial? Who has managed to do this in the creative industries and how did they do it?

With all of that in mind, we cluster the following chapters into three broad sections. The first section introduces and explores the ideas behind the creative industries and being entrepreneurial. For example, Chap. 2 examines the forces at work in the world which provide context for this crucial sector. It sets out some of the historical, social, cultural, economic, and political backgrounds of the sector and how it has developed internationally. Chapter 3 focuses on entrepreneurialism and its emergence. It provides a historical context for the theoretical evolution of the ideas that inform the concept of the creative industries and examines how a political ideology such as neoliberalism has led to the world that demands an entrepreneurial spirit of its workers. Chapter 4, the final chapter in this section, places the creative industries and entrepreneurship firmly within a systemic approach to creativity and cultural production. It provides a brief account of Pierre Bourdieu's ideas on cultural production and pairs these with the extant work on creative systems in an effort to set up an analytical framework to house the next two sections.

The second section of the book drills down into the pragmatics of undertaking entrepreneurial ventures. It discusses the practices, skills, business models, and plans necessary for one to be entrepreneurial. However, rather than focusing solely on the individual as entrepreneur, this section leads the reader to an understanding of how the social and cultural contexts they work in both enable and constrain an individual's foray into entrepreneurialism. It also details how individual agents go about taking care of business through deploying social, cultural, symbolic, and financial capital in an entrepreneurially focused world. It then provides a broad view of entrepreneurial practices by discussing individual skill sets, the actions of the gift economy, the effects of clusters, and the ongoing requirements of the state. A discussion of the nuts and bolts of running a business follows, with introductory material on business plans, SWOT and STEEPLE analysis, financing, intellectual property, ownership structures, bookkeeping, and human resources. We, of course, embed these ideas firmly in our theoretical framework as we apply it to creative industries entrepreneurship. These practically focused chapters will help those who wish to work in the creative industries to develop skills and a deep understanding of how creative and innovative agents, operating within and dependent on the structures of the world, attempt to bring novel and valued products and ideas into being. That is what creative entrepreneurs do. This section provides a springboard to the next, which analyses the stories of creative individuals who have effectively engaged in actual entrepreneurial activity.

The final section, as noted, takes all of these ideas and the practical detail we have talked about and applies them to successful entrepreneurs and intrapreneurs who work in the creative industries. We want to show how this knowledge has been leveraged in the real world. It therefore provides a set of case studies setting out the profiles of creative practitioners who have managed to gain an ongoing income as they operate locally and globally—glocally—in a variety of creative industries contexts. Part of the purpose of presenting these case studies is to provide evidence of how these entrepreneurs learn, understand, and interact with the structures they are embedded in and how those structures both constrain and enable their creative practice, as a means for them to achieve the success they have. Each chapter in this final section focuses on a sector of the creative industries: film and screen; writing, publishing, print media, and radio; public relations, advertising, and fashion; the music industry; and gaming and design. We examine practitioners who have blazed their own trail as well as who have continued to work in the traditional system but with an intrapreneurial spirit. Based on interviews and secondary data, we detail their practical experiences as they negotiate their way through the systems that affect their ability to gain an income through their own creative practice. In doing so we hope to demonstrate how theory illuminates practice and practice informs theory.

But before we begin that journey we want to see whether we can keep us all on the same page by setting out a few key terms we think are central to any exploration of creative industries entrepreneurship.

If we are dealing with creative industries entrepreneurship, the terms to be addressed here must include 'creativity', 'innovation', 'industry', and most importantly, what we mean when we put them together and say 'creative industries' since, we believe, these latter terms must encompass something about the prior two terms in its own definition. Of course, what we mean by 'entrepreneurship' and its derivatives such as social entrepreneurship, technopreneur, intrapreneur, journopreneur, and a host of others is also important if we are dealing with creative industries entrepreneurship. These following brief explanations will provide a baseline, a set of operational definitions if you like, that will be used throughout the book. They will be expanded on in future chapters, but for now the definitions are a good starting point.

In the first instance, as Keith Sawyer asserts, we need to 'look critically at our own cultural assumptions about how creativity works, and scientific studies of creativity fail to support our most cherished beliefs about creativity' (2006, p. 33). However, if we examine the extant peer-reviewed, authoritative, well-reasoned empirical research into 'creativity' (for extensive summaries of the literature see Alexander, 2003; McIntyre et al., 2018; Negus & Pickering, 2004; Pope, 2005; and Sawyer, 2006, 2011) we can see that most serious researchers now agree that creativity is the bringing into being of novel objects or processes that are valued in at least one social setting (Hennessey & Amabile, 2010, p. 572). We can extend this definition to indicate that creativity is:

> a productive activity whereby objects, processes and ideas are generated from antecedent conditions through the agency of someone, whose knowledge to do so comes from somewhere and the resultant novel variation is seen as a valued addition to the store of knowledge in at least one social setting. (McIntyre, 2008, p. 1)

To go in the opposite direction, as Raymond Williams did with his definition of culture, we can, as fraught with potential danger as this is, formularize the notion of creativity into a simple equation:

$$\text{Creativity} = \text{Novelty} + \text{Value}$$

Furthermore, Beth Hennessey argues that creativity emerges from a 'complex web of interrelated forces operating at multiple levels that can only be modeled and understood via multidisciplinary investigation' (2017, p. 342). She goes on to suggest that 'only with the adoption of a truly integrated systems perspective' (2017, p. 343) can we ever hope to understand the complexities of creativity.

Closely related to creativity, *innovation* tends to be more overtly linked to entrepreneurship. We will deal with the latter term shortly. In the meantime, Mazzarol asserts that 'innovation is not just about new technology, but also about doing things better to enhance value to customers, employees and shareholders' (2011, p. i). Everett Rogers has been far more precise:

> An *innovation* is an idea, practice, or object that is perceived as new by an individual or other unit of adoption. It matters little, so far as human behaviour is concerned, whether or not an idea is 'objectively' new as measured by the lapse of time since its first use or discovery. [Italics in original] (2003, p. 12)

McIntyre has claimed that this way of thinking about innovation 'has come quite close to recent definitions of "creativity"' (2011, p. 4), especially in regard to both novelty and value.

While scholars have tended to argue over the differences between innovation and creativity, there is a tendency to adhere to a naïve and simplistic view where creativity is thought to involve merely having an idea and innovation is presumed to be carrying it out. Brian Arthur suggests the idea is 'too diffuse, too nebulous' (2009, p. 90) and consequently takes the popular route preferring to invoke the term innovation 'wherever some improvement is put into practice or some new idea is tried out, no matter how trivial' (Arthur, 2009, p. 89). Rosenfeld and Servo (1991) are also typical in claiming that creativity is the generation of new ideas while innovation refers to the process of making money off those ideas. Furthermore, to add a discursive element to this appraisal, creativity is historically associated with the arts, while the term innovation tends to be affiliated with business, engineering, technology, and the sciences (Godin, 2013; McIntyre, 2011). That differentiation, especially at a national policy level, goes some way to explaining why innovation is still considered, outside a research understanding, as different to creativity. In fact, one could argue that creativity subsumes innovation within itself, inasmuch as creativity must involve both innovation and tradition (Negus & Pickering, 2004). More on these debates later.

The next term that also needs some brief unpacking here is that of the notion of an 'industry'. This term is often used to categorize 'a group of companies that are related in terms of their primary business activities' (Investopedia, 2021) and, by extension, products. In the broad sweep of time, it is a relatively new term. It emerged and solidified around the time of the Industrial Revolution but the solidity of that world has now given way to a certain imprecision. The claim has been made that 'industry and market boundaries are porous and "fuzzy" especially where globalization is taking place' (McGee et al., 1995, p. 261) since the merging of:

> trans-industrial products and service activities inside diversified corporations is especially striking among information sector firms, which operate in the telecommunications, broadcasting, entertainment, software, data processing, and related manufacturing industries. (Todeva et al., 2007, p. 3)

What's more, the notion of a solid objectifiable entity, an industry, is increasingly giving way to the idea that we are looking at 'loosely coupled systems of production' (Dubois & Gadde, 2010). The idea of the fuzziness of systems is of particular relevance in the creative industries where horizontal integration (Croteau & Hoynes, 2019, p. 74) has led to diversification, for example, where a telecommunication company such as Comcast has expanded into broadcasting and cable television, movie and television production, and theme parks. As another example, Apple has expanded from a technology company into television, and consequently one could ask which industry it should be placed within. Regardless of these definitional issues, if, as Smith (1998) notes, fish is the primary product of the fishing industry and the steel industries produce steel, it follows that creative outputs must be the primary 'product' of the creative industries. But there are dragons here too.

The first real example of the use of the term 'creative industries' is often associated with the United Kingdom's Department for Culture, Media and Sport (DCMS). In 1998, as a result of a policy desire, they defined the creative industries as 'those industries which have their origin in individual creativity, skill and talent which have a potential for job and wealth creation through the generation and exploitation of intellectual property' (1998, p. 3). This definition is not without its criticisms (e.g. Hesmondhalgh, 2019; O'Connor, 2012).

To put this simply, as we have seen above, the extant research into creativity indicates that creativity is not just applicable to artistic activity alone. It also applies to the sciences and just about every other area of human endeavor. If this is the case, then it is hard to argue that creativity is the sole distinguishing factor of the creative industries. All industries, by definition, must be creative. Further, we can argue that all industries originate in some form of creativity, skill, and talent. From there they are all engaged in pursuing wealth creation. And to compound the problem, not all industries create wealth through the specific exploitation of intellectual property. And herein lies another concern. The concept of intellectual property does not just refer to copyright but also to patents. A number of industries engage in wealth creation through developing and owning patents but many of these industries do not sit comfortably within our common-sense understanding of what constitutes the creative industries. The industries hinged on patents must include pharmaceuticals, biotechnology industries, the electronics industry, financial services in their use of business methods patents, and petroleum and refining industries, to give just a few examples. While John Howkins (2001) does assert that many of these must be included in the creative industries, none of them could be accepted from a 'common sense' point of view, as 'creative' industries. The DCMS definition, on consideration, may be too loose to be useful. This situation leaves us asking, how do we move closer to a satisfactory and useful operational understanding of the creative industries?

Davies and Sigthorsson argue that the notion of the 'creative industries' must be seen as an umbrella term, one that encompasses a broad set of sectors connected by three defining features. Firstly, they 'all require some input of *human creativity*; second, they are *vehicles for symbolic messages*, that is, they are carriers of *meaning*; and third, they contain, at least potentially, some *intellectual property* that belongs to an individual or group' [italics in original] (2013, p. 1).

There are problems here too. Given this is obviously an adaptation of the DCMS definition, points one and three must also be problematic, as discussed briefly above. However, for us, the definition's significance lies in the second point, that is, the creative industries are vehicles for symbolic messages. Given symbolic creativity is of a different order to other forms of creativity, we can logically argue that this industry must have, as its primary function, the task of intentionally generating meaning through its use of symbolic creativity. For Davies and Sigthorsson 'a tremendous range of economic activity arises from the creation of *pleasure* and *meaning*. These experiences, when they take the form of *goods* and *services* provide work for a host of people' [italics in original] (2013, p. 1). David Hesmondhalgh, a critic of the term creative industries, also favors the idea of 'symbolic creativity', using it to move beyond a Romantic emphasis on artistic activity and everything that entails. He suggests that:

> The invention and/or performance of stories, songs, images, poems, jokes and so on, in no matter what technological form, involves a particular type of creativity—the manipulation of symbols for the purposes of entertainment, information and perhaps even enlightenment. (2019, p. 9)

In this case we can say that the creative industries engage in the creation of symbolic meaning as their industrial output. This understanding gives some solidity to the production, management, circulation, and selling of, as Raymond Williams sets out, signifying practices. We can thus see that the umbrella term creative industries has come to represent a 'seemingly heterogeneous set of industries possessing an underlying commonality around creativity as a primary driver' (Flew, 2012, p. 83) but only insofar as the creativity is symbolic creativity generating meaning as its primary driver of profit.

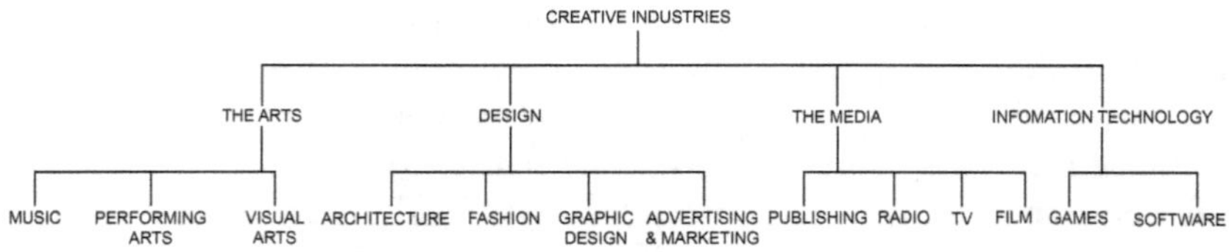

Fig. 1.1 Creative industries list represented as a hierarchical structure (McIntyre et al., 2019, p. 9)

These industries include the four broad sectors of the media, design, the arts, and information technology in games-based and app development forms (Flew, 2012) and, to provide a finer delineation, includes those professions that exist inside music, radio, publishing, advertising and design, fashion, visual arts, performing arts, film, television, electronic games and interactive content, and architecture (2019) (Fig. 1.1).

To consolidate the above, it is argued that 'the creative industries are thus those industries that use signifying practices to intentionally bring meaning into being via audio, visual and text based artefacts in order to create value' (McIntyre et al., 2019, p. 10). Note the term *value*, which may mean cultural or social value that may be convertible to financial value. This inclusion brings the definition closer to accepted understandings about creativity and innovation. It is worth noting here as well, that these creative industries have become far more entrepreneurial than they used to be.

Writing in *Key Concepts in Creative Industries*, John Hartley et al. assert that:

> Entrepreneurs are key agents in the creative industries. The *entrepreneur* (the agent) or *entrepreneurship* (the process) is the action of doing new things in the market context of uncertainty with respect to existing value-seeking to create and realise new value. The entrepreneur seeks to discover new sources of value by uncovering contradictions (i.e. opportunities) in extant value structures or by proposing new value structures (i.e. innovations). The entrepreneur's incentive is to claim some fraction of that value added. [Italics in original] (2013, p. 92)

Thomas Mazzarol also provides a very practically focused definition when he states:

> … entrepreneurship deals with the process of developing new business ventures and/or promoting growth and innovation in existing firms. Innovation is not just about new technology, but also about doing things better to enhance value to customers, employees and shareholders. (2011, p. i)

Hartley et al. claim that the most well-known understanding of entrepreneurship comes from Joseph Schumpeter who, according to them, sees:

> The entrepreneur as the economic agent who introduced *new ideas* into the *economic order*, in the face of uncertainty, and in pursuit of *profit*. The Schumpeterian (i.e. evolutionary economics) entrepreneur is an agent who disturbs the existing economic order with a new idea that may become an innovation. Entrepreneurship is the process of imagining, creating and realising economic opportunities profit in the face of uncertainty and in carrying the risk for this uncertainty themselves. [Italics in original] (2013, p. 94)

Leading on from this, the European Commission asserts that entrepreneurship is primarily a mindset which 'covers an individual's motivation and capacity, independently or within an organisation, to identify an opportunity and pursue it in order to produce new value or economic success' (EC, 2003). The Commission goes on to suggest that it takes 'creativity or innovation to enter and compete in an existing market, to change or even create a new market. To turn a business idea into success requires the ability to blend creativity or innovation with sound management' (EC, 2003).

This last definition complies with the simpler view of Davies and Sigthorsson who suggest 'entrepreneurship is sometimes regarded as a form of creative expression in the creative industries' (Daves & Sigthorsson, 2013, p. 64). They suggest that the career trajectory of an entrepreneur 'is to have an original idea, realize a gap in the market that it could fill and make money out of it' (2013, p. 65).

These ideas are all concerned in some way with developing something new or at least novel, mirroring the definitions of creativity and innovation discussed above. However, they do focus predominantly on what individuals do. David Hesmondhalgh (2019) asserts that *entrepreneurship* and *entrepreneurialism* have been romanticized and individualized and cites neoliberalism as a cause. Neoliberalism's emphasis on the role of the individual as entrepreneur and hero is seen as a reaction against the imposing structures of bureaucracy, the state, and large corporations. As a political ideology, it is resolutely individualist (Davies & Sigthorsson, 2013, p. 50). Despite this over-emphasis on the individual, there is now, in tandem with research in creativity and innovation, an increasing recognition that the social and cultural structures entrepreneurs work in are equally as important as individual action. We will return to these ideas shortly, but for now, we want to highlight the proliferation of terminology describing subvariants of the term entrepreneur. These include the idea of *intrapreneurship*, *social entrepreneurialism*, and the rise of terms like *technopreneur* and *journopreneur*.

An *intrapreneur*, in its simplest usage, is someone who is entrepreneurial *within* an organization—someone who sees opportunities and makes changes, particularly to enhance an organization's competitiveness:

> As levels of competition have accelerated, the creative and innovative nature of entrepreneurship has come to be seen as a way of enhancing the competitiveness of organisations and encouraging employees to view themselves as owners. This has seen organisations attempting to encourage employees to tap into their creative and innovative talents, and seeking to promote innovation. The word 'intrapreneur' is commonly used to describe entrepreneurs within large organisations. The word 'intrapreneurship' refers to entrepreneurs inside the established organisation and who—although employed in a corporate position—are nevertheless given the freedom to create and market their own ideas. The intrapreneur demonstrates a set of enterprising attributes in a wide variety of situations. They make things happen. (Mazzarol & Reboud, 2020, pp. 95–96)

However, the role of the intrapreneur is not universally accepted as a positive contribution to a firm's operation. For example, Elert and Stenkula (2020)

> challenge the outlook that intrapreneurship is always beneficial… firms do not necessarily perceive intrapreneurship in a positive light. Analysis of 2,000 medium-sized tech-businesses suggest that intrapreneurs often end up in an adversarial role: 'Intrapreneurs are very important to the company but they are seen as enemies because they question long-standing paradigms' (Baltes, 2016). (All in Elert & Stenkula, 2020)

Another derivative of entrepreneur is *technopreneur*, a portmanteau of technology and entrepreneur. As Bailetti states, the fundamental purpose of a technopreneur 'is to assemble a combination of specialized individuals and heterogeneous assets in order to create and capture value for the firm through collaborative exploration and experimentation' (2012, p. 12). For Fowosire et al.

> entrepreneurship forms the sub structure upon which science and technology are built. As we understand it, technopreneurship is, by a large part, still entrepreneurship. The difference is that technopreneurship is either involved in delivering an innovative hi-tech product (e.g. Microsoft) or makes use of hi-tech in an innovative way to deliver its product to the consumer (e.g. eBay), or both (e.g. most pharmaceutical companies). Technopreneurship is not a product but a process of synthesis in engineering the future.... (2017, p. i)

A *journopreneur*, on other hand, is a journalist 'who also identifies as an entrepreneur who is building a business on the side' (Evans, 2014). Ann Friedman, in an article for the *Columbia Journalism Review*, maintains that journopreneurs and other journalistic startups are concerned with traditional journalistic values such as 'informing the public and exposing injustice' (2014, n.p.) but are also interested in how to get this information to an audience by employing new technologies: 'Why wouldn't we try to find a way to produce the best journalism we can under modern circumstances?' (Friedman, 2014, n.p.). In a textual analysis of journalism trade publications, reviews, journalism institutions, and news outlets, Vos and Singer (2016) discovered that entrepreneurial journalism, while a vague concept, has been described as 'an emerging field, a set of skills, a spirit, a drive, and a serious act. The entrepreneurial journalist is depicted as a founder, an innovator, a trailblazer, a business creator, and a freelancer' (2016, p. 151).

Social entrepreneurialism is another matter altogether. According to Mair and Noboa, it involves 'innovative approaches to address issues in the domains of education, environment, fair trade, health and human rights and is widely regarded as an important building block of the sustainable development of countries' (2006, p. 121). This form of entrepreneurship, while it has several key characteristics in common with other forms, is not merely or fundamentally about turning a profit. Its primary goal is to undertake sustainable practices to better lives. Mair and Noboa continue by stating:

> SE differs from traditional business entrepreneurship in several aspects. First, social entrepreneurs are moved by different motivations to discover and exploit a distinct category of opportunities; second the way they pursue

> opportunities might diverge from typical business approaches; and third, the outcome social entrepreneurs aim for involves both social and economic aspects. (2006, p. 121)

An offshoot of social entrepreneurialism is *ecopreneurship*, which describes a business that values environmental concerns within a free market:

> A new term has been coined for entrepreneurs whose business efforts are not only driven by profit, but also by a concern for the environment. They are called ecopreneurs. Also known as environmental entrepreneurship and eco-capitalism, ecopreneurship is becoming more widespread. (Schuyler, 1998, p. 3)

A more recent derivative is *sustainopreneurship*, tentatively defined in 2006 by Anders Abrahamsson as a merging between social entrepreneurship and ecopreneurship, specifically aimed at sustainable solutions.

We can see from this brief foray into the notion of entrepreneurship, and its increasing number of derivatives, that it is an important way of being in the world. It is increasingly important in the creative industries. Many in these industries have original ideas, see how this could be exploited given a suitable gap in the market, and have become intent on gaining an income from it. For us, the definitions we have briefly explored here provide a baseline for the ongoing discussion throughout the book, where each chapter we present delves deeper into the creative industries, entrepreneurship, and the necessary creativity and innovation that supply the dynamic systems of action that hold it all together.

References

Abrahamsson, A. (2006). Sustainopreneurship – Business with a cause. *Science sustainable development – Starting points and critical reflections*. VHU – Föreningen Vetenskap för Hållbar Utveckling (Swedish Society for Sustainable Development), pp. 21–30.

Alexander, V. (2003). *Sociology of the arts: Exploring fine and popular forms*. Blackwell.

Arthur, B. (2009). *The nature of technology: What it is and how it evolves*. Free Press.

Bailetti, T. (2012). Technology entrepreneurship: Overview, definition, and distinctive aspects. *Technology Innovation Management Review, 2*(2), 5–12.

CIIC. (2013). Valuing Australia's creative industries: Final report. *SGS Economics and Planning for the Creative Industries Innovation Centre*. CIIC.

Comunian, R. (2019). Complexity thinking as a coordinating theoretical framework for creative industries research. In S. Cunningham & T. Flew (Eds.), *A research agenda for creative industries* (pp. 39–57). Elgar.

Croteau, D., & Hoynes, W. (2019). *Media/Society: Technology, industries, content, and users*. Sage Publications.

Curtin, M., & Sanson, K. (Eds.). (2016). *Precarious creativity: Global media, local labor*. University of California Press.

Davies, R., & Sigthorsson, G. (2013). *Introducing the creative industries: From theory to practice*. Sage.

DCMS. (1998). *Creative industries mapping document*. DCMS.

Deloittes Australia. (2012). *Digital disruption: Short fuse, big bang?* Retrieved May 24, 2017, from https://www2.deloitte.com/content/dam/Deloitte/au/Documents/Building%20Lucky%20Country/deloitte-au-consulting-digital-disruption-whitepaper-230217.pdf

Dubois, A. & Gadde, L. (2010). 'The Construction Industry as a Loosely Coupled System: Implications for Productivity and Innovation', *Construction Management and Economics, 20*(7), 621–631, published online: 21 Oct 2010, https://doi.org/10.1080/01446190210163543 (accessed 24/2/2022).

Dunlop, T. (2016). *Why the future is workless*. NewSouth Publishing.

EC. (2003). *Green paper – Entrepreneurship in Europe*. Commission of the European Communities.

EC. (2017). *Supporting cultural and creative industries*. European Commission. Retrieved July 21, 2017, from https://ec.europa.eu/culture/policy/cultural-creative-industries_en

Elert, N., & Stenkula, M. (2020). Intrapreneurship: Productive and non-productive. *Entrepreneurship Theory and Practice*, 1–17.

Evans, M. (2014). In Hue Magazine [Tumblr]. Retrieved April 3, 2014, from http://marissaaevans.tumblr.com/post/26833220688/journopreneur-n-a-journalist-who-also

Flew, T. (2012). *The creative industries: Culture & policy*. Sage.

Fowosire, R., Idris, O. & Opoola, E. (2017). Technopreneurship: A view of technology, innovations and entrepreneurship. *Global Journal of Research In Engineering, 17*(7). Retrieved March 21, 2022, from https://www.engineeringresearch.org/index.php/GJRE/article/view/1717

Frey, C. & Osborne, M. (2013). The future of employment: How susceptible are jobs to computerisation?' *Oxford Martin Working Papers*. Retrieved March 1, 2017, from http://www.oxfordmartin.ox.ac.uk/downloads/academic/The_Future_of_Employment.pdf

Friedman, A. (2014, July 31). No, 'journopreneurs' are not killing journalism. *Columbia Journalism Review*. Retrieved September 28, 2021, from https://archives.cjr.org/realtalk/response_to_the_baffler_journo.php

Godin, G. (2013). *Innovation contested: The idea of innovation over the centuries*. Routledge.

Hartley, J., Potts, J., Cunningham, S., Flew, T., Keane, M., & Banks, J. (2013). *Key concepts in creative industries.* Sage.
Hennessey, B. (2017). Taking a systems view of creativity: On the right path toward understanding. *The Journal of Creative Behavior – Special Issue: In Celebration of the Journal of Creative Behavior's 50th Anniversary, 51*(4), 341–344.
Hennessey, B. & Amabile, T. (2010) 'Creativity', *Annual Review of Psychology,* 61, 569–98.
Hesmondhalgh, D. (2019). *The cultural industries* (4th ed.). Sage.
Hesmondhalgh, D., & Baker, S. (2011). *Creative labour: Media work in three cultural industries.* Routledge.
Howkins, J. (2001). *The creative economy.* Allen Lane.
Investopedia. (2021). Retrieved September 6, 2221, from https://www.investopedia.com/terms/i/industry.asp
Lhermitte, M., Blanc, S., & Perrin, B. (2015). *Cultural times: The first global map of cultural and creative industries.* EYGM Ltd.
Mair, J., & Noboa, E. (2006). 'Social Entrepreneurship: How Intentions to Create a Social Venture are Formed', in *Social entrepreneurship* (Basingstoke UK: Palgrave Macmillan), 121–135).
Mazzarol, T. (2011). *Entrepreneurship and innovation.* Tilde University Press.
Mazzarol, T., & Reboud, S. (2020). *Entrepreneurship and innovation: Theory, practice and context* (4th ed.). Springer.
McGee, J., Thomas, H., & Pruett, M. (1995). Strategic groups and the analysis of market structure and industry dynamics. *British Journal of Management, 6*(4), 257–270.
McGrath, R. G. (2011). Failing by design. *Harvard Business Review, 89,* 77–83.
McIntyre, P. (2008, November). The systems model of creativity: Analyzing the distribution of power in the studio. *Journal of the Art of Record Production, Issue 4: Supplement to ARP08, The Peer – Reviewed Proceedings of the 2008 Art of Record Production Conference.* University of Massachusetts, Lowell: 4th Art of Record Production International Conference. Retrieved June 24, 2010, from http://www.artofrecordproduction.com/content/view/214/126/
McIntyre, P. (2011, July 6–8). Bringing novelty into being: Exploring the relationship between "creativity" and "innovation". In *ANZCA 2011 – Communication on the edge: Shifting boundaries and identities.* The University of Waikato, Hamilton, New Zealand. Retrieved April 26, 2015, from http://www.anzca.net/conferences/anzca11-proceedings.html
McIntyre, P., Balnaves, M., Kerrigan, S., Williams, C., & King, E. (2019). *Creativity and cultural production in the Hunter: An applied ethnographic study of applied entrepreneurial systems in the creative industries: Final report, ARC Grant LP130100348.* University of Newcastle.
McIntyre, P., Fulton, J., Paton, E., Kerrigan, S., & Meany, M. (2018). *Educating for creativity within higher education: Integration of research into media practice.* Palgrave Macmillan.

McRobbie, A. (2005). Clubs to companies. In J. Hartley (Ed.), *Creative industries* (pp. 375–390). Wiley-Blackwell.
McRobbie, A. (2016). *Be creative: Making a living in the new culture industries.* Polity Press.
Negus, K., & Pickering, M. (2004). *Creativity, communication and cultural value.* Sage.
O'Connor, J. (2012). Surrender to the void: Life after creative industries. *Cultural Studies Review, 18*(3), 387–410.
O'Donnell, P., & Zion, L. (2019). Precarity in media work. In M. Deuze & M. Prenger (Eds.), *Making media: Production, practices, and professions* (pp. 223–234). Amsterdam University Press.
Pope, R. (2005). *Creativity: Theory, history, practice.* Routledge.
Rogers, E. M. (2003). *Diffusion of innovations* (5th ed.). Free Press.
Rosenbaum, J. (2020, January 13). The role of purpose in the workplace of the future. *Nation Swell.* Retrieved February 23, 2020, from https://nationswell.com/purpose-work-gig-economy-aarp/
Rosenfeld, R., & Servo, J. (1991). Facilitating innovation in large organizations. In J. Henry & D. Walker (Eds.), *Managing innovation* (pp. 28–39). Sage.
Ross, A. (2009). *Nice work if you can get it: Life and labor in precarious times.* New York University Press.
Sawyer, K. (2006). *Explaining creativity: The science of human innovation.* Oxford University Press.
Sawyer, K. (2011). *Explaining creativity: The science of human innovation* (2nd ed.). Oxford University Press.
Schuyler, G. (1998). Merging economic and environmental concerns through ecopreneurship. *Digest, 98*(8), 3–4.
Smith, K. (1998). Innovation as a systemic phenomenon: Rethinking the role of policy. In K. Bryant & A. Wells (Eds.), *A new economic paradigm: Innovation-based evolutionary systems* (pp. 17–52). Department of Industry Science and Resources.
Standing, G. (2011). *The precariat: The new dangerous class.* Bloomsbury Academic.
Tahirsylaj, A. (2012). Stimulating creativity and innovation through intelligent fast failure. *Thinking Skills and Creativity, 7*(3), 265–270.
Todeva, E., Knoke, D., & Keskinova, D. (2007). Porous and fuzzy boundaries: A network approach to corporate diversification. Retrieved March 1, 2017, from http://assets.csom.umn.edu/assets/101202.pdf
Trembath, J., & Fielding, K. (2020). *Australia's cultural and creative economy: A 21st century guide.* A New Approach and the Australian Academy of the Humanities.
UNCTAD. (2008). Creative economy report 2008. U*nited Nations Conference on Trade and Development.* Retrieved June 27, 2017, from http://unctad.org/creative-economy
Vos, T. P., & Singer, J. (2016). Media discourse about entrepreneurial journalism: Implications for journalistic capital. *Journalism Practice, 10*(2), 143–159.

CHAPTER 2

Socio-Historical Context of Entrepreneurship in the Creative Industries

Entrepreneurship has become increasingly important to the creative industries. As it trades in a variety of signifying practices generated via symbolic creativity, as many exploit original ideas to fill a gap in the market, and as a number seek innovative means of gaining an income from it, we are reminded that nothing occurs in isolation, nobody exists in a vacuum, and nothing comes from nothing—nothing ever could. These ideas are generally regarded as truisms for most people, but from a dynamic systems perspective they are doubly so. As in all things, everything is interconnected and interrelated. This is why it is vitally important to understand the contexts the creative industries operate within.

For us, contexts are the spatial, temporal, and discursive spaces which are interconnected or woven together with other connected spaces or structures that are linked to, precede, or follow other discursive spaces that also operate hierarchically both above and below the ones we exist in. They are thus the ground of scalable and complex systems. From this perspective, contextual interconnections have an effect on the object that is located in that context. They have had an effect on the various sectors of the creative industries as they accommodate themselves, in a variety of ways, to the increasing dominance of entrepreneurship as a way of gaining an income in these industries. Without addressing the contexts of these industries and the varying actions taken there, we can only ever hope to gain a partial understanding of the object of our concern, that is, entrepreneurship in the creative industries in the twenty-first century.

P. McIntyre et al., *Entrepreneurship in the Creative Industries*,
https://doi.org/10.1007/978-3-031-19455-9_2

Given this assertion, this chapter sets out to provide the broad contexts of the development of the idea of the creative industries and its entwining with the notion of entrepreneurship. Like many ideas, objects, and processes, these were built on a set of complex antecedent conditions. The story of where the creative industries came from, and the necessity for entrepreneurship within them, is bound together with these antecedent conditions. For example, before the creative industries existed as a way to describe a set of industries that exploits signifying systems, 'the culture industry' was the common term used to describe a set of industries similar to them. This 'culture industry', of course, produces culture or cultural objects. Raymond Williams had identified two ways to think about culture. For him:

> There is some practical convergence between (i) the anthropological and sociological senses of culture as a distinct 'whole way of life'...and (ii) the more specialised if also more common sense of culture as 'artistic and intellectual activities', though these, because of the emphasis on a general signifying system, are now much more broadly defined, to include not only the traditional arts and forms of intellectual production but also all the 'signifying practices'—from language through the arts and philosophy to journalism, fashion and advertising—which now constitute this complex and necessarily extended field. (Williams, 1981, p. 13)

With this definition on board we argue that the introduction of the term 'culture industry', the precursor to the term 'creative industries', was the result of a reaction to some of the supposed deleterious effects on the various cultures in Europe that had produced the Industrial Revolution, as this change in the dominant mode of production took its toll over the long term.

The expression 'the culture industry' was coined by German sociologists Theodor Adorno and his compatriot Max Horkheimer. They and their colleagues were, in the 1930s, associated with the Institute for Social Research in Frankfurt, Germany, where they drew on thinkers like Kant, Hegel, Weber, Marx, and Freud in an effort to come to grips with the larger structural forces at play in various societies, and what individuals did as a matter of choice in response to them. The group of influential scholars located at this institute in Frankfurt and being predominantly Jewish, were in a particular situation that was shaped by historical forces well beyond their control. They had to flee from the Nazis as the forces of the Second

World War began to take shape. Adorno was lucky to be studying at Oxford. He eventually made his way to the United States where was offered a position initially with Paul Lazarsfeld at Columbia University in New York, where Horkheimer and the Institute for Social Research had relocated to. He was employed on Lazarsfeld's Radio Research Project but he was not happy with it. He then moved west to California where he began interacting with other eminent cultural producers and thinkers. From this potted history, we can say that in his personal life there were two forces at play driving Adorno's thinking. The first, of course, was totalitarianism of the type being displayed by the fascists, and the second was the culture shock he felt as a middle-class European Jewish intellectual now working in America. In regard to the latter, he could not for the life of him understand why the working class in the United States were so enamored of Hollywood movies and the popular music of the time, jazz, being played on the dominant medium of radio. Being an accomplished pianist interested in the avant-garde, Adorno did not hide his disdain for American popular culture. In other words, in his intellectual life Adorno had a personal need to explain why mass media and popular culture were so loved in this new land, especially by the working class. Drawing on the European intellectual tradition he was so steeped in, Adorno saw a negative dialectic at work between high culture and popular culture.

For him, high culture of the type he favored was potentially revolutionary through its encompassing of a high set of ideals. For him, forms like classical and avant-garde music had positive qualities which included order, harmonic integrity, balance, coherence, permanence, universality, complexity, and an underlying unity or wholeness. For him, low culture, such as the products of film, television, and popular music, had opposite qualities. They were trivial, base, and meretricious, that is, out for a fast buck, and were showily attractive as would befit a harlot. It was low culture, with all its negative attributes, that emanated from the culture industry. The term culture industry was not meant to be kind to this industry but was used instead as a pejorative by Adorno and his colleagues. They argued popular culture as produced by the culture industry was conformist and standardized, not unique as all great art is, as they saw it, and it was only significant because high culture was not as readily available to the working class or the masses. Low culture was used by the lower classes as a form of catharsis, a release from their arduous working week, which then allowed them to go back to their lives of drudgery each Monday morning. If only, reasoned Adorno, they could encounter high culture they would soon see how mistaken they were about how the world worked, and this awakening would lead them to throw off their bonds of servitude. For Adorno and Horkheimer and the Frankfurt School in general, 'the culture industry functioned as a powerful ideological and propaganda instrument' (Hartley et al., 2013, p. 78) for the governing elites, which adroitly used the new technological affordances provided by mass communication and the associated practices of mass production as a means to impose their ideological control over the population, which stripped of being citizens, used here in the fullest sense of the word, simply become mass consumers. As Adorno and Horkheimer argued 'under monopoly all mass culture is identical, and the lines of its artificial framework begin to show through…Movies and radio no longer pretend to be art. The truth that they are just business is made an ideology in order to justify the rubbish that they deliberately produce' (1979, p. 349).

As David Hesmondhalgh notes (2006, pp. 14–18), a number of French sociologists, including Bernard Miege, took these ideas, qualified them, and expanded the notion of 'the culture industry' in the singular, and pluralized it to that of 'the cultural industries' in an effort to delineate how complex these industries were. They were keen to emphasize and identify the differing logics at play, for example, in the broadcasting industry, as opposed to the press and other editorial or publishing modes of production. They also wanted to address these industries as they existed in this point in time, not in comparison to some idealized form of pre-industrial culture as the Frankfurt School was tending to do. They also saw the cultural industries as a contested space, not one where the forces of corporate oppression had won. However, in abandoning the cultural pessimism of Adorno, Miege and his colleagues were not simply celebrating the cultural industries but wanted to see them as complex and contested spaces (Hesmondhalgh, 2006, pp. 14–18).

Hesmondhalgh (2006, 2019) took these ideas further himself. He suggested there are core cultural industries (2019, pp. 14–17) and these may include television and radio, including the newer cable and satellite versions such as streaming; film, which can also be seen in the same digital light; content produced for the internet industry and its gaming equivalent; and print and electronic publishing ranging from newspapers, magazines, and books through to databases and other information services. He also includes the three sectors of the music industry, that is publishing, live performance, and recording. Apart from these core industries and their variable logics of production and consumption, he also set out what he calls peripheral industries which can be grouped around the idea that many of them use semi-industrial and at times non-industrial production methods. These include, in particular, theater and fine art. It was in reaction to many of these ideas, from Adorno onward, that the notion of the creative industries was born. We will return to that term shortly. For now, we will examine one of the other contextual elements that contributed to its birth as a useful idea.

One of the most important crucibles of the twentieth century was the Second World War. While intellectual movements like the critical theory espoused by the Frankfurt School and its thinkers like Adorno and Horkheimer were impacted by the conditions of the Second World War, this period in the middle of the twentieth century also proved to be a nursery for many of the technologies that were to sustain themselves right through into the next millennium. To name just a very few of these technologies, the development of walkie-talkies used to replace runners and signalers on the battlefield, which further debased wire-linked communication, led to the advent of transistorized radio and eventually the mobile phone. Tape-based technology was developed and refined in Germany for intelligence gathering and dissemination but it was to prove a boon as the later basis of both the North Atlantic film and music recording industries and eventually became the basis of digital software such as ProTools, which reflected the analogue world it grew out of. And if it wasn't for Alan Turing and the codebreakers at Bletchley Park in Britain working to decipher the Nazi's secret codes used during Second World War, the digital computers we take for granted in the twenty-first century, including laptops and mobile phones, now mainstays of the creative industries, would not have taken the eventual digital form they did.

Digitization, and the context it developed in, is significant for us. Once the fundamentals of computer networking were put in place and the protocols were defined for dial-up transmission, it became obvious to many that there were a myriad of benefits to be had from this process apart from what the universities and the military had envisaged. In just 10 years, the wider community embraced this world wholeheartedly. Very, very quickly these networks became crucial. As the NFSA reports 'by 1996 internet connections encircled the globe, networking public and private institutions, online communities, and the cyber citizens of the world' (2016, online). Once we arrived at cloud computing the globe opened up even more but it was still bound to, and dependent on, physical localities. The cloud, in reality a collection of server farms or data centers that are themselves massive arrays of drives designed to store and process vast amounts of digital information, were certainly geospatially situated. As earth bound electronic devices powered by electricity, which require significant cooling systems to keep them operating, server farms need to be located close to a means of providing both an adequate power supply and considerable sources of cooling since they generate vast amounts of heat in their daily operations. They also need the right kind of policy and regulation in place to allow them to do that (Williams, 2010, online). These factors illustrate the idea that the conditions of production a digitally oriented creative business operates in are vital to its ongoing sustainability and success. They also demonstrate the idea that technologies do not themselves exist in realms divorced from social, cultural, political, economic, physical, or geographical and environmental factors.

In order for technologies, like those that underpin the current digital realm, to exist, the necessary resources must be in place. One cannot make an axe and use it as a tool without access to iron ore to make the head or access to trees in order to make and shape an axe handle. Mobile phones, too, are made from something. It is important to understand that a number of resources they are made from are extremely rare. It is no surprise that in 2019

> Chinese president Xi Jinping suggested Beijing may use its position as the world's leading supplier of rare earth minerals (REMs)—metals that are critical for everything from mobile phones to fighter jets—as a means of pressuring Washington to ease or remove more than $300 billion in trade tariffs. (Cheng et al., 2019, p. 1)

From these very brief examples, we should be able to see that societies and the cultures that manifest their whole way of life through various signifying systems, or those who engage in the manufacture of symbolic messages such as in the creative industries, are inevitably dependent on the environmental conditions they exist within and have access to. This notion has been argued, in various ways, across the political spectrum over some time. For example, Karl Marx (2007) asserted that the conditions of production were fundamental to his base/superstructure model, a model we will delve into more fully in the next chapter. For now, we can say that Marx did not separate the environment from the society, culture, and economy that prevailed under those environmental conditions. He is not the only person to have made these connections. Adam Smith, seemingly from the opposite side of the political fence, also asserted in *An Inquiry into the Nature and Causes of the Wealth of Nations* that:

> Whatever be the soil, climate, or extent of territory of any particular nation, the abundance or scantiness of its annual supply must, *in that particular situation*, depend upon those two circumstances [author's italics], that is, the application of specialized skill employed and the proportion of people engaged in the divisions of labour. (2012 [1776], n.p.)

Smith made sure to stress that wealth creation is always 'in proportion to the extent and natural fertility of the ground' (2012 [1776], n.p.).

One of the more recent examples of connecting a way of life, or culture, with the environmental context it exists in is that of Jared Diamond (1997). He is a professor of physiology but has made contributions to ecology and evolutionary biology. Diamond argues that it is the climatic and geographical factors that a population exists within that produce its agriculture, its forms of civilization, and its technology. These ideas are not so far removed from Marx's understanding of the conditions of production or Smith's basis for his observations in *Wealth of Nations.* If this is the case then the creative industries, through the technologies that underpin their operations, are as dependent on the environmental contexts they exist in as they are on the sociocultural, economic, and political contexts they are interconnected with.

These contexts gave rise historically to another set of factors that have contributed to the rise of the necessity for entrepreneurial thinking in the creative industries. Globalization is not, however, as some 'communication scholars tend to identify … a recent phenomenon' (Servaes, 2015, p. 242). For example, in an edition of *Communication Research and Practice* Servaes writes that:

> the 1990s, with the fall of the Berlin Wall and the explosive growth of the World Wide Web as preludes, have been marked by the collapse of the physical, virtual and institutional barriers that have kept people apart. The ever closer trade relationships among nation-states, the growing power of transnational corporations, information and communication technologies (ICTs), Internet, and discussions on e-governance, the emergence of global health and environmental issues, and a common style of consumption of material and cultural products have all helped to bring about what is described as 'globalization' of our world or the world becoming a 'global village.' However, globalization is not a product of the 1990s, or even the

twentieth century, as many historians will explain (see, for instance, Hopkins, 2002). Therefore, Held, McGrew, Goldblatt, and Perraton (1999, p. 414) conclude that 'globalization is neither a wholly novel, nor primarily modern, social phenomenon. Its form has changed over time and across the key domains of human interaction, from the political to the ecological. (2015, p. 242)

This idea is reinforced by Timothy Havens and Amanda Lotz in their book *Understanding Media Industries*. They suggest that globalization 'involves a variety of complex and sometimes contradictory social and economic developments that have been taking place for centuries' (2016, p. 221). However, they observe that given the fundamentally global character of the Internet, the practices and forms of globalization 'may change profoundly as digitisation continues to change the media industries' (2016, p. 221). And it is not just the media industries that are being subject to disruption in this process. If you take yourself across to the Der Spiegel International website, you can see that there is no denying that things have been changing and changing fast:

> The technological advances made in the last decade have been breathtaking, but it is likely still just the beginning…We are witnessing nothing less than a societal transformation that ultimately nobody will be able to avoid. It is the kind of sea change that can only be compared with 19th century industrialization, but it is happening much faster this time. Just as the change from hand work to mass production dramatically changed our society over 100 years ago, the digital revolution isn't just altering specific sectors of the economy, it is changing the way we think and live. (Schulz, 2015, online)

Among all this, we can say that there have been seen startling and credible predictions that many waged positions will be lost across all industries. For example, Deloitte, one of the big four global accounting firms, produced a report in 2012 that projected the degree of what has been called 'digital disruption' (we will pick this idea up again in the next chapter) across eighteen major industries. Their next report called *Harnessing the "Bang": Stories from the Digital Frontline* states that they did not anticipate how much their original analysis would reverberate globally. In that report, they specifically warned that:

> two thirds of the Australian economy, both public and private, would experience significant digital disruption within the next five years. The stark

reality is that it has been more like five months for 65% of the Australian economy—including Deloitte's own professional services sector—to realise we are in the cross hairs of digital disruption. (Deloitte, 2014, online)

What is most intriguing about all of this movement is the core ideology that is underpinning these remarkable changes. For example, the founder and CEO of Uber, Travis Kalanick, has a 'vision' of Uber transforming itself into a global transportation service that will eventually, he hopes, see the end of car ownership in urban areas. He sees this process being just as applicable to the delivery of goods brought about by the introduction of driverless vehicles. But as Schulz identifies:

> Uber isn't the only company with ambitions of taking over the world. That's how they all think: Google and Facebook, Apple and Airbnb—all the digital giants along with the myriad smaller companies in their wake. Their goal is never a niche market; it's always the entire world. But far from being driven by delusional fantasies, their objectives are often realistic, made possible by a potent cocktail unique in economic history: globalization combined with digitalization. (2015, online)

The CEOs of these companies have been called 'the new masters of the universe' (Schulz 2015, online); and while they share a love of money with older capitalists, there is an identifiably fundamental difference from their predecessors. As Schulz argues, they want to determine not only what is consumed but how it should be consumed and how we should live as a result: 'They aren't stumbling haphazardly into the future, rather they are ideologues with a clear agenda' (2015, online). The beliefs that hold Silicon Valley together run much deeper than the values that drive Wall Street. Silicon Valley wants to reshape the world and they believe 'that technology can change humanity for the better' (Schulz, 2015, online). But they eschew the idea that they should be bound by any external interference or regulation put in place by policymakers they have little use for. State intervention, to them, is an anachronism:

> Their message seems to be: If societal values such as privacy and data protection stand in the way, then we simply have to develop new values. They see the roots of their technological crusade in the counterculture of the 1960s, the era that formed Apple cofounder Steve Jobs. But their worldview is a libertarian one, in the tradition of radical thinkers such as Noam Chomsky, Ayn Rand and Friedrich Hayek. (Schulz, 2015, online)

These names indicate a peculiar mix of ideas and thinkers who are almost at odds with each other. Chomsky is anti-corporate, seeming to favor a system that emphasizes the collectivist in some way—one that is oriented toward the group, oriented toward the benefits of the social, while others adhere to the primacy of the individual. As you will see, it is this latter thinking that has ramped up the competition between individuals that is characteristic of many twenty-first century economies and industries. However, under the current context, many younger citizens, particularly those in the democracies of the West, have only seen the second array of individualist thinking in operation. It is all they are familiar with. To these citizens, it is just the way the world is. But many of them have become locked into part-time, casual, or contract work as a result and they quickly become aware of the difficulties this situation creates in terms of them gaining full-time employment and all the benefits that spring from that. But many of them are also unaware that there is an ideological problem they must overcome if they are to find solutions to the issues they face in gaining an income. To return to Travis Kalanick and the new masters of the universe, we need to look closely at the ideology that underpins the control these new capitalists hope to wield. In this case, we can say that, running alongside globalization and digitization, another important contextual event was unfolding, this time based on a philosophical proposition that conflated freedom with the market. If we want to uncover the advent of that ideological change, we should start with the thinking of Friedrich August von Hayek.

Friedrich von Hayek, one of the founding figures of neoliberalism, was born into an academic family in Austria and served as a gunner in the Austro-Hungarian Army in First World War. This experience was instrumental in his early thinking, as was his family's connection to the philosopher Ludwig Wittgenstein. Second World War saw Hayek in London—he was studying at Oxford—where he became a British citizen rather than returning to Austria after the Nazis had taken control of the land where he was born. The Fascists and eventually the Communists, who took much of Eastern Europe as their just reward after shouldering the bulk of the fighting in Second World War, did not endear themselves to a thinker like Hayek. The fascists were repugnant to him and after a brief flirtation with Marxism, Hayek decided it was largely inflexible and unappealing to a thinker like him. He was invited to become a faculty member at the London School of Economics, itself dominated by Keynesian thinking that emphasized government intervention in stabilizing the economy, where it was hoped he would shake things up a little. He did.

The publication of his classic text *The Road to Serfdom* (Hayek, 1944) argued that 'the more the state plans, the more difficult planning becomes for the individual' (quoted in Low, 1991, p. 170). In this book, Hayek argued for the primacy of free-thinking individual agents, which he opposed to what were believed to be the deterministic structures of the state, seen most readily in fascism and communism but also, most importantly, in any form of state control. This thinking, which gave priority to freely choosing agents, was based in part on the phenomenological approach, which was understandably gaining significant traction in Europe at the time. The work of people like Edmund Husserl, who we will explore a little more fully in the following chapter, saw humans as free, self-determining beings (1970, p. 290). This idea can be seen as an important theoretical underpinning to what would become known through thinkers like Hayek as neoliberalism, since they favored individual agency and counterposed it with the supposedly negative characteristics of the imposition of deterministic and collective structures. Thinkers like Hayek were themselves seeing the results of collectivist action first-hand. With the Second World War coming to its bloody end, Stalinist communism was simply replacing the fascists, especially in Eastern Europe. When Hayek published *The Constitution of Liberty* (Hayek, 1960), it was obvious to Hayek that there should not be a repeat of what had just happened to them with the Nazis. Now Stalinism was gaining even more ground. For Hayek, 'all things collective had become anathema in one way or another. And on we went into the Cold War' (McIntyre, 2016, p. 444). This contextual information is critical to understand if we want to know why entrepreneurship has become so important. We will pick it up more fully shortly.

What we can say for now, by way of summary to this point, is that the current neoliberal ideology that dominates Western nations such as the US, the UK, and Australia, where the founding figures of neoliberal thought—as opposed to its application—took political ideals of human dignity and individual freedom as fundamental, plays a strong role in the strengths and weaknesses of the idea of the creative industries. However, neoliberalism's focus on individual business innovation and access to speculative capital to finance that entrepreneurship appears to eschew the necessary relationship all innovation has with the structures of what has been called the entrepreneurial state (Mazzucato, 2014; Janeway, 2012). It is the rise of entrepreneurship and its relationship to the state, particularly in the UK, that we need to turn to now.

In the late 1990s the Blair Labour Party was elected to govern in the UK and espoused what it called the 'Third Way'. The British sociologist Anthony Giddens was an advisor to Blair and the ideas underpinning the Third Way were largely based on his ideas. Giddens had argued, given the 'duality of structure', that you could combine agency, the ability to make individually based choices, with structural concerns, that is, the things that were thought to determine a person's or a society's actions. To put this in very simple terms, Giddens, now a Lord in the British Parliament, argued it was possible to synthesize socialism with capitalism and provide a third political option. Following this advice, Prime Minister Tony Blair tried to combine the socialist aspirations of the traditional labour movement in the UK, which in Giddens' terms were largely structural, with the capitalist tendencies of the Conservative party, which again in Giddens' terms was focused in general on individuals and their agency. One of the hallmarks of the Blair period was the idea that creativity and the creative industries were important. As Terry Flew writes:

> The formal origins of the concept of creative industries can be found in the decision in 1997 by the newly elected British Labour government headed by Tony Blair to establish a Creative Industries Task Force (CITF), as a central activity of its new Department of Culture, Media and Sport (DCMS). The Creative Industries Task Force set about mapping current activity in those sectors deemed to be a part of the UK creative industries, measuring their contribution to Britain's overall economic performance and identifying policy measures that would promote their further development. The Creative Industries Mapping Document, produced by the UK DCMS in 1998, identified the creative industries as constituting a large and growing component of the UK economy, employing 1.4 million people and generating an estimated £60 billion a year in economic value added, or about 5 per cent of total UK national income (DCMS, 1998). (2012, p. 9)

The Blair government, and later the government led by Gordon Brown, insisted that the creative industries were vital to the British economy and its future. Tony Blair was acutely motivated to invest in creativity since, 'our aim must be to create a nation where the creative talents of all the people are used to build a true enterprise economy for the twenty-first century—where we compete on brains, not brawn' (Blair quoted in Flew, 2012, p. 10).

The idea that the creative industries are important economically, underpinned by enterprising or entrepreneurial activity, has spread quickly around the globe (Flew 2018). As Curtin and Sanson indicate 'policymakers began to position their countries as hotspots of the "creative economy," reasoning that intellectual and cultural output had become distinguishing features of the world's wealthiest societies' (Curtin and Sanson, 2016, p. 7). In the light of this claim there have been a number of reports that have attempted to describe and, importantly, quantify the creative industries internationally, nationally, regionally, and locally (e.g. CIIC, 2013; Cox, 2005; Lhermitte et al., 2015; McIntyre et al., 2019; NESTA, 2006; Trembath and Fielding, 2020; Work Foundation, 2007). A broad review of these reports suggests that there is general agreement that, firstly, the creative industries deliver economic value and provide the foundation for other significant sectors; secondly, the creative industries play a key role in innovation and solving problems and challenges; and thirdly, cultural and arts sub-sectors of the creative industries are important in the personal and social lives of people, the development of ideas, and future-shaping.

Despite the ongoing attempts to report on these industries, the lack of a workable operational definition, an agreed nomenclature, and a common taxonomy of sectors, makes comparability between reports difficult. There is also a substantial crossover discernible between the idea of creative, cultural, and copyright industries (Hartley, 2005, pp. 30–31). In general, terminology labelling these industries 'changes across countries, with some referring to the cultural industries, the copyright industries, the digital content industries, and even the cultural and creative industries or—as in China—the cultural creative industries' (Flew, 2012, p. 4).

Despite these issues, as highlighted in our introductory chapter, the United Nations Conference on Trade and Development (UNCTAD) reported in 2008 that international trade in creative industries has shown sustained growth over the preceding decade, with traded creative goods and services (combined) at a record \$547 billion in 2012, as compared with \$302 billion in 2003. They went on to state that:

> Creative industries are among the most dynamic sectors in world trade. Over the period 2000–2005, international trade in creative goods and services experienced an unprecedented average annual growth rate of 8.7 per cent. The value of world exports of creative goods and services reached \$424.4 billion in 2005, representing 3.4 percent of total world trade,

> according to UNCTAD. Nowadays in the most advanced countries, the creative industries are emerging as a strategic choice for reinvigorating economic growth, employment and social cohesion. (UNCTAD, 2008, pp. 4–5)

Contrasted to the UNCTAD position, the figures provided by Marc Lhermitte, Solenne Blanc, and Bruno Perrin, the consultants from Ernst & Young Ltd who compiled the *Cultural Times: The First Global Map of Cultural and Creative Industries* (2015) report for the Confederation of Societies of Authors and Composers, are slightly different. They quoted Irina Bokova, the Director General of UNESCO, who stated that 'capitalising US$2,250 billion and nearly 30 million jobs worldwide, the creative and cultural industries are major drivers of the economies of the developed as well as the developing countries indicating that they are among the most rapidly growing sectors worldwide' (Lhermitte et al., 2015, p. 5).

For countries with emerging powerhouse economies driven by global demographic shifts, like Brazil, Russia, India, and China, *The Creative Industries and The BRICS* (2014) report reviewed the state of the creative economy in each of these countries and was carried out for the Confédération Internationale des Sociétés d'Auteurs et de Compositeurs [International Confederation of Societies of Authors and Composers] (CISAC). The report stated that 'the modern global economy today relies on creativity like never before and the creative economy makes up a growing proportion of national economic output and job creation in many countries around the world' (CISAC, 2014, p. 10). With this as the benchmark, the report declared that there is plenty of untapped potential in the creative industries.

While the idea of the creative industries was developed in the UK, it has been in East Asia where the strongest policy commitments to the creative industries have been made. In the early stages of the 2000s as Lee and Lim (2014) note, there was a shift in cultural policy concerns in East Asian nations toward engagement with the knowledge economy and the creative industries. Growing competition in manufacturing-based developing economies—most notably from China—meant that many East Asian nations identified a need to focus on innovation and creativity as a way of repositioning their increasingly post-industrial economies. At the same time, China moved rapidly to identify the economic benefits of culture and to promote its arts, media, design, and digital content industries, focusing on strategies for what were termed 'cultural creative industries' and 'digital creative industries' (Keane, 2013, pp. 36–43). Lee and Lim saw that these countries were 'taking a top-down, and hands-on approach to the development of their creative economy, regardless of how much bottom up entrepreneurialism is emphasized in the (Western) theory of creative industries' (Lee and Lim, 2014, p. 10).

In the bloc of countries that now constitute Europe, the European Commission had also been active in recognizing, understanding, and promoting their highly valuable creative sector. For example, in the *Innovative Instruments to Facilitate Access to Finance for the Cultural and Creative Sectors (CCS): Good Practice* (2016) report, the European Commission recognized that:

> Cultural and creative industries (CCIs) are, at the dawn of the 21st century, undergoing considerable change as a result of increased digital technologies, the economic crisis of the past several years, and considerable changes in the regulatory framework. Support to CCIs has, likewise, evolved rapidly, witnessing core changes in intellectual property law, increased support through state aid, and a greater recognition of their potential contribution to the economy. Despite the considerable potential of CCIs, estimated to be responsible for over 3% of the EU's gross domestic product and jobs, they remain undervalued and unrecognized, especially in terms of their ability to access start-up capital and financing. The challenges facing CCIs are compounded by a lack of clear evidence and information in the sector, which further limits the ability of financial backers to recognize their potential, as well as other legislative hurdles, such as intellectual property rights, varying tax regimes, and mobility issues. (EC, 2017, online)

In Australia the creative industries, an idea which was largely championed by the Centre for Creative Industries and Innovation at QUT in Brisbane, could be described as operating 'in the context of a small open economy operating unilaterally in an integrated world economy' (Justman, 2013, p. 272). In 2013 the then Federal Minister for Industry stated that:

> Our creative industries give our country a two-fold benefit. As this report shows, these industries contribute more than $90 billion to our economy annually in turnover, add more than $45 billion to GDP and generate annual exports of $3.2 billion. And quite separate is the intangible but undeniable worth of knowing our nation creates great software, films, TV, radio, music, theatre, dance, design, media, writing, marketing and architecture...These agile, sophisticated and digitally savvy businesses and the creative professionals they support are more significant in number than you might expect. In 2011 there were more than 600,000 people working in the

> creative industries in Australia and over 120,000 creative businesses. (CIIC, 2013, p. 5)

For the 2016–2017 period, the creative industries' contribution to national GDP stood at $111.7 billion (BCAR, 2018, p. 5). The NSW state government had also established a Creative Industries Taskforce to 'develop comprehensive strategies to drive growth, innovation and productivity in the NSW creative industries sector' (NSWT&I, 2012). Apart from the international, national, and state level reaction to the actuality and idea of the creative industries at the local level, the Newcastle City Council, for example, also identified the creative industries as central to the new knowledge economy and recognized that 'they are a key element in Newcastle's economic development strategy' (NCC, 2014, p. 38).

In 2015, in his initial statement as the newly elected Liberal Party leader, the future Prime Minister Malcolm Turnbull 'urged Australians to embrace disruption…The Australia of the future has to be a nation that is agile, that is innovative, that is creative' (Turnbull in Thomsen, 2015, online). He urged Australians to embrace 'the disruption that we see driven by technology' (ibid) and treat it like 'our friend if we are agile and smart enough to take advantage of it' (Turnbull in Thomsen, 2015, online). He then set out his plan to strengthen ties between the business community, universities, and scientific institutions by setting up an innovation fund.

> The $1 billion innovation statement is emblematic of how Prime Minister Malcolm Turnbull wants his Government to be defined, political editor Chris Uhlmann writes. A $200 million innovation fund will co-invest in businesses that develop technology from the CSIRO and Australian universities. Money has also been set aside to help students in years 5 and 7 learn coding. Early stage investors in start-up businesses will get a 20 per cent non-refundable tax offset and a capital gains tax exemption…Mr Turnbull said at the launch of the plan inside the CSIRO in Canberra. 'Our innovation agenda is going to help create the modern, dynamic 21st century economy Australia needs'. 'Unlike a mining boom, it is a boom that can continue forever, it is limited only by our imagination, and I know that Australians believe in themselves, I know that we are a creative and imaginative nation'. (Borrello and Keany, 2015, online)

Once this idea from Malcolm Turnbull himself had run its course, he was replaced as prime minister by Scott Morrison who, in an effort to distance himself from Turnbull's policies, downplayed the innovation agenda while ramping up the neoliberal agenda. Tech-led innovation was no longer *de rigeur*. Morrison 'took the local sector by surprise by dumping the Innovation portfolio from cabinet' (Bailey, 2018). However, Victorian state Innovation Minister Philip Dalidakis said, in response, that 'innovation is a way of life, it's a mindset, and encouraging it requires reaching out into lots of different industries and sectors' (quoted in Bailey, 2018). Later in 2020, Scott Morrison lauded tech innovation but not its creation. While he stated that digital technology is 'the biggest game-changer, arguably, the world has ever seen' (Sadler, 2020), he stated that his 'government wants to build an economy where sectors are at the global frontier of technological adaptation' (ibid) and noted that 'the digital economy is central to these tasks, to creating the jobs that Australians need' (ibid). But for many of those working in the creative industries, jobs in the traditional sense have all but disappeared. Curtin and Sanson summarize some of these changes and note that:

> Public policy research has explored ways to nurture a creative economy, but little has been written about the declining labor conditions within those economies. Much has been made of the challenges posed by media conglomeration, but little of it addresses the impact on creative employees and workplace practices. And while researchers have detailed the causes and effects of 'runaway production,' little of this work is framed by a global perspective, nor does it examine possibilities for building transnational labor alliances or regulatory frameworks that will be essential if conditions are to improve. (2016, p. 7)

As McIntyre et al. also note, '[t]here is a rapidly growing trend toward outsourcing, freelancing and the casualisation of the workforce which is having an effect on those who are members of this creative industries precariat' (2019, p. 17). More than a decade ago, Andrew Ross foresaw the precarity of employment in the creative industries:

> [N]o one, not even those in the traditional professions, can any longer expect a fixed pattern of employment in the course of their lifetime, and they are under more and more pressure to anticipate, and prepare for, a future in which they still will be able to compete in a changing marketplace. (2009, p. 2)

Fulton and Balnaves (2013) also noted that the blurring of boundaries across consumption and consumption of cultural goods has meant that creative practitioners must be multi-skilled across a range of areas from telling their stories in different formats and on different platforms, to understanding how to market and distribute those stories, to developing and maintaining an audience. Audience engagement needs to be actively encouraged with interactivity and connectivity, a key characteristic in a converged media environment (Fulton, 2017; McQuail and Deuze, 2020). It is increasingly important to become a 'business of one' (Gershon and Deuze, 2019, p. 297) where self-branding, competition, and contract-to-contract working are seen as the norm:

> Throughout the second half of the twentieth century, a general consensus emerged that people should indeed view themselves as a business—a bundle of skills, assets, qualities, experiences, and relationships that constantly had to be managed and enhanced. (Gershon and Deuze, 2019, p. 299)

Individual workers can, as Curtin and Sanson explain, no longer expect to have a single career nurtured within the arms of a corporate employer:

> instead they must ready themselves for iterative change and persistent contingency as standard employment and its associated entitlements become artifacts of a bygone industrial era. Precarious livelihoods are indicative of a new world order of social and economic instability. (2016, p. 6)

Rosenbaum wrote in 2020 that 'about a third of today's workforce is involved in the gig economy, in which freelancers and part-time contractors work job-to-job with little security and few employment rights' (2020, n.p.). He indicated that 'some are self-employed, while others work gigs on the side' (ibid.). Rosenbaum declared that this is a growing trend:

> A 2018 NPR/Marist poll predicted that contract workers and freelancers could make up half the workforce within the decade. But even as more people derive their income from the gig economy, they still make less than their peers in traditional jobs, according to a Deloitte analysis of more than 10 years' worth of survey data from the U.S. Bureau of Labor Statistics. Companies can save up to 30% by hiring contract workers and, as evolving technology replaces the need for human workers, more full-time jobs are likely to become part-time ones. (Rosenbaum, 2020, n.p.)

At the same time David Craig identified a new breed of creative practitioners:

> For a little over a decade, we have witnessed the rapid rise of creators, alternatively called content creators, influencers, YouTubers, vloggers, liver streamers, gameplayers, KOLS, and Wang Hong (in China). Forbes' annual list of the most successful creators extends across content...These comprise but a small portion of a vast global wave of online cultural producers fostering and blending old and new forms of media entrepreneurialism, management, creative labour, and user practices. (2019, p. 363)

In their book *Handbook on the Digital Creative Economy* (2013), Towse and Handke explained that the process of digitization, which was given a remarkable start with the technological developments of Second World War, has had 'a considerable impact on the creative industries' themselves (2013, p. 1). The advent of digitization transformed 'the way creative works are generated, disseminated and used. Digitization has also enabled the development of new types of creative goods and services' (Towse and Handke, 2013, p. 1). Dayan Thussu also contends that 'with the revolution in digital distribution, a whole range of new revenue earning opportunities have surfaced as the media and telecommunications sectors intersect globally. The expanding bandwidth, coupled with the rapid globalization of fixed and mobile networks, as well as the digitization of content and growing use of personal computers worldwide' (2006, p. 99), has helped 'a multitude of businesses capitalize on emerging markets and also experiment with new commercial products and business models' (Thussu, 2006, p. 99). He went on to suggest that globally active

> Corporations have widened and strengthened their presence worldwide through skilful localisation strategies...as well as 'outsourcing' their work to regional hubs of cultural and creative industries in a digitally linked globe. In the process, they seem to have refigured their hegemony, championing and legitimising the idea of a global free market...With the globalisation of the ideology of neo-liberalism, the market panacea has become a global mantra. (Thussu, 2019, p. xiv)

At the same time 'operatives in the creative industries, by necessity, are "glocally" oriented i.e. they are locally embedded but globally active. As such globalisation and digitisation provide the broad context of play for the creative industries' (McIntyre et al., 2019, p. 18). It is to the way many of these contextual factors have been theorized that we will now turn our attention.

References

Adorno, T., & Horkheimer, M. (1979). The culture industry: Enlightenment as mass deception. In J. Curran, M. Gurevitch, & J. Wollacott (Eds.), *Mass Communication and Society* (pp. 349–383). Verso.

Bailey, M. (2018, August 27). Industry concern as innovation goes missing in Scott Morrison government. *Financial Review*. Retrieved March 1, 2020, from https://www.afr.com/technology/industry-concern-as-innovation-goes-missing-in-scott-morrison-government-20180826-h14ja3

BCAR. (2018). *Cultural and creative activity in Australia 2008–09 to 2016–17*. Bureau of Communications and Arts Research.

Borrello, E., & Keany, F. (2015, July 12). Innovation statement: PM Malcolm Turnbull calls for "Ideas Boom" as he unveils $1b vision for Australia's future. *ABC News*. Retrieved December 12, 2015, from https://www.abc.net.au/news/2015-12-07/pm-malcolm-turnbull-unveils-$1-billion-innovation-program/7006952

Cheng, D., Loris, N., & Kitchen, K. (2019). *China is a paper tiger on rare earth minerals, Issue Brief No. 4968, 13 June 2019*. Heritage Foundation, Asian Studies Center. Retrieved January 14, 2022, from https://www.heritage.org/sites/default/files/2019-07/IB4968.pdf

CIIC. (2013). *Valuing Australia's creative industries: Final report*. Prepared by SGS Economics and Planning for the Creative Industries Innovation Centre. CIIC.

CISAC. (2014). *The creative industries and The BRICS: A Review of the state of the creative economy in Brazil, Russia, India, China and South Africa*. Communications Department of CISAC.

Cox, G. (2005). *Cox review of creativity in business: Building on the UK's strengths*. HM Treasury.

Craig, D. (2019). Creator management in the social media entertainment industry. In M. Deuze & M. Prenger (Eds.), *Making media* (pp. 363–386). University of Amsterdam Press.

Curtin, M., & Sanson, K. (Eds.). (2016). *Precarious creativity: Global media, local labor*. University of California Press.

DCMS. (1998). 'Creative Industries Mapping Documents' UK Department for Digital, Culture, Media & Sport, published 9 April 1998, http://www.creativitycultureeducation.org/creative-industries-mapping-document-1998

Deloitte. (2014). *Harnessing the "Bang": Stories from the digital frontline*. Deloitte Touche Tohmatsu Ltd.

Diamond, J. (1997). *Guns, germs, and steel: The fates of human societies* (1st ed.). W.W. Norton & Co.

EC (2017). *Supporting cultural and creative industries.* European Commission. Retrieved July 21, from https://ec.europa.eu/culture/policy/cultural-creative-industries_en

Flew, T. (2012). *The creative industries: Culture and policy.* Sage.

Flew, T. (2018). *Understanding global media* (2nd ed.). Palgrave Macmillan.

Fulton, J. M. (2017). Media entrepreneurship: Social networking sites, the audience and new media professionals. In J. M. Fulton & P. McIntyre (Eds.), *Creating space in the fifth estate* (pp. 47–60). Cambridge Scholars Publishing.

Fulton, J. M., & Balnaves, M. (2013, July 3–5). Australia and changes in Western media. In T. Lee, K. Trees, & R. Desai (Eds.), *Refereed proceedings of the Australian and New Zealand Communication Association conference: Global networks-global divides: Bridging new and traditional communication challenges*, ISSN 1448-4331, Fremantle, WA.

Gershon, I., & Deuze, M. (2019). A business of one or nurturing the craft: Who are you? In M. Deuze & M. Prenger (Eds.), *Making media* (pp. 297–306). University of Amsterdam Press.

Hartley, J. (Ed.) (2005). *Creative industries.*

Hartley, J., Potts, J., Cunningham, S., Flew, T., Keane, M., & Banks, J. (2013). *Key concepts in creative industries.* Sage.

Havens, T., & Lotz, A. (2016). *Understanding media industries.* Oxford University Press.

Hayek, F. (1944). *The road to serfdom.* George Routledge & Sons.

Hayek, F. (1960). *The constitution of liberty.* University of Chicago Press.

Hesmondhalgh, D. (2006). *The cultural industries* (2nd ed.).

Hesmondhalgh, D. (2019). *The cultural industries* (4th ed.). Sage.

Husserl, E. (1970). *The crisis of European sciences and transcendental philosophy.* Northwestern University Press.

Janeway, W. (2012). *Doing capitalism in the innovation economy.* Cambridge University Press.

Justman, M. (2013). 'The public economics of creativity: Economies of scope in technological infrastructure. In T. Burger-Helmchen (Ed.), *The economics of creativity: Ideas, firms and markets* (pp. 271–280). Routledge.

Keane, M. (2013). 'Creative Industries in China: Art, Design and Media', *China Today Series* (London: Polity Press), http://hdl.handle.net/20.500.11937/42140

Lee, H., & Lim, L. (2014). *Cultural policies in East Asia: Dynamics between the State, arts and creative industries.* Palgrave Macmillan.

Lhermitte, M., Blanc, S., & Perrin, B. (2015). *Cultural times: The first global map of cultural and creative industries.* EYGM Ltd.

Low, N. (1991). *Planning, politics and the state: Political foundations of planning thought*. Unwyn Hyman.
Marx, K. (2007). In F. Engels (Ed.), *Capital: A critique of political economy: The process of capital production, Vol 1 – Part II*. Cosimo Classic.
Mazzucato, M. (2014). *The entrepreneurial State: Debunking public vs. private sector myths*. Anthem Press.
McIntyre, P. (2016). What is the fifth estate and why does it matter?: Digitisation, globalisation, and neoliberalism and their part in the creation of a rapidly changing world. *Communication Research and Practice, 2*(4), 437–450.
McIntyre, P., Balnaves, M., Kerrigan, S., Williams, C., & King, E. (2019). *Creativity and cultural production in the Hunter: An applied ethnographic study of applied entrepreneurial systems in the creative industries: Final report, ARC Grant LP130100348*. University of Newcastle.
McQuail, D., & Deuze, M. (2020). *McQuail's media and mass communication theory*. Sage.
NCC. (2014). *Draft Newcastle economic development strategy*. Michael Connell & Associates Consulting for NCC.
NESTA. (2006). *Creating growth: How the UK can develop world class creative businesses*. NESTA. Retrieved July 23, 2014, from https://www.nesta.org.uk/report/creating-growth/
NFSA. (2016). *The fifth estate: A selective history of the internet in Australia*. National Film and Sound Archive. Retrieved May 3, 2016, from http://www.fromwirelesstoweb.com/
NSWT&I. (2012). *Industry action plans: Creative industries*. NSW Department of Trade and Investment. Retrieved May 30, 2014, from http://www.business.nsw.gov.au/doing-business-in-nsw/industry-action-plans/creative-industries
Rosenbaum, J. (2020, January 13). The role of purpose in the workplace of the future. *Nation Swell*. Retrieved February 23, 2020, from https://nationswell.com/purpose-work-gig-economy-aarp/
Ross, A. (2009). *Nice work if you can get it: Life and labor in precarious times*. New York University Press.
Sadler, D. (2020). Tech adoption not creation: The PM's digital plan. *InnovationAus*. Retrieved January 14, 2022, from https://www.innovationaus.com/tech-adoption-not-creation-the-pms-digital-plan/
Schulz, T. (2015). Tomorrowland: How Silicon Valley shapes our future. *Der Spiegel Online International*. Retrieved February 28, 2016, from http://www.spiegel.de/international/germany/spiegel-cover-story-how-silicon-valley-shapes-our-future-a-1021557.html
Servaes, J. (2015). Studying the global from within the local. *Communication Research and Practice, 1*(3), 242–250.

Smith, A. (2012 [1776]). *An inquiry into the nature and causes of the wealth of nations*. Project Gutenberg Index of files. Retrieved March 25, 2012, from http://www.gutenberg.org/files/3300/

Thomsen, S. (2015, September 15). Turnbull's vision for Australia: "Disruption is our friend". *Business Insider*. Retrieved February 27, 2016, from http://www.businessinsider.com.au/malcolm-turnbull-disruption-is-our-friend-2015-9

Thussu, D. (2006). *International communication: Continuity and change* (2nd ed.). Hodder Arnold.

Thussu, D. (2019). *International communication: Continuity and change* (3rd ed.). Hodder Arnold.

Towse, R., & Handke, C. (Eds.). (2013). *Handbook on the digital creative economy*. Edward Elgar.

Trembath, J., & Fielding, K. (2020). *Pre-release extract, Australia's cultural and creative economy: A 21st century guide*. Produced by A New Approach think tank with lead delivery partner the Australian Academy of the Humanities, Canberra.

UNCTAD. (2008). *Creative economy report 2008*. United Nations Conference on Trade and Development. Retrieved June 27, 2017, from http://unctad.org/creative-economy

Williams, A. (2010). First a data center, now free WiFi: Google, The Cloud and the significance of a small Oregon town. *ReadWriteCloud*, February 12, 2010 1:00 AM. Retrieved March 30, 2011, from http://www.readwriteweb.com/cloud/2010/02/google-and-a-small-town-in-ore.php

Williams, R. (1981). *Culture*. Fontana Press.

Work Foundation. (2007). *Staying ahead: The economic performance of the UK's creative industries*. The Work Foundation.

CHAPTER 3

Theoretical Contexts of Entrepreneurship in the Creative Industries

Having set the scene, as it were, with our prior chapters, this one explores the concept of entrepreneurship by deeply embedding it in its theoretical context, examining it through the development of the political ideology of neoliberalism, and exploring the duality of philosophical, political, and economic oppositions that it resides within.

After the problems of the Great Depression and Second World War, John Maynard Keynes' economic theories (Keynes, 1936, 1940) espoused state intervention to help troubled economies. These ideas were at first very successful. However, this approach to managing economies appears to have led, in the 1970s, to stagflation in some countries and rising unemployment and accelerating inflation in others. What was on offer to solve these crucial economic and social problems were two seemingly oppositional positions. These options included, according to David Harvey, 'social democracy and central planning on the one hand…and the interests of all those concerned with liberating corporate and business power and re-establishing market freedoms on the other' (2005, p. 13). The latter group became known as the neoliberals.

With the post-Second World War Bretton Woods Agreement, Keynesian ideas on the value of government intervention in the economy had come to dominate political thinking, based on the idea that free markets would not, if left unchecked, lead to full employment. At the same time, institutions such as the International Monetary Fund and the World Bank were

P. McIntyre et al., *Entrepreneurship in the Creative Industries*, https://doi.org/10.1007/978-3-031-19455-9_3

being established. Then, in 1947, immediately after the war, The Mont Pelerin Society was also formed. Thinkers like Friedrich Hayek, Karl Popper, Ludwig von Mises, George Sigler, and Milton Friedman were founding members. They came together to strengthen 'the principles and practice of a free society and to study the workings, virtues, and defects of market oriented economic systems' (MPS, 2016, online). The society still meets annually and its members include government officials, Nobel Prize winners, various journalists, and economic, legal, and financial experts from across the globe. It advocates for free expression, free markets, and the idea that private enterprise should replace many government functions. They are an active society.

They have been trying for some time, at the theoretical level, to displace the ideas of Adam Smith, David Ricardo, and, most notably, Karl Marx, that is, any form of economic or political thought alleged to interfere with the individual liberties supposedly manifest in the principles of the free market. Their line can be traced from Smith, as nearly all economists can, to Malthus, to (among others) Jevons, Pareto, and figures such as Milton Friedman. They did hang on to Smith's notion that the invisible hand of the market was the best way to mobilize human behavior, but it was John Maynard Keynes in particular, and his premise that state intervention was necessary to ameliorate the 'boom and bust' cycles typical of unfettered free markets, that neoliberals like Milton Friedman were primarily reacting to. The establishment of Franklin Roosevelt's New Deal, which was implemented as an antidote to the laissez-faire policies that led to the Great Depression and may have been stimulated by Keynes' open letter to Roosevelt proffering advice to him at this time, was seen as part and parcel of the same collectivist ideals that generated the centrally regulated Five Year Plans favored by communist governments. As the years wore on, the neoliberals proved to be implacably opposed to anything that might resemble collectivism. For example, Milton and Rose Friedman wrote in their book *Free to Choose* (1980) that:

> all the movements of the past two decades—the consumer movement, the ecology movement, the back-to-the-land movement, the hippie movement, the organic food movement, the protect-the-wilderness movement, the zero population growth movement, the 'small is beautiful' movement, the anti-nuclear movement—have had one thing in common. All have been anti-growth. They have been opposed to new developments, to industrial innovation, to the increased use of natural resources. (Quoted in Watson, 2000, p. 647)

Peter Watson, in his book *A Terrible Beauty: A History of the People and Ideas That Shaped the Modern Mind*, wrote that the Friedmans believed that the forces for 'rights' had gone too far down the collectivist path (Watson, 2000, p. 647). With Keynes in the ascendant, however, the nascent neoliberals thought their own ideas were doomed. Then in the 1970s, the West began experiencing crippling stagflation and, coupled with the Oil Embargo from OPEC states, many countries moved into recession. It seemed at that point that Keynesian economic thinking and its practical application had had its day. The first government to take neoliberal ideas seriously, under advice from Milton Friedman, was that of Augusto Pinochet's in Chile. We can see historically the effects that the adoption of these ideas had on that country but, despite the evident problems, neoliberal thinking was quickly picked up all over the world. As well as the more famous influence of Milton Freidman on the Thatcher and Reagan administrations in Britain and the USA respectively, these adoptions included the Australian polity as well, where, according to Jonathan Swarts in *Constructing Neoliberalism: Economic Transformation in Anglo-American Democracies* (2013), they were introduced into this country's fortunes primarily by the Labor Party and taken up wholeheartedly by all parties after the Labor Party's long electoral successes. It is during this period that the neoliberals 'discover and redefine the work of Joseph Schumpeter' (Plehwe & Mills, 2012, online).

Herbert Giersch, one of Germany's eminent neoliberal economists and then president of the Mont Pelerin Society, declared the new age of Schumpeterian thinking. It was to replace the age of Keynesian thinking but Schumpeter was, of course, no friend of neoliberalism. Giersch had to play an intellectual trick to make him so:

> he nominally adopted Schumpeter's concept of entrepreneurship and dynamism whilst divorcing it from Schumpeter's commitment to macroeconomic innovation. Giersch's entrepreneur then is an average guy. He follows von Mises who declared every person to be an entrepreneur if he or she carries responsibility. In this way, every dependent employee is easily turned into a self-employed entrepreneur. You can even redefine an unemployed youth as an entrepreneur, alone and fully responsible for his own fate! (Plehwe & Mills, 2012, online)

However, over his life's work, Schumpeter (e.g. 1994 [1942]) hadn't quite argued that. He had argued, initially, that innovation and change come from entrepreneurs, firstly focusing on what he identified as wild-spirited individuals—*unternehmergeist*—implicitly agreeing with a widespread Romantic understanding of how creativity and innovation were thought to come about. He quickly scaled up his thinking. Based on the evidence he was seeing, he had to accommodate himself to the idea that what we call meta-structural entities such as big business organizations, institutions, and corporations were possibly the major drivers of innovation, having the necessary capital to finance entrepreneurial change. He also saw, at an even larger mega-structural scale, that long-term economic cycles, such as those suggested by Kondraitev and others, were driven by innovation and, at exactly the same time, these innovations were also expressions of those cycles. As Brian Arthur, a recipient of the International Schumpeter Prize in Economics and the inaugural Lagrange Prize in Complexity Science, remarked:

> Only when we observe over decades do we see the arrangements and processes that form the economy coming into being, interacting, and collapsing back again. Only in the longer reaches of time do we see this continual creation and re-creation of the economy. (Arthur, 2009, p. 194)

The simple argument being put by the advocates of Schumpeterian economic thinking is that 'the economic order evolves because of the disruptive actions of entrepreneurs' (Hartley et al., 2013, p. 94). However, Schumpeter thought there may also be more complex forces at work. Capitalism must be understood in evolutionary terms, where continual innovation is endemic to it as a dynamically evolving system with no end point to its evolutionary process in sight. Drawing on Marx, without being as teleological as him, Schumpeter argued that the fundamental attribute of capitalism as it evolves was the 'perennial gale of creative destruction' (1994 [1942], p. 84), where each innovation in economic life destroys the old order to make way for a new one. While this process may necessitate the unshackling of these forces in a cycle of bust and boom, Schumpeter accepted that 'recognising the "engine's" fragility assists fundamentally in securing an ongoing role for the state and for government policymaking' (Hartley et al., 2013, p. 52), especially as markets fail as they do regularly and consistently.

Much of this thinking has been encapsulated in what has often been referred to as Schumpeter Mark I and Mark II. We discern for the first period that this was largely characterized by an agent-centered position, which is why neoliberals like Giersch were in favor of it. The second accounted for the influence of structural entities like organizations and institutions as well as the much broader evolutionary structures at play in any economy as innovation interacts with it. At a superficial level, Mark I and Mark II thinking may seem self-exclusive, but they are likely to be much more complementary than Schumpeter or his adherents at first realized. In this case, a brief examination of the notion of complementarity, a prime characteristic of systems, is in order.

To get there we need to understand that the world is often commonly divided by humans into what Kelso and Engstrøm (2006) call contraries or oppositions. These include, for example:

> the discrete and the continuous, the individual and the collective, the orderly and the random, the qualitative and the quantitative, the internal and the external, the persistent and the changing, the gradual and the abrupt, the reductionist and the holist—and yes, the certain and the uncertain. (Kelso, 2020, p. 78)

There are many more, as humans have tended to understand their world using a great deal of these oppositions or either/or dichotomies, and seen them as though they are mutually exclusive. Yet, the nature of complementarity 'says that two opposing tendencies are complementary and do coexist at the same time' (Kelso, 2020, p. 84). For our purposes, we could say, for example, that agency and structure are often seen as mutually exclusive. Agency is related to the ability to make choices, and the possession of enough free will to do so, while structures are those things that are thought to determine our action. This pair, agency and structure, appears at first glance to be mutually opposed to each other, but in reality they support and reinforce each other. We will pick this precise point up again in more detail in the next chapter, but for now we want to point out that, for many of the oppositions that have, in many ways, defined the latter half of the twentieth century and on into the twenty-first—'a world replete with either/or dichotomies' (Kelso, 2020, p. 83)—many of these pairs are 'inextricably related, yet each may retain their singular character' (ibid.). There are many such pairs but for now the following will suffice to illustrate the idea:

Capitalism	v	Communism
Free Market	v	Planned Economy
Democracy	v	Totalitarianism

Freedom	v	State Control
The Individual	v	The Collective
Free Will	v	Determinism
Agency	v	Structure

All of these seeming opposites were manifest in the twentieth-century world as part of the Cold War, an undeclared war which was played out between, primarily, the USA and its allies and the USSR and its allies. This way of seeing the world, as a set of rigidly opposed and mutually exclusive forces, meant it was the case that a choice often had to be made between either one or the other points of view.

So, let us briefly track our way down the path of structuralist thought, by way of Marx, and then backtrack down the path of agent-centered thinking, particularly manifest through phenomenological thinking. This exercise should, hopefully, enable us to see more clearly which path neo-liberalism was predominantly trekking on as it moved toward the future.

Structuralism proposes that surface events can be explained by looking at the underlying structures involved. It seeks to expose the underlying patterns believed to be the foundation of all societies and cultures. It is big picture oriented, as it explores the conceptual underpinnings of the world we live in. Structuralist thinkers, among many others, include Sigmund Freud, Ferdinand de Saussure, and, for our purposes, Karl Marx.

In simple terms, Marx (2007 [1867]) argued that it is the material factors in society which determine the way we think. He rejected Hegel's notion that thought or ideas drove history in a dialectical process but kept Hegel's basic idea, inverting the cause and the effect, thus coming up with the process he called dialectical materialism. The largely deterministic structure Marx proposed to reveal this process was seen in his base/superstructure model. For him it is primarily the material and economic forces in society that form the base of that society and it is these forces that drive change.

The base is made up of three levels. These are, firstly, the conditions of production, that is the climate, geography, and raw materials each society has access to. These conditions of production not only determine the type of production undertaken in a society but also the nature of the society itself and the way the people in that society think. Secondly, there are the means of production, that is, the society's various kinds of equipment, tools, and machinery, as well as the raw materials to be found there, which spring from the available conditions of production. For Marx, the next level of the base could be identified in those who owned the means of production. The division of labor, or the distribution of work and ownership, was what he called society's production relations. Marx was convinced that whoever owns the means of production controls the ideas of a society:

> the class which is the ruling material force of society, is at the same time its ruling intellectual force. The class which has the means of material production at its disposal, has control at the same time over the means of mental production, so that thereby, generally speaking, the ideas of those who lack the means of mental production are subject to it. (Marx & Engels, 2022 [1846])

The superstructure, on the other hand, which like a house was built on top of the base, could be seen in the modes of thinking a society espouses, what kind of political institutions arise there, which laws it has, and what there is of religion, morals, art, philosophy, and science. All of these are reflections of the material base. Marx was convinced that the superstructure could not exist independently of the base, but the material base did not just govern the superstructure; it operated in relation to it. Marx saw a process of interaction between the base and the superstructure in terms of a dialectic relation, hence the term 'dialectical materialism'.

With this structure in place, Marx then began to pursue the idea that the phases of history were predictably similar. He saw there was always a conflict between two dominant classes of society, dependent on the type of society involved. For the slave societies of antiquity, the antagonists were the free citizens and slaves, for feudal societies they were the feudal lord and their serfs, for the agrarian or pre-industrial ones the conflict was between the aristocrats and citizens. Once societies developed into a bourgeois or capitalist mode, the conflict was between capitalists and the workers or proletariat. The structural proposition was that the conflict was always between those who own the means of production versus those who don't, and since the ruling class does not voluntarily relinquish their power, change can only come about through revolution. He predicted that societies would inevitably move beyond capitalism and become communally or collectively oriented.

Louis Althusser, who was involved in a later re-reading of Marx, coined the term *ideological state apparatus* to describe the ideological role the media, and by extension the creative industries, play in a capitalist society. Antonio Gramsci refined these ideas. He argued, like Marx, that:

> Military force was not necessarily the best instrument to retain power for the ruling classes, but that a more effective way of wielding power was to build consent by ideological control of cultural production and distribution. According to Gramsci, such a system exists when a dominant social class exerts moral and intellectual leadership over both allied and subordinate classes through its control of such institutions as schools, religious bodies and mass media. (Thussu, 2019, p. 52)

This dominant group not only requires consent but educates the people it governs toward this consent until it appears to be the 'natural' order—this is called establishing hegemony. This notion of hegemony is 'widely used to conceptualize political functions of the mass media in propagating and maintaining the dominant ideology' (Thussu, 2019, p. 53). This fundamental idea also underpinned the work of the Frankfurt School of critical theorists.

Phenomenologists, however, largely rejected deterministic views of this type. They opted for another more subjectivist, agent-centered, and less deterministically oriented one. They wanted to understand humanities perception of phenomena, the sensory data available to humans, as it presented itself to us in our own subjective experience. They wanted knowledge derived primarily from the experiences and perceptions held first-hand by individuals, rather than the real or noumenal objects themselves. How the individual experiences or understands the object they are consciously engaging with or directing their attention to is the ground of meaning given to that object. Following on from Franz Brentano's (1995 [1874]) work on intentionality and consciousness and Wilhelm Wundt's (2016 [1874]) proposition that introspection—formally examining our own mental states—was a valid method for research, Edmund Husserl (1962 [1913]) set the framework for this approach by insisting that one could examine the content of consciousness and arrive at the essential immediacy of a person's experience. He was thus deeply interested in the subjective experience of the individual agent and believed it could be described objectively. In short, Husserl's argument held that one could know the objective content of subjective acts of consciousness—of perceptual experience. His quest was for the essence of an individual's consciousness.

Martin Heidegger, one of Husserl's former students, took matters further. He believed that looking for the essence of consciousness would lead us to an even deeper question; that is, what is the nature of being? Heidegger (2008 [1927]) had argued that, as humans, we are not wholly constrained by our thinking about the world but by our own mortal being. This question led him to the idea of a fundamental ontology, raising the idea of what makes us real, a question at the core of our existence as humans. Our existence is compared to non-existence or, in Heidegger's terms, 'nothingness'. But being or existing in the world, what he called 'dasein', was not quite the same thing as being conscious of the world. For Heidegger, a human being's existence in the world is made up of the choices they make. Who we are, our being, is made up of the totality of these choices. If the decisions we make are forced on us, rather than coming from our own free choices, then we must be acting inauthentically. It follows that if we assume the roles society pushes us toward, then we are also acting inauthentically.

While Jean-Paul Sartre (2018 [1943]) was also concerned with authenticity, his existential phenomenology was grounded in the idea that the universe is primarily absurd, having no essential design given to it by an almighty God figure who holds it all together. If this is the case, there can also be no such thing as an essential human nature manufactured according to this universal and all-pervasive plan. For Sartre, this situation, one where existence precedes essence, can only lead to the idea that we must accept that we are our own personal projects, self-made through our own personal choices. With this realization comes ultimate freedom and ultimate responsibility—responsibility for ourselves and our choices. Drawing on his own experiences in the French Resistance during Second World War, Sartre argued that we cannot, in all good faith, slip into pre-ordained social roles and use these as excuses for our life decisions, but we must take full responsibility for our choices and live accordingly. This was the only authentic existence one could have.

It's not surprising then that this phenomenological approach, particularly Husserl's argument that an individual human is a free, self-determining being who exists in a state of rational subjectivity, was an important theoretical precursor to neoliberalism, as it tended to emphasize individual agency over what can be seen as collectivist and deterministic structures. According to Glendinning, liberal political thought, a forerunner to neoliberalism, had aimed 'to optimize opportunities for free performance in different and autonomous domains of human life' (2015, p. 4). In this case, 'power should aim to organise the social world in such a way that each person's capacity freely to perform (if and where proper) in each of these domains is optimised' (Glendinning, 2015, p. 5). Thus, the neoliberals aligned themselves with a way of thought that idealized free will and free choice. This situation had its advantages. As David Harvey makes clear:

> For any way of thought to become dominant a conceptual apparatus has to be advanced that appeals to our intuitions and instincts, to our values and our desires, as well as the possibilities inherent in the social world we inhabit. If successful, this conceptual apparatus becomes so embedded in common sense as to be taken for granted and not open to question. The founding figures of neoliberal thought took political ideals of human dignity and individual freedom as fundamental, as 'the central values of civilization'. In so doing they chose wisely, for these are indeed compelling and seductive ideals. These values, they held, were threatened not only by fascism, dictatorships, and communism, but by all forms of state intervention that substituted collective judgements for those of individuals free to choose. Concepts of dignity and individual freedom are powerful and appealing in their own right...these ideals appeal to anyone who values the ability to make decisions for themselves. (Harvey, 2005, p. 5)

Unfortunately, the pragmatics of the neoliberal program, operating under the cover of an appealing set of utopian ideals centered on an individual's freedom, worked mainly to safeguard the freedoms of businesses, assuming that if business did well all would benefit. This pragmatic program, rather than the utopian ideal of neoliberalism, came to dominate, seeking the privatization of all industries including education, public services, the media, manufacturing, transportation, finance, construction, the military, and so on, as well as market deregulation, abolition of trade barriers, a flat tax system, freeing the labor market through abolishing the collective right to strike, and the promotion of an entrepreneurial spirit centered on creative action, in order to innovate and move an economy forward in an unending process of growth. Despite the promotion of individual freedoms, the neoliberals argue that these diminutions of collective activity are all necessary actions for the creation of individual wealth. It is noteworthy that Margaret Thatcher, UK prime minister and an early implementer of this neoliberal program, declared that there was no such thing as society (McSmith, 2011).

While this notion may be true conceptually and somewhat naive, society being argued to be a simple abstraction rather than a concrete object, there is more to all of this than that easy political slogan offers. As Pierre Bourdieu was to assert, agency, the ability to make choices for ourselves, was always and everywhere, contingent on the structures humans inhabit and which also inhabit them. In short, we argue that there is a complementarity to what appear to be binary opposites—free markets and planned economies, the individual and the collective, free will and determinism, agency and structure. For us the notion of complementarity rises to the challenge of describing how either/or thinking obscures the in-between dynamic realities that constitute life itself and in turn how these realities rest on complementary rather than oppositional pairs. To uncover this further, the ideas presented by Pierre Bourdieu (1977, 1993, 1996) on cultural production are coupled here with the systems model of creativity developed by Mihaly Csikszentmihalyi (1988, 1999, 2014), which allows us to apply a solid theoretical framework to this investigation into how entrepreneurship works. With this framework at our disposal, we harness the structural possibilities offered by the historical, social, cultural, economic, and political contexts they work within, reveal what they can bring to this endeavor from their own background and personal attributes, and see what strength can be gained from developing a strong social network. While remnants of Romanticism still exist within the creative industries, we argue that successful creative practitioners such as those included as exemplar entrepreneurs in the third part of this book understand and embrace the structures and contexts that enable and constrain their own creative agency.

References

Arthur, B. (2009). *The nature of technology: What it is and how it evolves*. Free Press.

Bourdieu, P. (1977). *Outline of a theory of practice*. Cambridge University Press.

Bourdieu, P. (1993). *Field of cultural production*. Columbia University Press.

Bourdieu, P. (1996). *The rules of art: Genesis and structure of the literary field*. Polity Press.

Brentano, F. (1995 [1874]). *Psychology from an empirical standpoint*. Routledge.

Csikszentmihalyi, M. (1988). Society, culture, and person: A systems view of creativity. In R. Sternberg (Ed.), *The nature of creativity: Contemporary psychological perspectives* (pp. 325–329). Cambridge University Press.

Csikszentmihalyi, M. (1999). Implications of a systems perspective for the study of creativity. In R. Sternberg (Ed.), *Handbook of creativity* (pp. 313–335). Cambridge University Press.

Csikszentmihalyi, M. (2014). *The systems model of creativity: The collected works of Mihaly Csikszentmihalyi*. Springer.

Friedman, M., & Friedman, R. (1980). *Free to choose*. Harcourt Press.

Glendinning, S. (2015). Varieties of neoliberalism. *Graduate Faculty Philosophy Journal, 36*(2), 2–27.
Hartley, J., Potts, J., Cunningham, S., Flew, T., Keane, M., & Banks, J. (2013). *Key concepts in creative industries.* Sage.
Harvey, D. (2005). *A brief history of neoliberalism.* Oxford University Press.
Heidegger, M. (2008 [1927]). *Being and time.* Harper Perennial.
Husserl, E. (1962 [1913]). *Ideas: General introduction to pure phenomenology* (B. Gibson, Trans.). Macmillan.
Kelso, S. (2020). The complementary nature of coordination dynamics: Toward a science of the in-between. In R. McDaniel Jr. & D. Driebe (Eds.), *Uncertainty and surprise in complex systems* (pp. 77–85). Springer.
Kelso, S., & Engstrøm, D. (2006). *The complementary nature.* MIT Press.
Keynes, J. M. (1936). *The general theory of employment, interest and money.* Palgrave Macmillan.
Keynes, J. M. (1940). *How to pay for the war: A radical plan for the Chancellor of the Exchequer.* Macmillan & Co.
Marx, K. (2007 [1867]). *Capital: A critique of political economy: The process of capital production* (Vol. 1). Cosimo Classic.
Marx, K., & Engels, F. (2022 [1846]). *The German ideology: Critique of modern German philosophy according to its representatives Feuerbach, B. Bauer and Stirner, and of German Socialism according to its various prophets.* Watkins/Penguin.
McSmith, A. (2011). *No such thing as society: A history of Britain in the 1980s.* Constable & Robinson.
MPS. (2016). *Home.* The Mont Pelerin Society. Retrieved August 21, 2016, from https://www.montpelerin.org/
Plehwe, D., & Mills, T. (2012). *Defending capitalism: The rise of the neoliberal thought collective (Part 2).* New Left Project. Retrieved February 6, 2016, from http://www.newleftproject.org/index.php/site/article_comments/defending_capitalism_the_rise_of_the_neoliberal_thought_collective_part_2
Sartre, J. P. (2018 [1943]). *Being and nothingness: An essay in phenomenological ontology.* Routledge.
Schumpeter, J. (1994 [1942]). *Capitalism, socialism and democracy.* Routledge.
Swarts, J. (2013). *Constructing neoliberalism: Economic transformation in Anglo-American democracies.* University of Toronto Press.
Thussu, D. (2019). *International communication: Continuity and change* (3rd ed.). Hodder Arnold.
Watson, P. (2000). *A terrible beauty: A history of the people and ideas that shaped the modern mind.* Phoenix.
Wundt, W. (2016 [1874]). *Principles of physiological psychology.* Wentworth Press.

CHAPTER 4

Systems of Creative Industries Entrepreneurship: A Framework

The previous chapters have provided a macro context for understanding creative industries entrepreneurship, both in spatiotemporal terms and in relation to ideas that helped theories develop about it. It is now time to bring that contextual work down in scale, to set out a very specific and useful theoretical framework we can apply to the pragmatics of entrepreneurship in the creative industries. It will help us understand and act on the way individual agents are both enabled and constrained—that is, constrabled (Criticos, 2021; Kerrigan et al., 2021)—by the structures of the creative industries system. It will help explain how creative practice works within those systemic structures. In setting it out here in this chapter, we introduce you, the reader, to a usable concept of the social field; the importance of individual decision-making agents who should be cognizant of the power structures that operate in that field; and how cultural knowledge, skills, and techniques are crucially important to gaining an income through being successful entrepreneurs in the creative industries. In other words, we are going to provide a well thought-out, evidence-based explanation of how you, as a choice-making entity, negotiate a place in the sociocultural systems you want to, or currently do, work in.

Anthony Giddens (1979), advisor to Tony Blair's UK government, asserted that a social system is 'simply a pattern of relations that exists over a period of time and space' (Haralambos & Holbern, 2013, p. 985). To understand a social system and the patterns of relations between the

P. McIntyre et al., *Entrepreneurship in the Creative Industries*,
https://doi.org/10.1007/978-3-031-19455-9_4

people it contains, as well as the ways of life that a particular society engages in and the symbolic artefacts it produces—that is, its culture—two things need to be understood: firstly, the ability of individuals to freely choose, that is, enact human agency; and, secondly, some understanding of the determining structures those individuals exist within. Both, in combination, lead to a sense of how practice works within creative industries and how and why things are done in the way they are in those industries. Pierre Bourdieu's work on cultural production provides us with a very practical way to do that, and then we will link this work to Mihaly Csikszentmihalyi's views on how creativity and innovation, central elements to being an entrepreneur in the creative industries, work.

Pierre Bourdieu's theory of practice, according to David Swartz, 'may be seen as a probing reflection on one of the oldest problems in the Western intellectual tradition, namely, the relationship between the individual and society' (1997, p. 96), or, to put it another way, the relationship between free will and determinism or agency and structure: the ability to make choices and those things that predispose actions. Bourdieu himself stated that 'all of my thinking started from this point: how can behavior be regulated without being the product of obedience to rules?' (in Swartz, 1997, p. 95). As Randall Johnson explains:

> Bourdieu sought to develop a concept of agent free from the voluntarism and idealism of subjectivist accounts and a concept of social space free from the deterministic and mechanistic causality inherent in many objectivist approaches. (Johnson in Bourdieu, 1993, p. 4)

In pursuing these ideas, Bourdieu concluded that agency and structure are not diametrically opposed but are intimately linked. They are, in fact, not opposed to each other at all but are, from our point of view, another case of a complementary pair at work (Kelso & Engstrøm, 2006). Schirato and Yell, summarizing Bourdieu's conclusion, stated:

> Bourdieu, reading across both approaches simultaneously, insists that practice is always informed by a sense of agency (the ability to understand and control our own actions), but that the possibilities of agency must be understood in terms of cultural trajectories, literacies and dispositions. (1996, p. 148)

What Bourdieu is saying is that those larger structures we engage with—the social and cultural world, the language we use, the political, environmental, technological worlds entrepreneurs must interact with—all have some impact on the decisions that we as creative practitioners make. It is the interplay between structure and agency that makes that creative practice possible. Bourdieu coined the term *habitus* to provide an explanation for the interdependency of structure and agency seen in creative and cultural practice. Habitus is defined as:

> ...a 'feel for the game', a 'practical sense' (*sens pratique*) that inclines agents to act and react in specific situations in a manner that is not always calculated and that is not simply a question of conscious obedience to rules. Rather it is a set of dispositions which generates practices and perceptions. The habitus is the result of a long process of inculcation, beginning in early childhood, which becomes a 'second sense' or a second nature. (Johnson in Bourdieu, 1993, p. 5)

As such habitus is a term that deals with the way people 'like to be' and accounts for their preferences, their tastes, values, desires, and ideas they express and the narratives they hold to. These of course are produced by their family, religion, class, gender, education, and the social institutions they engage with, as well as the broader society and culture they exist in. Given the inculcation that is involved, we can say that people develop a long-term way of seeing themselves and others that is unique to them but shared by many others. In simple terms, habitus consists of knowledge about the world, a disposition or inclination to do things in a certain way, a set of tendencies in problem solving and in how to resolve conflict, and in our unconscious desires, which are manifest in the way we talk, the way we dress, and the mannerisms we adopt, along with our cultural taste. All of these come about partly because of the structures that have been absorbed by the agent, who is therefore disposed to act in certain ways.

Habitus is one part of Bourdieu's cultural production model, a model that includes several other elements: various forms of capital, a field of works, and fields themselves. Fields are structured social situations governed by a set of objective social relations. They are characterized by relations between agents, which are always in flux. A field is thus dynamic: 'a change in agent's positions necessarily entails a change in the field's structure' (Johnson in Bourdieu, 1993, p. 6). Bourdieu described a field as an 'arena of social contestation where struggles for dominance take place' (Swartz, 1997, p. 117). They are dynamic spaces which 'denote arenas of production, circulation and appropriation of goods, services, knowledge, or status, and the competitive positions held by actors in their struggle to accumulate and monopolize...different kinds of capital' (Swartz, 1997, p. 117).

Given that competition and struggle are central to Bourdieu's thinking on fields, the use of capital within fields can be seen as the pivot point around which power relationships resolve themselves within that field. However, this is not a simple process as, for Bourdieu, there are crucial distinctions to be made between various forms of capital including economic, cultural, social (Bourdieu, 1986), and symbolic capital (Johnson in Bourdieu, 1993). To simplify these, *in extremis* these forms of capital consist of the possession of cash, skills, contacts, and experience. There are, of course, critical distinctions to be made between these various forms of capital but it can also be demonstrated that there is a crucial interplay at work between them.

Economic capital can be described as the money, the *cash* and assets an individual agent amasses throughout their lifetime. For Bourdieu, economic capital is 'immediately and directly convertible into money and may be institutionalised in the form of property rights' (1986, p. 243). In terms of the creative industries, assets include the possession of intellectual property rights, which in turn underpin the structure of many sectors in these industries, such as the music, television, publishing, and filmmaking sectors.

Cultural capital 'is convertible, on certain conditions, into economic capital' (Bourdieu, 1986, p. 284) but consists of an understanding of how the culture of a field works, that is, an acquired knowledge of the intellectual artifacts and the way of life pertinent to a particular culture. This requires a certain level of cultural literacy. This ability to read and decipher cultural clues consists of formally and informally acquired *skills* used in 'deciphering cultural relations and cultural artefacts' (Johnson in Bourdieu, 1993, p. 7). It is 'what an individual knows and understands about the field, including the knowledge and skills required to work successfully' (Fulton, 2019, p. 70), whether that is within a national culture or a professional work culture pertinent to a creative field.

Social capital, according to Bourdieu, is 'made up of social obligations (connections)' (1986, p. 284), 'contacts and networks with well-placed individuals' (Grenfell, 2004, p. 28), which, again, can be converted to economic capital. According to Schugurensky (2008), it consists of 'all actual or potential resources linked to possession of a durable network of more or less institutionalised relationships of mutual acquaintance or recognition (connections to certain individuals and groups)' (Schugurensky, 2008, online). It is an asset which 'provides tangible advantages to those individuals, families or groups that are better connected' (Schugurensky, 2008, online) and entails an understanding of how the social order works and how to use that knowledge to advantage. It is the power derived from knowing crucial players in the game, how important and skilled they are, and who is best to contact in various situations as these develop and change within a dynamic field. As an entrepreneur, a reliable and complex network of *contacts* can often be the difference between entrepreneurial success or failure.

Randall Johnson indicates that *symbolic capital* addresses the degree of 'accumulated prestige, celebrity or honor' (in Bourdieu, 1993, p. 7) one acquires and also displays within a field. It is reputational. It can be seen in awards, prizes, and other markers of prestige that are recognized by the field. It can be seen in gold records or the possession of an Oscar or a Pulitzer Prize. One's professional *curriculum vitae* also acts as a form of symbolic capital, since it demonstrates, or symbolizes, the level of *experience* one has in the relevant field.

Each of those forms of capital can be used to 'trade' in the field, and possession of capital gives a person a certain degree of power. For example, those with a high degree of cultural capital generally govern what constitutes taste within a society. The distinctions one makes between objects, between one song, one film, one book or another, are founded on a dialectic of knowledge (connaissance) and recognition (reconnaissance). We make distinctions and judgements based on what we know about and recognize in works we encounter. In making these distinctions we tend to overvalue our own tastes, and as a consequence, we generally see as valuable or authentic the things we ourselves value (Bourdieu, 1984).

Bourdieu also asserts that the possibility of action occurs within, or is produced in, a *space of works* (sometimes called a field of works). The space/field of works consists of all the accumulated cultural work done by all actors to this time in a particular field. According to Jason Toynbee (2000), it also includes techniques and codes of production. The space of works is thus made up of every cultural product ever produced and, as seen in the works themselves, also the techniques used in producing those artefacts. As an example, for filmmaking it includes every film ever made and embedded in all those films are the techniques used in making them, such as shot types, camera angles, lighting effects, set decoration, and soundtracks, which provide the tools for action. In this case, we can see that 'the heritage accumulated by collective work presents itself to each agent as a space of possibles, that is as an ensemble of probable *constraints* which are the condition and counterpart of a set of *possible uses*' (Bourdieu, 1996, p. 235). It presents itself to each agent as a space of what it is possible to do (Bourdieu, 1996, pp. 234–239).

From all of this, we can say that:

> [I]t is the interplay between a *field [space] of works* which presents possibilities of action to an individual who possesses the necessary *habitus*, partially composed of personal levels of *social, cultural, symbolic and economic capital* that then inclines them to act and react within particular structured and dynamic spaces called *fields*. (McIntyre, 2009, p. 161)

As demonstrated in Fig. 4.1, an agent that has a particular idiosyncratic habitus has access to and learns from a space of works, and interacts with

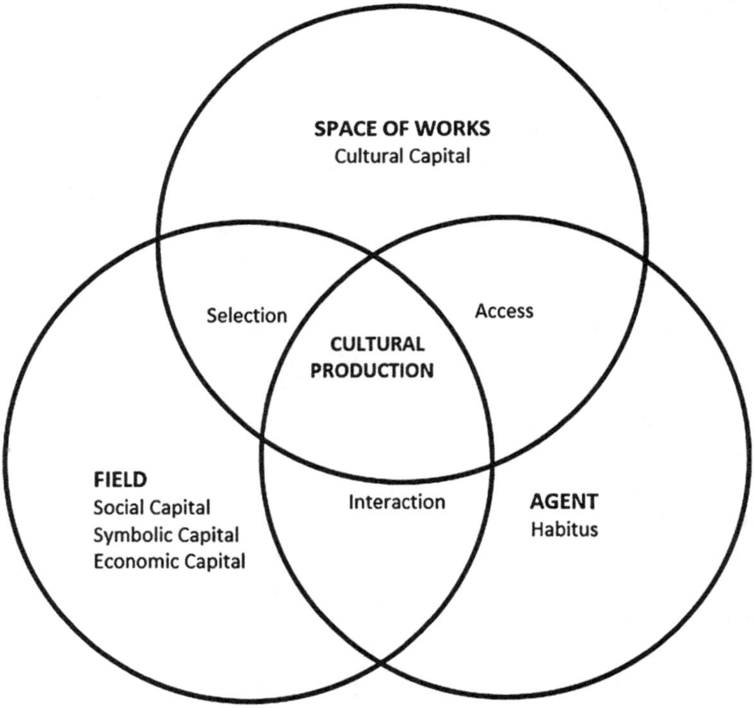

Fig. 4.1 A representation of Pierre Bourdieu's ideas on cultural production (McIntyre, 2021, p. 8)

a field that selects a developed cultural product to include in the space of works. It is the intersection of all those themes, and the interplay between them, that allows creative practice to actually occur. It both enables and constrains creative and innovative action. This interplay is evident across all professions in the creative industries.

Arguments have been made elsewhere (e.g. McIntyre, 2008a, 2008b, 2011; McIntyre & Thompson, 2021) that there is a close correspondence between Bourdieu's ideas on cultural production (1984, 1993, 1996) and the systems model of creativity developed by Mihaly Csikszentmihalyi (1988, 1997, 1999, 2014). Csikszentmihalyi's initial model has been modified a number of times, but for the Revised Systems Model of Creativity developed by Susan Kerrigan (2013), as demonstrated in Fig. 4.2, creative practice occurs when an agent with an idiosyncratic background learns from a domain of works, develops a creative contribution, and presents it to a field of experts, and that contribution is confirmed by that field as creative and appropriate. If selected by the field as novel, the

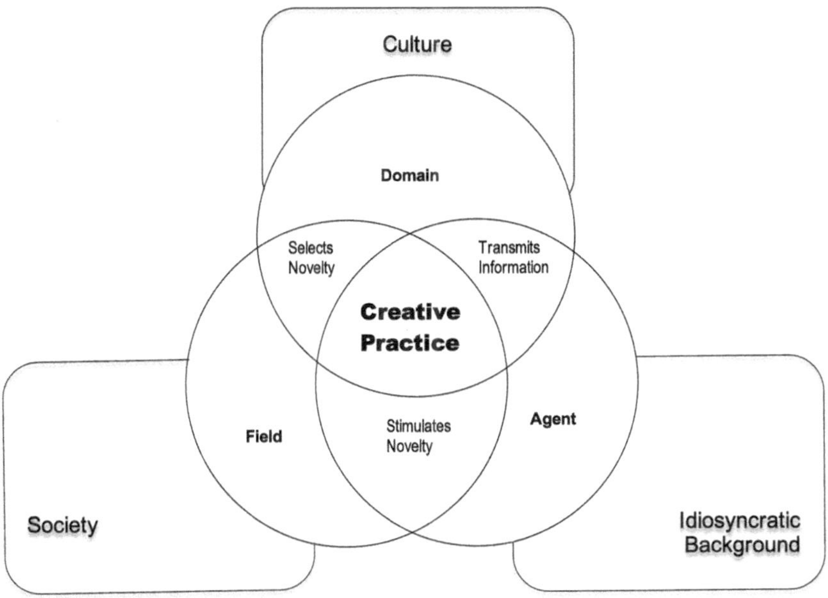

Fig. 4.2 Revised systems model of creativity incorporating creative practice (Kerrigan, 2022)

creative contribution is included in the domain for future generations to use in their practice and the process continues. The model provides a simplified explanation of 'how culture transmits information to an individual, a society stimulates an individual's novelty and a social group is then able to select the novelty offered by the individual via the community' (Kerrigan, 2011, p. 11).

It is the interaction of these elements, summarized as a system consisting of a field, domain, and agent, that provides the ideal environment for creative practice and innovation to emerge, and, by extension, entrepreneurialism.

The domain element of the systems model 'consists of a set of symbolic rules and procedures' (Csikszentmihalyi, 1997, p. 27) that an individual agent engages with. This description has been expanded by Sawyer to include, in a similar vein to Bourdieu's notion of the space of works, 'all of the created products that have been accepted by the field in the past' (Sawyer, 2012, p. 216). In early writing on creativity, Csikszentmihalyi (1988) made the point that without an understanding of what has gone before, what is stored in a domain of knowledge, an individual would find it difficult to produce a variation and members of the field would have nothing to compare that variation to, confirming the idea that nothing occurs in a vacuum, as both Csikszentmihalyi (1999, pp. 314–315) and Bourdieu according to Johnson (in Bourdieu, 1993, p. 6) have asserted.

What an individual agent brings to the system is their background, a set of personal attributes and their own motivations for creating work, as well as an understanding of the domain of knowledge and their take on the 'criteria of selection, the preferences of the field' (Csikszentmihalyi, 1997, p. 47). The individual immerses themselves in the domain, learning the structures, the rules and procedures, and produces a variation. This variation is then presented to the field, a group that is knowledgeable to varying degrees in the domain, for judgment and possible acceptance into the domain for future generations of creators to learn from and adapt their work to.

For Csikszentmihalyi, the field, similar in many ways to Bourdieu's formulation of the field, is the social element in the creative system. He notes that the field has 'the power to determine the structure of the domain. Its major function is to preserve the domain as it is, and its secondary function is to help it evolve by a judicious selection of new content' (1990, p. 206). In other words, the field interacts with the individual and the domain as a necessary but not sufficient part of the system, demonstrating the system's circular causality and, thus, nonlinearity. The field is defined in this system as the social structure that 'selects from the variations produced by individuals those that are worth preserving' (1988, p. 325). Members of a field include 'experts in a given domain whose job involves passing judgment on performance in that domain' (Csikszentmihalyi, 1997, p. 42) and, according to Sawyer (2012), these experts can have differing levels of expertise ranging from intermediaries, those with an intimate knowledge of a domain and the most power in deciding creativity, through to a broad audience ranging from connoisseurs, to fans or amateurs, to the general public (Sawyer, 2012, pp. 218–221). Each wields varying degrees of power in the field.

As Bourdieu has suggested, the state of power relations in the field—who wields effective authority in any conflict about what is or isn't to be included as acceptable to the field—'depends on the degree of overall autonomy possessed by the field, that is, the extent to which it manages to impose its own norms and sanctions on the whole set of producers' (Bourdieu, 1993, p. 40). Power is thus dependent on the constitution of fields of knowledge, a situation which works in the reverse as well. This summation is very similar to Michel Foucault's understanding of power as a productive network which permeates all sociocultural systems. Rather than seeing the operation of power as primarily negative, Foucault insisted that

> if power were never anything but repressive, if it never did anything but to say no, do you really think one would be brought to obey it? What makes power hold good, what makes it accepted, is simply the fact that it doesn't only weigh on us as a force that says no, but that it traverses and produces things, it induces pleasure, forms knowledge, produces discourse. It needs to be considered as a productive network which runs through the whole social body much more than as a negative instance whose function is repression. (Foucault in Jordan & Weedon, 1995, p. 479)

Power from this perspective is not hierarchical and 'top down' but is instead diffuse and, one could claim, nonlinear. Power also has a 'transformative capacity', as Anthony Giddens (1979) has argued. This capacity can be used by choice-making agents to enable change in either things or the actions of other people they come into relations with. This means certain agents are not just making choices but in doing so they also 'exercise power over other people, and so constrain people and reduce their freedom. At the same time though, power also increases the freedom of action of the agents who possess it. What restricts one person, enables another to do more' (Haralambos & Holbern, 1995, p. 906). Understanding how this works is incredibly important to entrepreneurs working inside this dynamic system. For example, it bodes well to understand who holds the power in the networks entrepreneurs must work within in order to practice effectively. Who are these people? Where do they exist in the network? What do they do? How do I get to know them?

To pursue the importance of networks in the field a little further and to start answering the question raised above, Vaidhyanathan argued that another 'more significant process inherent in the "digital moment" is the rise of networks' (Vaidhyanathan, 2001, p. 152). As Manuel Castells also argued in his influential work *The Rise of the Network Society* (1996), as interpreted by Flew:

> the development of a global and decentralized communications network with the Internet, combined with the growing importance of information and knowledge as the basis of competitive advantage in the economy as well as other spheres, means that the network increasingly shapes the logic of social interaction. (Flew, 2005, p. 16)

To bring this down in this case to the level of creative agents, those looking to gain an income within the network society, we can see that there are many things to learn about networks. Davies and Sigthorsson assert that searching for work in any creative sector 'involves looking for work through informal channels, more often than not friends and acquaintances in the business' (2013, p. 104). Added to this process is the fact that:

> most creative teams are put together from a network of contacts. So in order to find work, it's important to be a part of other people's networks, know what you want and need, identifying the people who might be helpful, and then contacting them…creative professionals tend to rely more on their networks of contacts the more experienced they get. (Davies and Sigthorsson, 2013, p. 104)

In this case, it is necessary for any creative practitioner, and especially entrepreneurs, to network strategically in order to engage in, as Randle and Culkin explain, 'creating, maintaining and extending a network of contacts in order to maximize the opportunities to work' (quoted in Davies & Sigthorsson, 2013, p. 109).

Davies and Sigthorsson pragmatically and helpfully suggest that to develop a network, first start with what you already have: that is, family, friends, teachers, and other people around you. Secondly, research the professional sector you want to be part of. Look at trade magazines and blogs that cover developments in the field, find out what professionals read, jot down names of people, and get to know the field. Thirdly, make sure you have a business card. Fourthly, be as socially generous as you can be. Help others and pass on their details, ideas, and contacts. Recommendations are important. Fifth, socialize and make good use of the encounters socializing brings (Davies & Sigthorsson, 2013, pp. 109–110). This will help you negotiate the exigencies of the field.

Using this advice, we can expand on this perspective by saying, a little more formally, that a field operates like a game where strategic and tactical maneuvering take place in order to better one's position in relation to others in the field. Positions within the field are related to roles that are ascribed or adopted in these structured social spaces. People and organizations (active agents) deploy certain resources they have in their possession that give them competitive orientations in the game. They are committed to the game, thus giving it value, and consequently they immerse themselves in the space of works, which helps constitute the game. People strategize their moves in the game, based on their habitus, in a manner calculated to guarantee success and they deploy various forms of capital, be it social, cultural, symbolic, or financial, that is, contacts, skills, experience, or cash, to improve their position in the field. Practitioners have levels of social capital in the form of contacts; levels of cultural capital and the skills necessary to take part in that culture; levels of symbolic capital, demonstrating their experience in the field in the form of reputation; and cash or economic capital. To overlay the creative system onto these actions, we can put all of this another way:

> This system consists of three interlocking and interactive subsystems. These include a structured knowledge system manifest in all the collected works pertinent to that symbol system. This is called a domain. It also consists of a field, that is, a structured social organisation that operates using domain knowledge in a process of coopetition. This field is populated by all those who can act upon and effect the symbol system, that is those with varying expertise including other produsers, gatekeepers, cultural intermediaries and audiences. The third subsystem we will call an agent. This agent is an active choice making entity which may be scaled outward from individuals to dyads, groups and other collective entities such as institutions who make

> 'changes to the stored information that pre-exists them' (Csikszentmihalyi, 1988, p. 329). These agents necessarily have a unique but shared background and bring their distinctive characteristics to bear on the entire system. (McIntyre, 2021, p. 9)

All of the subsystems, the domain, the field, and the agent, are necessary for the system to work but they are not sufficient, in and of themselves, to enable novel and valued products to come into being. These emerge from the nonlinear interactions of all three.

With this as our framework, we will now use it to describe, explain, and understand how entrepreneurialism is enacted in the creative industries. The next section of our book sets out the necessary nuts and bolts of running an entrepreneurial enterprise in the creative industries and demonstrates how an understanding of, and immersion in, the social and cultural contexts this system is part of and draws from can provide a pragmatic set of functions for entrepreneurial activity to emerge. From this, we hope to demonstrate how theory illuminates practice and, in the spirit of complementarity, how at the same time practice informs theory.

References

Bourdieu, P. (1984). *Distinction: A social critique of the judgement of taste* (R. Nice, Trans.). Harvard University Press.

Bourdieu, P. (1986). The forms of capital. In J. Richardson (Ed.), *Handbook of theory and research for the sociology of education* (pp. 241–258). Greenwood Press.

Bourdieu, P. (1993). In R. Johnson (Ed.), *Field of cultural production*. Columbia University Press.

Bourdieu, P. (1996). *The rules of art: Genesis and structure of the literary field*. Polity Press.

Castells, M. (1996). *The rise of the Network Society, the Information Age: Economy, society and culture* (Vol. 1). Blackwell.

Criticos, H. (2021). The constrabling effect of internet radio. *Journal of Radio & Audio Media, online*, 1–12. https://doi.org/10.1080/19376529.2021.1937629

Csikszentmihalyi, M. (1988). Society, culture, and person: A systems view of creativity. In R. Sternberg (Ed.), *The nature of creativity: Contemporary psychological perspectives* (pp. 325–329). Cambridge University Press.

Csikszentmihalyi, M. (1990). The domain of creativity. In M. A. Runco & R. S. Albert (Eds.), *Theories of creativity* (pp. 190–212). Sage Publications.

Csikszentmihalyi, M. (1997). *Creativity: Flow and the psychology of discovery and invention*. Harper Collins.

Csikszentmihalyi, M. (1999). Implications of a systems perspective for the study of creativity. In R. Sternberg (Ed.), *Handbook of creativity* (pp. 313–335). Cambridge University Press.

Csikszentmihalyi, M. (2014). *The systems model of creativity*. Springer.

Davies, R., & Sigthorsson, G. (2013). *Introducing the creative industries: From theory to practice.* .

Flew, T. (2005). *New media: An introduction* (2nd ed.). Oxford University Press.

Fulton, J. (2019). Media entrepreneurship: Preparing students for work in a creative profession. *Australian Journalism Review, 41*(1), 67–83. https://doi.org/10.1386/ajr.41.1.67_1

Giddens, A. (1979). *Central problems in social theory: Action, structure, and contradiction in social analysis.* Macmillan.

Grenfell, M. (2004). *Pierre Bourdieu: Agent provocateur. Continuum.*

Haralambos, M., & Holbern, M. (1995). *Sociology: Themes and perspectives* (4th ed.). Harper Collins.

Haralambos, M., & Holbern, M. (2013). *Sociology: Themes and perspectives* (8th ed.). Harper Collins.

Jordan, G., & Weedon, C. (1995). *Cultural politics: Class, gender, race and the postmodern world.* Blackwell.

Kelso, S., & Engstrøm, D. (2006). *The complementary nature.* MIT Press.

Kerrigan, S. (2011). *Creative documentary practice: Internalising the systems model of creativity through documentary video and online practice.* Doctoral dissertation, University of Newcastle, NOVA.

Kerrigan, S. (2013). Accommodating creative documentary practice within a revised systems model of creativity. *Journal of Media Practice, 14*(2), 111–127. https://doi.org/10.1386/jmpr.14.2.111_1

Kerrigan, S. (2022, May 3). *Creative Practice as a Revised Systems model.* https://susankerrigan.wordpress.com/2022/05/03/creative-practice-as-a-revised-systems-model/

Kerrigan, S., Criticos, H., Kerrigan, V., & Ritchie, S. (2021). Podcasting as a creative practice and the spirit of radio: Local histories of Maitland. *Journal of Radio & Audio Media,* (online). https://doi.org/10.1080/19376529.2021.1897986

McIntyre, P. (2008a). The Systems Model Of Creativity: Analyzing The Distribution Of Power In The Studio. *Journal on the Art of Record. Production, 3.* https://www.arpjournal.com/asarpwp/the-systems-model-of-creativity-analyzing-the-distribution-of-power-in-the-studio/

McIntyre, P. (2008b). Creativity and cultural production: A study of contemporary western popular music songwriting. *Creativity Research Journal, 20*(1), 40–52.

McIntyre, P. (2009). Rethinking communication, creativity and cultural production: Outlining issues for media practice. In T. Flew (Ed.), *Communication, creativity and global citizenship: Refereed proceedings of the Australian and New Zealand Communication Association annual conference* (pp. 156–172).

McIntyre, P. (2011). Rethinking the creative process: The systems model of creativity applied to popular songwriting. *Journal of Music, Technology and Education, 4*(1), 77–90.

McIntyre, P. (2021). Songwriting practice and production: The past, present and future. *The Songwriting Studies Journal, 1*, 5–26.

McIntyre, P., & Thompson, P. (2021). *Paul McCartney and his creative practice: The Beatles and beyond*. Palgrave Macmillan.

Sawyer, K. (2012). *Explaining creativity: The science of human innovation* (2nd ed.). Oxford University Press.

Schirato, T., & Yell, S. (1996). *Communication and cultural literacy: An introduction*. Allen & Unwin.

Schugurensky, D. (2008). 1986: Pierre Bourdieu's 'The forms of capital' is published In English. *History of Education*. Retrieved December 16, 2008, from http://fcis.oise.utoronto.ca/~daniel_schugurensky/assignment1/v1986bourdieu.html

Swartz, D. (1997). *Culture and power: The sociology of Pierre Bourdieu*. University of Chicago Press.

Toynbee, J. (2000). *Making popular music: Musicians, creativity and institutions*. .

Vaidhyanathan, S. (2001). *Copyrights and copywrongs: The rise of intellectual property and how it threatens creativity*. New York University Press.

PART II

How You Do It: Taking Care of Business

CHAPTER 5

Entrepreneurial Practices and Skills: Personal Skill Sets, the Gift Economy, Clusters, and the State

The previous chapters have examined the macro structures that practitioners work within—the contexts so important to an entrepreneur—as well as the broad theoretical antecedents of the ideas underpinning entrepreneurship in the creative industries. We have discovered where those big picture ideas come from as we explored the interconnections between entrepreneurialism, creative industries, creativity, and systems and how they have developed. This chapter embeds the individual agent, the entrepreneurial person, within some of the larger structures they may need to deal with. These include the gift economy, creative clusters of fellow professionals, and the actions of the state. It does this by also focusing on what the individual, a decision-making agent, brings to this creative system. We emphasize again that while it can be seen that this individual is not at the center of the system, and previous chapters have clearly shown the interconnections between social, cultural, and individual structures, it can also be demonstrated that personal and often idiosyncratic skill sets are still a necessary part of this creative entrepreneurial system in action. The individual remains a factor in entrepreneurial and intrapreneurial practices. As Vlad Glaveanu asserts, when talking about creativity distributed across a system, it would be easy to assume that refocusing the role of individuals 'does away with the individual or downplays his/her role in creative production' (2014, p. 9). However, he argues that we can't lose the

P. McIntyre et al., *Entrepreneurship in the Creative Industries*,
https://doi.org/10.1007/978-3-031-19455-9_5

individual in the creative act but equally we cannot return to a focus on the individual alone. Instead, we need to give them 'a new status and value' (2014, p. 9). The self and the sociocultural are mutually constituting, as Bourdieu's notion of habitus indicates. Creative action, in this case the specific actions of being an entrepreneur, bears the mark of both the individual agent and the structures that enable and constrain their actions. This means we must ultimately 'recognize the self as an agent within an ever-changing world' (2014, p. 9).

Perhaps the set of questions we could direct at an understanding of these agents could include the following: what does it actually take to be an entrepreneur, and are there common characteristics for individual entrepreneurs? As Mazzarol and Reboud (2020) point out, it was initially thought, in research terms at least, and is still done so in a commonsense way, that an entrepreneur is 'an enterprising person with enterprising attributes or traits' (2020, p. 36). They examined early research on entrepreneurship and discovered that much of that research focused on the individual alone, by looking predominantly at entrepreneurial traits, particularly of those who founded a business, rather than entrepreneurialism as a systemic whole. As they note, 'an almost endless list of entrepreneurial traits was suggested' (2020, p. 36), including initiative, flexibility, persuasiveness, problem-solving ability, risk-taking, creativity, and imagination. What has been found more recently though is that it is just as important to take personal background into consideration (2020, p. 36) as well as those social and cultural contexts discussed earlier. In other words, research into entrepreneurship has taken a similar path to research into creativity and innovation, where research investigations focused initially on particular individuals. The research focus then moved, in a largely socioculturally reductionist approach, to looking at the influence of the broader structures on entrepreneurial activity, before discovering that the actions of both agents and sociocultural structures needed to be accounted for.

The kinds of personality characteristics, if there are indeed such things, that have been attributed to many entrepreneurs can be boiled down to four fundamental categories: entrepreneurs are seen to be (1) creative and innovative people who are (2) motivated, (3) risk takers and, in taking those risks, they have learned to be (4) resilient.

To tease out these ideas further, we can firstly focus on creativity. In doing so, we draw on research by Mihaly Csikszentmihalyi, the same researcher who first identified the idea of a creative system, and his ideas about creativity, motivation, and personality. He stated that:

to be creative, a person has to internalize the entire system that makes creativity possible. So what sort of person is likely to do that? This question is very difficult to answer. Creative individuals are remarkable for their ability to adapt to almost any situation and to make do with whatever is at hand to reach their goals. If nothing else, this distinguishes them from the rest of us. But there does not seem to be a particular set of traits that a person must have in order to come up with a valuable novelty. (1997, p. 51)

While Csikszentmihalyi was hesitant to write about the supposed deep personality of creative people, he did contend that creative people tend toward complexity (1997, p. 57). By this he meant that creative people seem to exhibit a range of personality traits that included apparent paradoxes. They may be energetic but also often quiet, smart yet naïve, playful and disciplined, imaginative but rooted in reality, extroverted and introverted, humble and proud, not stereotyped to either masculine or feminine but with attributes of both, rebellious and independent but a traditionalist regarding the rules of the domain, passionate about work but also dispassionate and objective, and, finally, suffering and sensitive but also able to derive enjoyment from their work (1997, pp. 58–76). In other words, the creative personality is complex, ranging across dichotomous behaviors and difficult to generalize about. Csikszentmihalyi was willing to say that:

[C]reative persons are characterized not so much by single traits as by their ability to operate through the entire spectrum of personality dimensions...What dictates their behavior is not a rigid inner structure, but the demands of the interaction between them and the domain in which they are working. (1999, p. 331)

We would add 'the field' to that statement. In this case, we can restate it, saying that creativity emerges when an individual's personality and background interact with the domain and field in a complex system. None of the elements in the system—the domain, individual, or field—can explain, by themselves alone, how an entrepreneur carries out their innovative activity.

The second trait generally mentioned in research that is thought to describe entrepreneurs is that of motivation, since motivated people tend to be tenacious, that is, determined and persistent. They appear to have a feeling that they make their own destiny, coupled with a desire for autonomy. While personal ambition or competition may drive their pursuit of success, and therefore both internal or external motivation may be present for them, it can be argued that autotelic motivation, or to use its more common name, flow, may be a very significant motivator for those working in the creative industries. Autotelic experience can be explained as the experience where an individual is so absorbed in what they are doing that time seems to fly by for them; they are in a state of flow.

> Concentration is so intense that there is no attention left over to think about anything irrelevant, or to worry about problems. Self-consciousness disappears, and the sense of time becomes distorted. An activity that produces such experiences is so gratifying that people are willing to do it for its own sake, with little concern for what they will get out of it, even when it is difficult, or dangerous. (In Csikszentmihalyi & Csikszentmihalyi, 1988, p. 71)

In setting out the conditions of this state, Csikszentmihalyi (1997) posited that if the level of challenge faced by, in our case, an entrepreneur working in the creative industries, and the skills they possess are up to it, a state of flow could be achieved. If the challenge is too great, anxiety occurs, sometimes overwhelmingly, and not much will be achieved. If, on the other hand, the challenge is low in comparison to the skill level the entrepreneur possesses, boredom may ensue, and again not much will be achieved. But when the goals and incoming information are in harmony, a state known as 'flow' occurs (Fig. 5.1).

Janet Fulton, discussing flow in journalism in particular, found in her own research that a journalist's engagement with the entire system, that is, their understanding of the expectations of the field and rules of the domain, meant a flow state could be achieved by that agent:

> it can be seen that if a journalist possesses the 'skills' that are provided by the system, that is knowledge from the domain and field, and works at a level that is commensurate with those skills, a journalist could feasibly enter the flow channel. But, a journalist must also continue to find challenges within the work environment or risk boredom. On the other hand, when a journalist is expected to write without adequate knowledge of the expectations of the field or domain, anxiety will most likely occur and this distraction may lead to a less optimum outcome. (2013, p. 244)

To apply these ideas to the entrepreneurial mindset, when an individual instigates a startup or is developing an idea at work, at some point they will

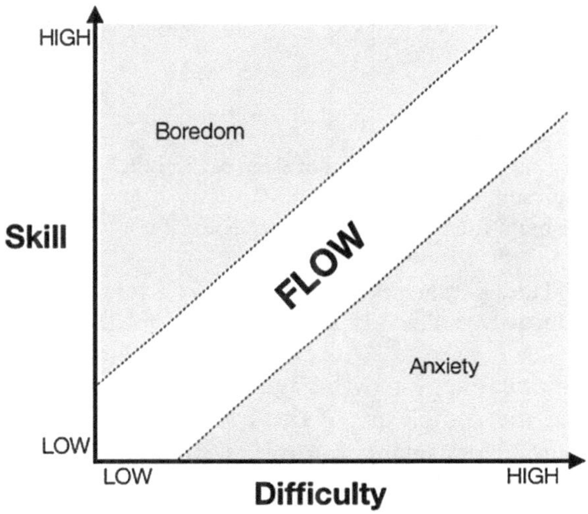

Fig. 5.1 The flow diagram

experience flow: their skills and skill level will equal the challenge they are dealing with. They will be absorbed in what they do and, given the passions at play, that experience, the pure joy or love of doing it, becomes the motivator:

> When we step beyond motivations based on pleasure, power, and participation, we open up consciousness to experience new opportunities for being that lead to emergent structures of the self. This is autotelic motivation, because its goal is primarily the experience itself, rather than any future reward or advantage it may bring. (Csikszentmihalyi, 1988, p. 29)

In this case we can say motivation is important, but this can be difficult to maintain if the agent is operating at less than their optimal capacity. If entrepreneurship has anything to do with maintaining a certain mindset, as the European Commission claimed, then it is also necessary to take account of how to maintain not only motivation but also health. As Josh Kaufman explains:

> Coffee and all-nighters can only take you so far. If you want to do good work, taking care of yourself isn't optional...Your body has Performance Requirements. If you don't give your body what it needs to run, you'll stop

functioning before you reach your goals. You need nutrition, rest and exercise to be productive. Here are some tips:

1. Eat high-quality food.
2. Exercise regularly.
3. Get at least seven to eight hours of sleep each night.
4. Get enough sun, but not too much.
5. Feed your brain the raw materials it needs to run.

It's a good idea to experiment to see what works for you to improve your energy, productivity and mood. (Kaufman, 2020, pp. 218–220)

While these ideas appear to be agent centered, it would be wise to remember that the complexity of the system demands we look further afield. For example, risk-taking, our third entrepreneurial attribute, is not just attributable to the individual alone. Risk-taking leads to either failure or success and, as a result, the development of resilience.

To explore these interconnections further, we can see that entrepreneurs are generally seen to be willing to fail in order to succeed. And there are, more often than not, failures to be dealt with. However, Western culture has a tendency to valorize success without taking into consideration the high number of failures an individual may have overcome to enjoy that success (Kerrigan et al., 2019). But for entrepreneurs, failure and success go hand in hand—particularly if these bedfellows are framed within the notion of complementarity, rather than the typical understanding of failure and success as diametrically opposed. We should be able to say that 'creative failure is intimately related to creative success' (Kerrigan et al., 2019, p. 11). As a part of this process, entrepreneurs, as a matter of course, tend to weigh up the opportunities and benefits (opportunity costs) that can be derived, and calculate the risks before acting. This is not to say they are all overly cautious. Many know when to leap. *Carpe diem* seems to be their call to arms. What can be said in research terms though is, there tends to be a strong correlation between risk-taking and a tendency for entrepreneurialism (Mazzarol & Reboud, 2020).

John Stuart Mill (1848) had stated that risk-taking was a major difference between someone who was a manager and someone who took an entrepreneurial leap. Joseph Schumpeter argued against this contention and claimed, instead, that both took risks, albeit at different levels. Risks born by the entrepreneur, as Liles (1974) also suggests, include 'financial, career opportunities, family relations and well-being' (Mazzarol & Reboud, 2020, p. 39). But in the face of risks to these areas of our life, many people exhibit what is called loss aversion (Kaufman, 2020). They 'hate to lose things more than they like to gain them...people respond twice as strongly to potential loss than they do to the opportunity of an equivalent gain' (Kaufman, 2020, p. 245). This type of thinking is understandable, as identifying and acting on immediate threats take precedence in most survival situations for most people. However, according to entrepreneur and media publisher Felix Dennis, the unwillingness to assume risk often leads to a variety of excuses and evasions that have been erected by many to justify not acting. He claims these excuses 'are the children of fear and the parents of a thousand "if onlys"' (2011, p. 301). On the other hand, entrepreneurs, as risk-takers, tend to reinterpret situations of potential loss into situations of potential gain. For them, it is about reinterpretation and perception: do you see this situation in a positive way or a negative way? To put that simply, they can convince themselves failure is 'no big deal' (Kaufman, 2020, p. 245). This habit of mind is coupled with our fourth characteristic, an ability to be resilient.

Resilient people are able to recover from failure well, leading to eventual self-confidence and a generally optimistic outlook about their own survival. They have learned to be adaptable, gaining a flexible approach to uncertainty. One way to describe this is to say they are ego resilient, that is, they have 'the capacity to overcome, steer through, or bounce back from adversity' (Zolli & Healy, 2012, p. 167). George Bonnano from the University of Michigan uses the term resilient 'to identify people capable of functioning with a sense of core purpose, meaning and forward momentum in the face of trauma' (Zolli & Healy, 2012, p. 165). This description echoes Andrew Zolli and Ann Marie Healy's explanation that resilience is 'the capacity of a system, enterprise, or a person to maintain its core purpose and integrity in the face of dramatically changed circumstances' (2012, p. 126).

At this point, having connected resilience and systems, we can now start to bring the ideas of structure and agency back together. In order to be resilient, it is not only how an individual agent behaves, but also how the structures they are operating within either support or deny that process of being resilient. As a study by Werner and Smith indicated, 'the ability of members from certain communities to bounce back from adversity is also aided by high-functioning social networks' (Zolli & Healy, 2012, p. 169). Werner and Smith's comment here ties agency and structure together nicely as a series of interrelationships. As they argue, 'correlates to personal resilience are rooted in our beliefs and our experiences' (Zolli & Healy, 2012, pp. 170–171) since 'even the hardiest individual cannot go it alone—our resilience is rooted in that of the groups and communities in which we live and work. In turn at the core of social resilience are two factors...cooperation and trust' (Zolli & Healy, 2012, p. 188). What we can note here is that for the creative industries much of this cooperation and trust are established inside what is called a gift economy. The lesson is, you need to give some things away in order to get some things back.

There is little doubt that the gift economy is a significant part of the creative industries, and one that entrepreneurs in this field are adept at drawing on. However, as has been noted by several eminent scholars, gift giving itself is a very ancient form of exchange (Bourdieu, 1977; Cheal, 1988; Malinowski, 1922; Mauss, 1990[1925]) and it has persisted into the twenty-first century. Offner, in summarizing gifting, states that '[f]oremost is exchange within the household. But gift giving also motivates much retail purchasing. Reciprocity abounds at work; it affects management, agriculture, marketing, entrepreneurship, and politics' (1997, p. 450). The media industries and the broader creative industries need to understand this actual process, the symbolic, social, and cultural exchange so prevalent in a sector such as the creative industries, and that it occurs in a context of reciprocity.

Veale, referring to the internet, claimed there are three fundamental principles of the gift economy: 'exchange in the Internet gift economy facilitates reciprocity; reciprocity in the form of intangible rewards; and, intangible rewards leading to the tangible' (2003, n.p.). Veale states that 'reciprocity can be in the form of intangible rewards, such as reputation, anticipated reciprocity and self-esteem' (2003, n.p.). Enhanced reputation, for example, is an example of the working of symbolic capital, as is prestige, but these intangible rewards may also lead to economic capital in the form of tangible rewards such as fees and the possession of copyright (Veale, 2003). However, as Offner notes, in a gift exchange:

> [T]he price is indeterminate. 'Delivery' and 'payment' can be separated by the exercise of discretion and the passage of time. Something else is acquired, over and above the material gains from trade. Exchange is not only an economic transaction, it is also a good in itself, a 'process benefit', usually in the form of a personal relationship. Personal interaction ranks very high among

> the sources of satisfaction. It can take many forms: acknowledgement, attention, acceptance, respect, reputation, status, power, intimacy, love, friendship, kinship, sociability. To wrap it all into one term, interaction is driven by the grant and pursuit of regard...It is not costless. (1997, pp. 451–452)

The importance of regard can be seen as just as great as economic capital, but the evidence is that it needs to be natural and unforced to have value in the field. It must be seen as authentic to be effective.

To summarize, gift giving occurs in a context of reciprocity, but that reciprocity is subject to social and cultural norms:

> Reciprocity is usually delayed. Both the value of the reciprocal gesture, and its timing are left to discretion, though often regulated tightly by convention and custom. When the exchange is completed, a new sequence can begin. Take the practice of hospitality. The middle-class exchange of dinner invitations, and the small gifts that accompany them, are an example of delayed reciprocity. Reciprocity can also be indirect, with no return from the beneficiary (who may be unknown), but a credit with the community, to be reciprocated at some other time and place. (Offner, 1997, p. 451)

This last is an important point and one creative and innovative entrepreneurs wishing to activate their ideas would do well to consider. It is this form of indirect reciprocity that drives much important activity within what are called creative industries clusters.

Clusters are aggregations of similar businesses and their affiliated sectors within one geographical locality, to paraphrase Michael Porter, the C. Roland Christensen Professor of Business Administration at the Harvard Business School. Porter writes that 'untangling the paradox of location in a global economy offers insights into how companies continually create competitive advantage' (1998, p. 78). He argues that proximity 'amplifies all of the pressure to innovate and upgrade' (1998, p. 90). Clusters drive competition in three ways: first, 'by increasing the productivity of businesses based in the area; second by driving the direction and pace of innovation; and third, by stimulating the formation of new businesses, which expands and strengthens the cluster itself' (Porter, 1998, p. 80).

Famous creative industries clusters include Hollywood, where film companies and all of the ancillary workers they interact with have gathered to make films for over a century; Silicon Valley, the area close to San

Francisco and Stanford University that has generated a collection of very successful information technology firms; in the United Kingdom, the famous journalism cluster on Fleet Street; and the collection of music publishers, recording studios, and retail outlets in Denmark St in London, commonly referred to as Tin Pan Alley. What makes these notable clusters effective is the social aspect of human behavior. Porter argues that the very human qualities of 'peer pressure, pride and the desire to look good in the community spur executives to outdo one another' (Porter, 1998, p. 83), while cooperative networking is fundamental to their complementary operation since 'tapping into the competitively valuable assets requires personal relationships and "insider" status' (Porter, 1998, p. 88). Relationships are thus critically important. Perhaps more importantly, smaller businesses, including microbusinesses, benefit from clusters because of their scalability (Porter, 1998), since clusters may operate beside other related clusters and, at the intersection of these clusters, 'insights and skill from various fields merge, sparking new businesses' (Porter, 1998, p. 84). There is far more to be gained from people sharing and gift giving, in terms of the gift economy, than in keeping people and businesses separate. An example of this type of synergy exists in Ballarat, Australia, where, supported by Federation University, itself partially funded by the Federal Government, a cluster of technology industries has been developing for 30 years at what is called Federation University Technology Parks (FUTPs). There are four FUTPs in the Ballarat region with IBM as the principal employer, but with 64 enterprises included overall in these parks (Kerrigan et al., 2020). The primary focus is to develop ICT industries, but other businesses such as design, architecture, and health are also necessarily part of the FUTPs. They not only contribute to these clusters but also take advantage of the training, skills, and technology built up in Ballarat because of the success of the parks. As noted by Kerrigan, McIntyre, and McCutcheon, the 'Tech Park is focused on building partnerships to create a clustered "ecosystem"' (2020, p. 30).

At a much larger scale, sitting astride all of this activity is the state, enabling and constraining business activity by instituting legal frameworks, supplying infrastructure, education, R&D, and tax incentives. It operates as a seemingly deterministic structure providing a set of possible, and at times forced, choices to the agents working within that system.

Typically, when we think of the state, we think of a top-down hierarchical monolith, but that is a narrow way of understanding the concept. While it has been defined simply and bluntly by Max Weber as any 'human community that (successfully) claims the monopoly of the legitimate use of physical force within a given territory' (1948, p. 78), Kelly provides a more complex understanding by asserting that it has 'grown into a complicated network of related organizations with varying degrees of apparent autonomy' (1984, p. 44), which is another way of saying that the state is a very large cluster, in Porter's terms, while also recognizing that the 'basic principles and motivations which fuel the network of the state still belong to the most powerful groups in society' (Kelly, 1984, pp. 44–45). Carol Gould adds that

> ..though it sometimes appears that such institutions have an independent existence apart from social relations among persons, it should be evident that such institutions or objectified forms are socially constituted, that is, they have been brought into being by the decisions and actions of agents and can also be changed by them. (1988, p. 113)

Kelly asserts that, 'although the state is not a Leviathan-like machine, neither is it a neutral and passive instrument. It is a series of active relationships between organisations; and a way of organizing those relationships which are rooted in specific assumptions and beliefs' (1984, p. 45). In other words, it is an expression of complementarity; it has the qualities of an agent at the same time as it exhibits the qualities of a structure.

As various governments around the world make the choice to adopt neoliberal ideologies and naturalize them for their citizen populations, there is a committed belief that private enterprise operates best in a deregulated market environment, that this set-up will deliver more positive innovation without significant intervention from the state. In other words, entrepreneurs need to keep the state at a distance, and the belief is that then more innovation will occur. This claim, while now a central dogma for many neoclassical economists and the policy makers who adhere to these ideas around the world, appears to run counter to the empirical evidence. Dawson and Holmes, for example, assert that 'the state has always played a vital role in overseeing and, in some instances, determining systems of media production' (2012, p. 8). Furthermore, academic and entrepreneur William Janeway supports the claim that the state has long reinforced innovation and, in fact, has been central to it:

> From the First Industrial Revolution on, the state has served as an enabler—sometimes as the engine—of economic development, subsidizing if not

> directing the deployment of transformational technology and, more recently, taking responsibility for funding the advanced science and engineering from which economically significant innovation has come to be derived. (2018, p. 241)

William Janeway (2018) notes the importance of the state to entrepreneurs, suggesting there are three things required for entrepreneurship to occur: business innovation; speculative capital to support that business innovation; and a state to put the larger infrastructure processes in place as well as supply the grants, the subsidies, and the policies that allow venture capitalists and startup and ongoing businesses to do what it is that they do. The macrostructures provided by the state are as crucial to the individual as they are to the social apparatus, the society they are designed to serve. They are certainly crucial to entrepreneurship. Janeway argues that government investment builds the platform on which venture capitalists and entrepreneurs can 'dance' (Parramore, 2013). He insists that, counter to the neoliberal understanding of the so-called free market, the three-player game, the 'complex, reciprocal interactions between the state, financial capitalism and the market economy' (2018, p. xix), is an historical, necessary, and ongoing relationship. Out of this dynamic interaction 'successive technological revolutions have transformed the conditions of life over more than 200 years' (Janeway, 2018, p. xix).

An example of how the state is involved in innovation can be seen in the ongoing development of the radio sector of the creative industries in Australia. This sector is regulated by the Broadcasting Services Act 1992, a legal framework emanating from the Australian Parliament, and operates under the auspices of the Department of Infrastructure, Transport, Regional Development and Communications. This Department, an organ of the state, regulates communication and media infrastructure, services and content. The Act of Parliament it enforces allows commercial broadcast licenses to be granted and managed through the organizational structure of the Australian Communication and Media Authority (ACMA). Public broadcasters such as the ABC and SBS are covered by their own Acts as well as the ACMA and 'are accountable to the Parliament through annual reports, corporate plans, financial and performance audits and appearances before Parliamentary Committees' (Australian Government, 2022). Community radio has self-regulating Codes of Practice, developed by the Community Broadcasting Association of Australia, but is still overseen by the ACMA and must abide by those regulations. Digital radio is also overseen by the state, with reviews and reports conducted into the technology and how it should be regulated. Apart from these industry-specific regulations, the radio sector is also subject to the general laws of the land such as defamation, discrimination, incitement, vilification, and sub judice.

To take this example further, we can now include the development of the National Broadband Network (NBN) as an important piece of infrastructure provided by the state. It has not only enabled a wider reach for many radio stations as they exploit their digital potential through their websites and podcasts, but it has also enabled innovative radio-like formats such as Pandora and Spotify to enter the Australian market and compete with others in this sector. Audience access to these music-sharing platforms would not be as feasible without the NBN.

This technological infrastructure, the NBN, provided by the state, offers the affordances necessary to conduct business in the twenty-first century. The legal infrastructure, The Broadcast Services Act in particular and the ACMA, set up to administer and oversee this Act of Parliament, provides the regulatory structure that ensures equitable access to the licenses many radio networks, such as Austereo and the SRN, rely on to give them access to audiences. At each station, complying with and using these structural necessities, a station manager controls the activity occurring at the station. They do so through a Program Director, who actively decides the overall sound of the station, along with a Music Director, often using software like Selector to help them, making active decisions about what music to include or not include, and keeping within the format of the station, a format that is often decided on at the network level. The DJ carries out the directives, injecting their on-air personality into the creative system that produces the radio that audiences interact with. The whole system is an example of the intermingling of active decision-making agents working within the possibilities presented by the multiple structures they interact with, including the structures supplied by the state.

Contrary to the ideals of neoliberalism, there are numerous other examples across the creative industries where state support, regulation and intervention, either positive or negative, has been integral to how that creative system operates. These range from the provision of grants and subsidies through government instrumentalities such as Creative Victoria or Create NSW, as well as the institution of necessary legislation to support the reasonable collection of copyright fees. Without the Australian Copyright Act and the government being a signatory to the Berne

Convention, this action would be quite difficult to police. In other words, the state is part of a structure that constrains and enables those practicing agents who operate within the creative industries.

These creative agents are often the subject of myth-making. Mariana Mazzucato has engaged in a detailed process of myth-busting in order to reveal the inherent problems with the ideals of neoliberalism and its emphasis on the freedoms of individuals. Mazzacuto draws on extensive empirical evidence to demonstrate that the private sector, rather than being hamstrung by the state, depends on it to make bold, high-risk investments in innovative processes and technologies before private sector venture capitalists and entrepreneurs take steps to capitalize on what the state has provided for them. As one example, she notes that Apple developers Steve Jobs and Steve Wozniak are often cited as great entrepreneurs who manifest the ideals of the independent innovator, or what Schumpeter called wild-spirited individuals before he realized that organizational structures were just as important to innovation. But the story that is seldom told is not only did they have access to public funds, which helped them start their company, but they also used the 'technologies that resulted from major government research programmes, military initiatives, public procurement contracts, or that were developed by public research institutions, all backed by state or federal dollars' (Mazzucato, 2014, p. 93). This dependence on the state in any entrepreneurial activity is often downplayed in favor of classic neoliberal myth-building.

In summary, we can say that in all creative and innovative activities there are a series of structures at play that are unavoidable. The innovative agent must take those structures into consideration and work with them to be able to practice successfully. While there are some structures, for example legislation, or events such as the GFC of 2008, that are out of the control of the agent, there are many others that can be used beneficially to ensure the success of entrepreneurial activity. As such, there is a direct correlation between the times we live in, the places we live in, and the choices we can make inside this game. As stated prior, the game is located inside a field, the social organization deployed around certain domain knowledge where strategic and tactical maneuvering takes place in order to better one's position in relation to others in the field. People and organizations, both choice-making entities, deploy certain resources they have in their possession that give them competitive and cooperative orientations in this game. There are risks involved. Sometimes there is success, sometimes there is failure, and through this they learn to be adaptable and resilient as they gain more experience in the game. They strategize their moves, based on their habitus, in a manner calculated to help achieve success, as they deploy—often in the gift economy, where reciprocity rules—various forms of capital, be it social, cultural, symbolic, or financial, that is, contacts, skills, experience, or cash, to improve their position in the field and in relation to the structures they encounter and exist within. While this description outlines the actions of the field very well, it is the domain of entrepreneurship that now needs some exploration.

References

Australian Government. (2022). *ABC and SBS radio*. Department of Infrastructure, Transport, Regional Development and Communications. Retrieved January 19, 2022, from https://www.infrastructure.gov.au/media-technology-communications/radio/abc-sbs-radio

Bourdieu, P. (1977). *Outline of a theory of practice* (R. Nice, Trans.). Cambridge University Press.

Cheal, D. (1988). *The gift economy*. Routledge.

Csikszentmihalyi, M. (1988). The flow experience and its significance for human psychology. In M. Csikszentmihalyi & I. Csikszentmihalyi (Eds.), *Optimal experience: Psychological studies of flow in consciousness* (pp. 15–35). Cambridge University Press.

Csikszentmihalyi, M. (1997). *Creativity: Flow and the psychology of discovery and invention*. Harper Collins.

Csikszentmihalyi, M. (1999). Implications of a systems perspective for the study of creativity. In R. Sternberg (Ed.), *Handbook of creativity* (pp. 313–335). Cambridge University Press.

Csikszentmihalyi, M., & Csikszentmihalyi, I.S. (Eds.). (1988). *Optimal experience: Psychological studies of flow in consciousness*. Cambridge University Press.

Dawson, A., & Holmes, S. (2012). *Working in the global film and television Industries: Creativity, systems, space, patronage*. Bloomsbury Academic.

Dennis, F. (2011). *How to get rich: The distilled wisdom of one of Britain's wealthiest self-made entrepreneurs*. Ebury Press.

Fulton, J. (2013). Communication joy: Print journalists and the experience of flow. In M. Pitts & T. J. Socha (Eds.), *Positive communication in health and wellness*. Peter Lang.

Glăveanu, V. (2014). *Distributed creativity: Thinking outside the box of the creative individual*. Springer.

Gould, C. (1988). *Rethinking democracy: Freedom and social cooperation in politics, economy and society*. Cambridge University Press.

Janeway, W. (2018). *Doing capitalism in the innovation economy* (2nd ed.). Cambridge University Press.
Kaufman, J. (2020). *The personal MBA: Master the art of business 10th anniversary edition*. Penguin.
Kelly, O. (1984). *Community, art and the state: Storming the citadels*. Comedia.
Kerrigan, S., McIntyre, P., Fulton, J., & Meany, M. (2019). The systemic relationship between creative failure and creative success in the creative industries. *Creative Industries Journal*, 1–15. https://doi.org/10.1080/17510694.2019.1624134
Kerrigan, S., McIntyre, P., & McCutcheon, M. (2020). *Australian cultural and creative activity: A population and hotspot analysis: Ballarat*. Digital Media Research Centre.
Liles, P. (1974). Who are the entrepreneurs? *MSU Business Topics, 22*(1), 5–14.
Malinowski, B. (1922). *Argonauts of the Western Pacific*. Routledge & Sons.
Mauss, M. (1990 [1925]). *The gift: The form and reason for exchange in archaic societies* (W. Halls, Trans.). Routledge.
Mazzarol, T., & Reboud, S. (2020). *Entrepreneurship and innovation: Theory, practice and context* (4th ed.). Springer.
Mazzucato, M. (2014). *The entrepreneurial state: Debunking public vs. private sector myths*. Anthem Press.
Mill, J. S. (1848). *The principles of political economy with some of their applications to social philosophy*. Longmans.
Offner, A. (1997). Between the gift and the market: The economy of regard. *Economic History Review, 3*(3), 450–476.
Parramore, L. (2013, April 20). *Meet the visionary venture capitalist inspired by Marx and Keynes*. Alternet. Retrieved January 20, 2022, from http://www.alternet.org/economy/meet-visionary-venture-capitalist-inspired-marx-and-keynes
Porter, M. (1998, November–December). Clusters and the new economics of competition. *Harvard Business Review*, 77–90.
Veale, K.J. (2003). Internet gift economies: Voluntary payment schemes as tangible reciprocity. *First Monday, 8*(12). Retrieved December 30, 2021, from https://firstmonday.org/ojs/index.php/fm/article/download/1101/1021
Weber, M. (1948). Politics as a vocation. In H. H. Gerth & C. W. Mills (Eds. & Trans.), *From Max Weber: Essays in sociology* (pp. 77–128). Oxford University Press.
Zolli, A., & Healy, A. (2012). *Resilience: Why things bounce back*. Headline Publishing.

CHAPTER 6

Entrepreneurial Business Plans and Models: The Nuts and Bolts of Running a Business

The domain of knowledge in any creative system consists of formal and informal knowledge, the conventions, codes of practice, and techniques one uses to operate successfully in any field. This chapter details many of the things that all those engaging in entrepreneurial activity would be wise to know. It highlights what you need in your compendium of knowledge in order to successfully run a business in the creative industries. Before we pursue that in earnest though, we need to remind ourselves that many businesses in the creative industries, apart from the corporate megaliths, can be classified as nano, micro, or small to medium operations. These are usually identified in a number of ways: by looking at the 'number of employees, the size of annual turnover, size of payroll, size of assets or size of business debt' (Mazzarol & Reboud, 2020, p. 132). Mazzarol and Reboud define nano enterprises as 'independent contractors, independent professionals (iPros), and freelancers working within the so-called "gig economy"' (2020, p. 2). A micro-business, on the other hand, is formally defined by the Australian Bureau of Statistics as one that employs less than five people. Small businesses employ between five and 19, while medium enterprises employ between 20 and 199 people (ABS, 2001). To further differentiate these categories, a micro-business in Australia is classified as such if it is not registered for Goods and Services Tax (less than $75,000 income), while a small to medium enterprise (SME) is registered for GST and earns over $75,000. Understanding the business you set up or are

P. McIntyre et al., *Entrepreneurship in the Creative Industries*, https://doi.org/10.1007/978-3-031-19455-9_6

already running has taxation and regulation implications for you. In addition, as this chapter discusses, there are different types of business models to get to know as well as how to put together business plans, the use of business analysis tools such as SWOT and STEEPLE, the importance and effect of copyright and other legal information, and of course knowledge of financing and bookkeeping.

Apart from these things, starting a business is very simple. There are really only three things needed for you to get underway: a product or service, and this could be as simple as personal skills; customers; and a way to get paid. According to Guillebeau, if you have those three things in play, you can be considered to be entrepreneurial:

> If you have a group of interested people but nothing to sell, you don't have a business. If you have something to sell but no-one willing to buy it, you don't have a business. In both cases, without a clear and easy way for customers to pay for what you offer, you don't have a business. Put the three together, and congratulations—you're now an entrepreneur. (2012, p. 18)

There is, of course, much more to say about those three things, with a myriad of permutations of each. For example, Josh Kaufman asserts that '[e]very business is fundamentally a collection of five interdependent processes. And you can see here the development of the business model coming out of these processes, each of which flow into the next' (2020, p. 38). Kaufman lists these five key processes as value creation, marketing, sales, value delivery, and finance. For him, value creation consists of finding a gap in the market—finding out what people want and making or delivering that for them. Marketing is understanding how to make the product or service attractive and generating demand for it. Sales is self-explanatory for most, and entails turning interested parties into paying customers. Value delivery means living up to what you promised the customer. Finance is, of course, '[b]ringing in enough money to keep going and make your effort worthwhile' (Kaufman, 2020, p. 38).

> If these five things sound simple, it's because they are. Business is not (and never has been) rocket science—it's simply a process of identifying a problem and finding a way to solve it that benefits both parties...The five parts of every business are the basis of every good business idea and business plan. If you can clearly define each of these processes for any business, you'll have a complete understanding of how it works. If you're thinking about starting

a business, defining what these processes might look like is the best place to start. (Kaufman, 2020, p. 39)

A good place to start a business is to identify the above five processes, use them to understand how the business will work, and from there develop a business plan—'a written document that describes the current state and the presupposed future of an organisation' (Honig & Karlsson, 2004, pp. 29–48). A more detailed discussion of business plans is contained further in the chapter, but the following sections will help in developing the kind of information needed for a plan.

As part of the business plan, it is worthwhile developing a value proposition, a way to think about the benefits to the person who is going to give you money for the object, product, or service. Its value is to the customer: what do they get out of this deal, what can they expect from your product or services, and what do you think they might get? As Guillebeau describes it:

> Value is something desirable and of worth, created through exchange or effort. In our context, an easier way to think about it is; Value means helping people. If you're trying to build a microbusiness and you begin your efforts by helping people, you're on the right track. When you get stuck, ask yourself: How can I give more value? Or more simply: How can I help my customer more?... A business ultimately succeeds because of the value it provides to end users, customers, or clients. More than anything else, value relates to emotional needs. Many business owners talk about their work in terms of the features it offers, but it's much more powerful to talk about the benefits customers receive. A feature is descriptive; a benefit is emotional. (2012, p. 29)

Recognizing the benefit, or emotional satisfaction, can help in that exchange between a business and customer, helping to provide value for the customer and generate an income. Again drawing on Kaufman, for a business to engage in the provision of value to a customer, 'that value must take on a form they're willing to pay for. Fortunately there's no need to reinvent the wheel—economic value takes on one of twelve standard forms' (2020, p. 49).

The first is *Product*, where an item or entity is sold for a higher amount than it costs. In the music industry, musicians include merchandising such as clothing to increase revenue. *Service* is the next form and consists of providing a benefit to someone for a fee. An architect developing plans is an example, as is charging for personal appearances and taking part in panels and workshops, which writers have done for many years. *Shared Resource* is where an asset is created and customers are charged to access that asset. Museums, rehearsal spaces, and music studios fit into this category. The *Subscription* model is one where you charge an ongoing fee for an ongoing benefit, such as is current for news organizations, which are attempting to introduce a subscription model in an online environment. The Netflix business model is another example of subscription at work. *Resale* is a form where a wholesaler acts as a middleman between the producer and the customer, and companies such as Amazon follow this model. The *Lease* model is where an asset is rented out to another for a set fee and an agreed amount of time. Spotify and iTunes are examples of successful users of the lease model. A business that follows an *Agency* model doesn't have their own product but rather sells someone else's product and charges a percentage of the sale price. Parts of the music industry follow this model, as does the agent who works on behalf of authors in the book publishing industry. *Audience Aggregation* is an older model in that it gathers together people with particular characteristics and sells those on to third parties. This is the model traditionally used in media organizations such as newspapers, magazines, and radio, but is also used effectively by social media giants such as Facebook. A *Loan* business collects interest on money that has been lent, and this model is prevalent in banking but it is also used by film companies that lend money to filmmakers with the expectation that the money will be paid back along with a nominated percentage of the profits. An *Option* form of income generation is 'the ability to take a pre-defined action for a fixed period of time in exchange for a fee' (Kaufman, 2020, p. 59) and Kaufman uses the example of movie tickets to demonstrate this model in action. *Insurance* takes money from people to protect their assets, and the final form is *Capital*, where ownership in a business is purchased and money is generated by dividends.

Michael Rappa specifically discusses online business models typical in the digital world. Demonstrating that all creative and innovative action rests on a set of antecedents, Rappa asserts that:

> In the most basic sense, a business model is the method of doing business by which a company can sustain itself—that is, generate revenue. The business model spells-out how a company makes money by specifying where it is positioned in the value chain. Some models are quite simple. A company produces a good or service and sells it to customers. If all goes well, the

> revenues from sales exceed the cost of operation and the company realizes a profit. Other models can be more intricately woven. Broadcasting is a good example. Radio and later television programming has been broadcast over the airwaves free to anyone with a receiver for much of the past century. The broadcaster is part of a complex network of distributors, content creators, advertisers (and their agencies), and listeners or viewers. Who makes money and how much is not always clear at the outset. The bottom line depends on many competing factors. Internet commerce will give rise to new kinds of business models. That much is certain. But the web is also likely to reinvent tried-and-true models. (2022, online)

Rappa notes a set of nine models often used for online businesses. These are listed as: Brokerage, Advertising, Infomediary, Merchant, Manufacturer (Direct), Affiliate, Community, Subscription, and Utility.

Amazon and eBay are examples of the *Brokerage* model, where that business facilitates transactions between a business and a customer. *Advertising* is similar to the traditional model where customers are onsold to advertisers, and in an online environment, numbers are seemingly easier to generate due to analytics. An *Infomediary* model provides data about consumers and their habits, and this data is sold to third parties. Nielsen ratings is an example of this model. The *Merchant* model covers retailers and wholesalers who sell online and/or offline, while the *Manufacturer (Direct)* model bypasses the middleman and sells directly to consumers. Pay-per-click revenue generators are covered under the *Affiliate* model, often used by bloggers, and a *Subscription* model is similar to Kaufman's thinking on this, with users charged a fee for a service/product. This model is used by the more traditional media (e.g. news organizations) but has been updated with 'subscription-based crowdfunding' (Dalla Chiesa & Handke, 2020, p. 160), on which platforms such as Patreon operate. A *Community* business model 'is based on user loyalty... Revenue can be based on the sale of ancillary products and services or voluntary contributions; or revenue may be tied to contextual advertising and subscriptions for premium services' (Rappa, 2022). Public broadcasting such as the Australian Broadcasting Corporation (ABC) and the Special Broadcasting Service (SBS) are examples of how this model is applied. Finally, the *Utility* model is an approach that depends on pay-as-you-go. An example of this business model is metered subscription, where customers are able to access particular content by purchasing portions, for example articles in scholarly journals.

Rappa contends that these models can be combined within a business's strategy: 'For example, it is not uncommon for content driven businesses to blend advertising with a subscription model' (Rappa, 2022). The SBS, for example, has a hybrid public funding/advertising approach to revenue raising. In an entrepreneurial sense, several of these models fit into the practice of creative industries practitioners, but other forms of funding, particularly in the creative production sectors, have also developed over a number of years and can be considered under a *Patronage* model. For example, grants, personal and corporate donations, and philanthropy all form part of the suite of income streams drawn on by sectors such as theater, film, publishing, and the writing of literature. As McIntyre notes, the action of patronage, an old form of support, 'is vitally important…It has certainly been crucial to the development of much of what we call "Art" in the West' (2012, p. 191). Mihaly Csikszentmihalyi (1997) points out that patronage in Florence during the Renaissance and the close relationship between Florentine elites and artists such as Brunelleschi, Ghiberti, Donatello, Masaccio, and da Fabriano were vitally important products of their art works. Without the financial support of bankers, royalty, and churchmen, many of Florence's masterpieces would not have been made. Bringing this idea into the twenty-first century, grants, sponsorships, and subsidies from governments and philanthropic donors for creative practitioners are providing similar support, as are crowdfunding platforms such as Patreon and KickStarter.

If a business model is the method of generating revenue, then a business plan is a map of how to get there. It is a rational exercise in stepping you through from the beginning to the end of the process of achieving the business's particular objective. As part of starting up a business, particularly if the intention is to apply for some form of funding or other support, a business plan should be developed. It is a formal written document that 'is a communications tool, designed to inform, guide and sometimes sell a business concept or case to a third party' (Mazzarol & Reboud, 2020, p. 192). While Mazzarol and Reboud (2020) claim that many small entrepreneurial enterprises often do not have formal business plans, often due to a lack of business skills, having a business plan does assist in strategic planning for 'long-range thinking and systematic screening of opportunities' (2020, p. 193) and helps reduce the likelihood of failure. Business plans, according to Mazzarol and Reboud, have the following key elements and often use the following format:

1. Executive summary: 1–2 pages outlining the key elements of the plan.
2. Company overview: description of the business, including a mission statement.
3. Product or services: what the business is selling.
4. Market opportunity: demand for the services or product, SWOT analysis.
5. Competition and threats: the main competitors and other threats, including regulatory, political, legal.
6. Economics of the business: KPIs, anticipated profit margins, cash flow.
7. Marketing strategy: how the business will make itself known to potential customers, pricing, marketing, and promotion.
8. Operations: how the product or service will be produced.
9. Management team: structure of the personnel, if necessary.
10. Financial plan: profit and loss projections, balance sheet, and future growth forecasts.
11. Appendices: any other documentation to support the above.

For a micro entrepreneurial startup, a simple plan can be developed. For example, The *One-Page Business Plan* available at The $100 Startup lists five key areas to consider: overview, hustling, ka-ching, success, and obstacles/challenges/open questions (The $100 Startup, 2022). In other words, a plan needs an overarching section that includes what is for sale, the intended customer, and why the business is a good idea, but can also include a mission statement and vision for the business, as well as how to market the business, that is, how customers can learn about what the business does and pass on referrals. The plan can include how much to charge and how to get paid, how to measure success via numbers of customers or income, and a note of any anticipated issues.

Some fundamental common elements can be built into these plans. You want to know yourself very well and know what it is that you're going to sell. There must be a marketing plan, that is, some sort of strategy around marketing. Make sure you know who your competitors are, what your own strengths and weaknesses are, and what your competitors' strengths and weaknesses are. How is the business going to be financed? How are you going to work your way through the details and how are you going to keep control of all of that? What mechanisms do you have in place to make sure that all of the actions that you want to occur actually occur?

Understanding the target market is one consideration and, in turn, lends itself to how to reach that target. Kotler and Lee (2007) list three factors to understanding a market: geographic, demographic, and psychographic factors. *Geographic* variables can be as broad as a nation location, to as narrow as a specific worksite. *Demographics* include age, sex, occupation, family circumstances, religion, nationality, and ethnic background of your customers. *Psychographics* are an extension of this, providing finer details by also including 'value, lifestyle, or personality characteristics' (2007, n.p.). *Lifestyles* research is another rapidly rising factor in understanding a target audience: 'Lifestyle relates to how people live, how they spend their money, and how they allocate their time among different types of activities' (Watkins et al., 2021, p. 1). Any or all of these factorial analyses can be used to understand the target market or audience.

The data provided from those analyses will enable an entrepreneur or established business person to develop a targeted marketing plan. This plan can take on the form of word of mouth, advertising, direct marketing, a business website, promotional events, brochures and flyers, and social media engagement and blogging. Fulton, in a project that examined media entrepreneurs, found that social media engagement targeting their specific audience worked very well, outlining how each participant in the study has 'carefully chosen the form/s of social media and digital dissemination that their audience would find appropriate' (2017, p. 49).

A further key component of a business plan is a SWOT analysis. This acronym stands for: Strengths, Weaknesses, Opportunities, and Threats. Kolb notes that a SWOT analysis is a 'tool for organizing the data obtained through scanning and research into information that will then result in knowledge of what action to take' (2016, n.p.). The first two are aimed internally and include analysis of what the business is particularly good at and what can be improved. Opportunities and Threats are aimed at external forces and can include scrutiny of market trends that can be capitalized on, but also an understanding of the broader context in the form of what competitors are doing. Mazzarol and Reboud (2020) prefer an inversion of SWOT, that is, a TOWS analysis (Threats, Opportunities, Weaknesses, and Strengths), because this gives early focus on the external elements in the first instance. The core idea remains the same, that is, analyzing the environment and taking action as required. To help, the Australian Government (2022a) business site provides the following questions to aid in developing a SWOT framework:

Strengths: What do we do well? What do we do better than our competition? What unique assets do we have internally (such as knowledge, background, network, reputation or skills) and externally (such as customers, patents, technology or capital)? What positive aspects of the business give us a competitive advantage?

Weaknesses: What and where can we improve? What do our competitors do better? Where are the gaps in our assets and resources (such as knowledge, cash or equipment)? Is the thing that sets us apart from our competition obvious? How can we improve business processes?

Opportunities: What trends can we use to our advantage to increase use of our product or service? Are there any changes or events that might positively impact us (such as consumer behaviour, regulation, policies or new technology)? Has anything changed in the market that creates opportunity for us? Do the public like us?

Threats: What factors beyond our control could place us at risk? What potential competitors may enter the market? Are our resource and material supplies unstable or insecure? Are there any changes or events that might negatively impact us (such as consumer behaviour, regulation, policies or new technology)?

Ongoing SWOT analysis also helps a business to keep on top of any issues that may arise or possibilities that emerge. In saying that, another analysis tool that gives a deeper analysis of the external opportunities and threats is the acronym STEEPLE. The factors inside this analytical tool include: socio-cultural, technological, economic, environmental, political, legal, and ethical factors.

Socio-cultural factors examine behavioral and cultural trends, such as population and demographics, level of education, diversity, and traditions. *Technological* factors can affect how business is done, and includes understanding current and potential infrastructure and equipment as well as understanding such things as social media. *Economic* factors include how the business can be impacted by fiscal decisions such as interest rate rises, while *Environmental* factors include how your business impacts the environment and, most significantly, how changes in the environment impact your business. *Political* factors include an understanding of how political changes can impact the business in areas such as legislation and taxation. *Legal* factors cover any new legal requirements to ensure compliance, including health and safety, contracts, employment and competition laws, and IP regimes, including international if necessary. The *Ethical* factor is about the social values that govern business behavior and act as the foundation for what is right and wrong.

Businesses need funding. Funding requirements and levels depend on the type of business structure used, from nano, to micro-businesses, through to SMEs and large corporations. Kaufman (2020) discusses what he calls the 'Hierarchy of Funding', with ten options that range from personal cash at the top through to public stock offering, as ways of raising funds for a business. He notes that to access funding, 'it's often necessary to give up a certain amount of control over the business's operations. Businesspeople won't give you money for nothing' (2020, p. 207). The hierarchy demonstrates that the further down the hierarchy you operate, the more money you can get, but the less control you have.

At the top of the hierarchy is *personal cash*, which Kaufman claims to be the best, and this is using your own cash to invest in your own business. This option also gives you the most control over any decisions. Next on the list is *personal credit* and includes such options as credit cards, which, while still giving control over business decisions, can lead to issues with a personal credit rating if payments cannot be met. It is, however, an '[e]asy and quick option if your needs don't exceed a few thousand dollars' (Kaufman, 2022). *Personal loans* are the third on the list and entail asking friends and family for money, a sometimes fraught process if the loan cannot be paid back, which could lead to breakdown in relationships and a curtailing of vital reciprocity.

The next elements depend on a number and variety of what we call outside players. The first is an *unsecured loan* from a bank or credit union. These loans are referred to as personal loans in the banking industry and are typically for smaller amounts, as they do not require collateral. Personal loans often have a higher interest rate because of the risk the bank is taking if a borrower defaults. The second type of loan from banks is a *secured loan* and does require collateral, often property such as a house, and, while this option is useful, there are anecdotal stories about filmmakers who have lost their houses when the film they financed using collateral on their house flopped. The next two are not typical in the creative industries, only usually activated at the corporate level. *Bonds* are where businesses onsell their debt to individuals, and *receivable financing* is using receivables (or how much customers owe a business) as collateral for a loan.

While the abovementioned funding options typically leave the running of the business in the hands of the owner, the following three provide a way for investors to become part of the business. *Angel Capital* is a form of investment where an 'angel' in the form of an investor provides funding for part ownership of a business. Angels are typically 'high net wealth individuals who make a significant investment in start-up companies' (Rijanto, 2021). While the business ownership is partially relinquished, this form of funding usually does not mean that the investor is part of the day-to-day running of the operation. However, *venture capital* funding, the ninth level of the hierarchy set out by Kaufman (2022), provides a large amount of funds and a correspondingly large amount of sway in the business decisions. Similarly, a *Public Stock Offering* means less control, as it invites investors to take a stake in a business via an open market, thus ownership can be in many hands and control belongs to whoever owns the most shares. This option can be particularly risky if the owner has less than a 51% share, as they can be voted out by stockholders.

Kaufman uses the example of Steve Jobs as someone who started a company (Apple) and was voted out:

> The more control you have to give up, the less attractive the funding. More opinions means slower operations [and] it's also not uncommon for investors to remove executives of a company that's not performing well, even if those executives are the founder of the company. Even high-flying executives aren't immune: when Apple was performing poorly in the 1990s, the board of directors fired Steve Jobs from the company he cofounded. (2020, pp. 209–210)

As Felix Dennis also strongly asserts, '[n]o founder of a business who surrenders control in exchange for capital is ever likely to retrieve control of their business. Their financial destiny is in the hands of others and the entrepreneur has lost their way on the narrow road' (2010, p. 61).

While the above forms of funding are available to practitioners in the creative industries, especially those who are freelancers and contractors, they may find it difficult to raise money using these resources, particularly those that involve banks or investors (Rijanto, 2021). However, there are other forms of funding available. Crowdfunding, for example, is a more recent entry into the suite of investment options that involves 'online contributions by the general public, above all, to a diverse pool of creative projects' (Buff & Alhadeff, 2013, p. 28). Parhankangas et al. provide a simple definition when they say that it is a 'recent movement where the general public, or "the crowd", is invited to participate in the process of value creation traditionally conducted within more closed systems' (2019,

p. 1). One crowdfunding platform, Kickstarter, has raised more than USD6.3 billion since its inception and funded over 200,000 projects (Kickstarter, 2022). An analysis of the categories funded by Kickstarter shows that, apart from 'Food' all the funding is relevant to the creative industries, with the highest number of successful projects in music (33,059) and film and video (29,985) (Kickstarter, 2022).

While this practice of raising money has been a way of allegedly democratizing investment in creativity and cultural production (Parhankangas et al., 2019), other benefits include low transaction costs, broader access to an audience, the ability to test the market, and increased visibility (Lazzaro & Noonan, 2021). However, others are more cautious about the pitfalls. It provides an upfront injection of cash, which is particularly helpful in areas that are cost-intensive at the beginning of a project, but the ethos behind crowdfunding is that funds are not forthcoming if the nominated target is not met. Lazzaro and Noonan also note what they call the 'moral hazard problem' (2021, n.p.), where 'creators fail to adequately deliver to their backers' (2021, n.p.), or scammers who promise but disappear. Another, more subtle pitfall is the issue of discrimination (Lazzaro & Noonan, 2021), including bias toward well-known creators (Dalla Chiesa & Handke, 2020).

Buff and Alhadeff (2013) identify four types of crowdfunding: *equity-based* and *lending-based*, where funders expect a financial return in the form of shares in the business or interest; *reward-based*, which provides a 'reward' such as access to the developed product; and *donation-based*, where the contributor expects nothing in return. Massolution (2012) and De Buysere et al. (2012) add *royalty-based*, which provides payment when the product shows a profit.

Another form of funding under the crowd sourcing banner is 'subscription-based crowdfunding' (Dalla Chiesa & Handke, 2020, p. 160) or 'digital patronage' (Wohn et al. 2019) models such as Patreon, which was established in 2013 to 'establish a longer-term association between founders and backers, beyond the scope of a single project' (Dalla Chiesa & Handke, 2020, p. 160). It provides regular payments:

> On Patreon you can let your fans become active participants in the work they love by offering them a monthly membership. You give them access to exclusive content, community, and insight into your creative process. In exchange, you get the freedom to do your best work, and the stability you need to build an independent creative career. (Patreon, 2022)

The success of a campaign using the digital patronage model depends on communication between the practitioner and funder, but analysis demonstrated that the top 1% of creators received more than $2500 per month in income and the top 5% received more than $750 (Regner, 2020).

Regardless of which model is used, some form of funding for creative industries start-ups is required. Once that is in place, keeping track of how the business is performing is critical. The two simplest and most valuable ways to do this are through the regular monitoring of income and expenditure, and, most importantly, cash flow:

> Many good businesses cease to operate because of poor cash flow. You might have good ideas, they might be well marketed and profitable, but if the money isn't coming in regularly, you'll starve and the business will go bust! You must learn to anticipate and resolve poor cash flow. (Chessell & Edwards, 1984, p. 53)

A positive cash flow involves the art of ensuring more money comes in than goes out, and this is crucially important for any size business, from micro-enterprises to publicly listed companies.

> The easiest part of managing your cash flow is by regular billing...although you may expect to be paid on completion of the job, often this does not happen. Organize all financial arrangements before you begin a project. A contract may be required. Deposits or progress payments must be arranged. (Chessell & Edwards, 1984, p. 53)

In other words, and referring to the beginning of the chapter, this is a way to get paid. Construct an invoice, agree on payment schedules, collect all debts as soon as you can, and plan ahead. Part of the idea of maintaining a positive cash flow is in understanding how to charge for the product or service you deliver. One of the critical things you must do is decide on a price. For products, calculate all costs and add 50%, leaving a price mark-up of 33.3% of retail. But it is important to remember that in setting fees for services you must also take account of all costs, as well as factoring in your level of expertise and skill set. Costs such as overheads (ongoing business expenses) need to be included in any pricing. Overheads include all ongoing business expenses not including or related to direct labor, direct materials or third-party expenses that are billed directly to customers, and include expenses such as accounting, banking and legal fees, insurances, advertising, rent, taxes, telephone and internet expenses, travel and utilities. It is worth repeating that value for money is very important for both yourself and the client. Do not undersell yourself or overcharge the client. Some work will undoubtedly need to be done for free, as suggested earlier in our discussion of the gift economy, but most work requires you to decide on an hourly rate or a set fee for the job. One quick method of pricing yourself, that is, setting an hourly rate, was developed by Chessell and Edwards (1984). The calculation they suggested goes something like the one provided in Table 6.1.

As part of this client interaction, there may be the need to put a written contract in place. But be wary. According to Chessell and Edwards, 'an oral contract is not worth the paper it's written on!' (1984, p. 48). That said, particularly when it comes to smaller transactions, a handshake is often the extent of the agreement. Nevertheless, a formal contract is an agreement between parties that lays out obligations between a practitioner and a client:

> Contracts have an economic dimension and not just when money is involved: they record an agreement between people to exchange something of value, they offer an incentive and a reward, and they can be enforced, either formally in court, settled out of court or enforced informally through social pressure. (Towse, 2020, p. 115)

Table 6.1 Calculation of hourly rate for sole operator

Gross salary required per week	$600
Hours to be worked	30 hours per week
Wage rate = 600 ÷ 30	$20 per hour
Cost of overheads and personal expenses	$10,000
Relating to business	
Plus: Two weeks holiday for owner	$1200
Subtotal	$11,200 per annum
Overhead per week working 50 weeks per annum	
Overhead rate	$224
224 ÷ 30	$7.50 per hour
Investment in business	$15,000
Return on investment required	20% per annum
Return required (profit)	$3000 per annum = $60 per week
Profit rate 60 ÷ 30	$2 per hour
Total hourly rate: $20 + $7.50 + $2 = $29.50	$30 per hour

Source: Based on Chessell and Edwards (1984, p. 49)

Ruth Towse (2020) explains the complexity of contracts in the creative industries by noting that they can range from a 'handshake' deal, as mentioned, between an individual artist and a gallery to exhibit work, to a band that has a written contract with a record label, right through to a film producer that has multiple contracts with multiple professionals including actors, designers, stunt people, writers, and directors. They can also be a one-off event or cover an ongoing relationship. McMahon (2013) notes that contracts can cover such things as publishing rights, access to royalties, and international obligations. Regardless of the size and complexity of the venture you are undertaking, contracts have a simple thing in common: 'The contract lays down each party's commitments' (Towse, 2020, p. 117). However, it is wise to remember that there is often a power imbalance within the contract process where one party, say a large corporation, has a higher leverage than the other. The general rule of thumb is the one with the most money has the most power. But leverage may also come in the amount of symbolic, cultural, or social capital one has, and that depends on the importance placed on each of these forms of capital within the field you are working in. This is why your reputation, in part, is incredibly important. In the case we are talking about here, it gives you leverage in contract negotiations.

Other legal matters are to do with the protections afforded to you in such things as intellectual property (IP), that is, 'the property of your mind or exclusive knowledge. If you develop a new product, service, process or idea it belongs to you and is considered your IP. IP rights provide IP owners with the time and opportunity to commercialize their creations' (Australian Government, 2022b). IP rights relevant to the creative industries include protection for patents, trademarks, design, and copyright. These are considered a key asset to a creative industries business:

> Ownership of IP—or the rights associated with IP—allows individuals or companies to enjoy financial benefits from the sale or licencing of this IP. This is similar to how the ownership of physical property allows it to be sold or leased. In a world that is increasingly yielding value from knowledge-based assets, the role of IP is becoming crucial to economic success. (Mazzarol & Reboud, 2020, p. 432)

Patent protection ensures a third party won't manufacture an invention without permission. Trademark protection looks after logos, words in set fonts, unique phrases, and so on that identify a brand. Design rights protect 'the overall visual appearance of new and distinctive products' (IP Australia, 2022) and can be a combination of shape, configuration, pattern, or ornamentation that gives a product a unique appearance. The fourth important right for creative industries practitioners is copyright.

Copyright is automatically awarded in the Australian system and there is no need to register and no fee payable to assume copyright. When something is expressed, it is covered by copyright. According to Straubhaar et al., '[c]opyright is the legal right to control intellectual property' (2016, p. 181). It is a way to generate income from one's own work: 'It formalizes in law the entitlement of a creative originator to be recompensed for their intellectual labour, in order that such efforts be encouraged by sufficient reward' (Athique, 2013, p. 149). And while copyright law doesn't protect an idea but the form of expression (Pearson, 2011) there are plenty of forms of expression it does protect: text (e.g. in books, journal articles, reports, webpages, news, and magazine articles), images (e.g. photographs, artistic works, graphs), video and moving images (e.g. films, videos, television commercials, vodcasts), audio recordings (e.g. music recordings, radio programs, podcasts), and computer programs.

While each of these products of the creative industries requires both formal and informal domain knowledge in music, film, journalism, photography, television, design, information technology, and so on in order to put them together, to make them, to produce them, something similar occurs for the necessary business activity and systems of patronage that underpin them. The knowledge we set out briefly above, the conventions, rules, and typical methods stored in the space of works, the preceding knowledge used to start, build, and continue an innovative business in the creative industries, we describe here as entrepreneurial domain knowledge. These are the fundamental things that constitute the domain of entrepreneurial activity in the creative industries. It is this set of components, described above, that constitutes the conventions of the symbol system that creative industries entrepreneurs currently draw on to produce the work they do. This is the basic domain knowledge one must engage with in order to become an entrepreneurial creative agent.

We argue that this entrepreneurial domain knowledge must intersect with the domain knowledge of how to make specific cultural products in order for creative agents to gain and maintain an income. We can see that intersection in the lives of those who have succeeded, in various ways, to actively do just that, that is, gain an income in the creative industries using an entrepreneurial approach to their creative activities. As we move into setting out case studies of successful and entrepreneurial creative practitioners, we remind you to consider *all* of the things we have been talking about, as they help to demonstrate the deep interconnectedness that exists within the creative system we are detailing in this book. The crucial thing to remember is that nothing occurs in isolation from anything else. Creative industries entrepreneurs in the twenty-first century are deeply connected socially, technologically, economically, environmentally, politically, legally, and ethically to the worlds that surround them.

References

ABS. (2001). 1321.0 – Small business in Australia, 2001. *Australian Bureau of Statistics*. Retrieved January 24, 2022, from https://www.abs.gov.au/ausstats/abs@.nsf/mf/1321.0

Athique, A. (2013). *Digital media and society: An introduction*. Polity.

IP Australia. (2022). What a design right is. *Australian Government: IP Australia*. Retrieved January 21, 2022, from https://www.ipaustralia.gov.au/designs/understanding-designs/what-design-right

Australian Government. (2022a). Develop your SWOT analysis. *Business.gov.au*. Retrieved January 14, 2022, from https://business.gov.au/planning/business-plans/swot-analysis

Australian Government. (2022b). Intellectual property. *Business.gov.au*. Retrieved January 14, 2022, from https://business.gov.au/planning/protect-your-brand-idea-or-creation/intellectual-property

Buff, L. A., & Alhadeff, P. (2013). Budgeting for crowdfunding rewards. *Journal of the Music and Entertainment Industry Educators Association, 13*(1), 27–44.

Chessell, P., & Edwards, H. (1984). *Being your own boss: How to work successfully for yourself*. Penguin.

Csikszentmihalyi, M. (1997). *Creativity: Flow and the psychology of discovery and invention*. Harper Collins.

Dalla, C. C., & Handke, C. (2020). Crowdfunding. In R. Towse & T. Navarrete-Hernandez (Eds.), *Handbook of cultural economics* (pp. 158–167). Edward Elgar.

De Buysere, K., Oliver, G., Ronald, K., & Dan, M. (2012). A framework for European crowdfunding. Retrieved February 12, 2022, from https://www.fundraisingschool.it/wp-content/uploads/2013/02/European-Crowdfunding-Framework-Oct-2012.pdf

Dennis, F. (2010). *The narrow road: A brief guide to the getting of money*. Penguin.

Fulton, J. (2017). Media entrepreneurship: Social networking sites, the audience and new media professionals. In J. M. Fulton & P. McIntyre (Eds.), *Creating space in the fifth estate* (pp. 47–60). Cambridge Scholars Publishing.

Guillebeau, C. (2012). *The $100 startup: Fire your boss, do what you love and work better to live more*. Pan Books.
Honig, B., & Karlsson, T. (2004). Institutional forces and the written business plan. *Journal of Management, 30*(2), 29–48.
Kaufman, J. (2020). *The personal MBA: Master the art of business 10th anniversary edition*. Penguin.
Kaufman, J. (2022). *The personal MBA: Master the art of business*. Retrieved January 11, 2022, from https://personalmba.com/hierarchy-of-funding/
Kickstarter. (2022). *Stats*. Retrieved January 12, 2022, from https://www.kickstarter.com/help/stats
Kolb, B. M. (2016). *Marketing strategy for the creative and cultural industries*. Routledge.
Kotler, P., & Lee, N. (2007). *Marketing in the public sector: A roadmap for improved performance*. Pearson Education, Inc.
Lazzaro, E., & Noonan, D. (2021). A comparative analysis of US and EU regulatory frameworks of crowdfunding for the cultural and creative industries. *International Journal of Cultural Policy, 27*(5), 590–606. https://doi.org/10.1080/10286632.2020.1776270
Massolution. (2012). *Crowdfunding industry report: Market trends, composition and crowdfunding platforms*. Crowdsourcing LLC. Retrieved January 12, 2022,fromhttp://ncfacanada.org/wp-content/uploads/2012/10/Massolution-Full-Industry-Report.pdf
Mazzarol, T., & Reboud, S. (2020). *Entrepreneurship and innovation: Theory, practice and context* (4th ed.). Springer.
McIntyre, P. (2012). *Creativity and cultural production: Issues for media practice*. Palgrave Macmillan.
McMahon, J. (2013). Contracts in media and entertainment: Show me the CLM!. *Determine*. Retrieved April 17, 2016, from http://www.determine.com/blog/entry/contracts-in-the-media-and-entertainment-industry-show-me-the-clm#.VxMM40au87F
Parhankangas, A., Mason, C., & Landström, H. (2019). Crowdfunding: An introduction. In A. Parhankangas, C. Mason, & H. Landström (Eds.), *Handbook of research on crowdfunding* (pp. 1–22). Edward Elgar.
Patreon. (2022). *What's Patreon?* Retrieved January 12, 2022, from https://www.patreon.com
Pearson, M. (2011). *Blogging and tweeting without getting sued: A global guide to the law for anyone writing online*. Allen & Unwin.
Rappa, M. (2022). Business models on the Web. *Managing the Digital Enterprise*. Retrieved January 14, 2022, from http://digitalenterprise.org/models/models.html
Regner, T. (2020). Crowdfunding a monthly income: An analysis of the membership platform Patreon. *Journal of Cultural Economics, 45*, 133–142. https://doi.org/10.1007/s10824-020-09381-5

Rijanto, A. (2021). Creative industries project financing through crowdfunding: The roles of fund target & backers. *Creative Industries Journal*, (online). https://doi.org/10.1080/17510694.2021.1899489

Straubhaar, J., LaRose, R., & Davenport, L. (2016). *Media now: Understanding media, culture and technology* (9th ed.). Wadsworth.

The $100 Startup. (2022). *The one-page business plan.* Retrieved January 13, 2022, from https://100startup.com/resources/business-plan.pdf

Towse, R. (2020). Contract for creators and performers in the creative industries. In T. Bille, A. Mignosa, & R. Towse (Eds.), *Teaching cultural economics* (pp. 115–121). Elgar.

Watkins, L., Aitken, R., Robertson, K., Williams, J., & Thyne, M. (2021). New Zealand consumer lifestyles. *Aotearoa New Zealand Journal of Social Issues, 1*, 1–17. https://doi.org/10.24135/anzjsi.v1i.50

Wohn, D. Y., Jough, P., Eskander, P., Siri, J. S., Shimobayashi, M., & Desai, P. (2019). Understanding digital patronage: Why do people subscribe to streamers on Twitch? *Proceeding of ACM CHI PLAY* (pp. 99–110).

PART III

Case Studies: Profiles of Successful Entrepreneurs in a Variety of Creative Industry Contexts

CHAPTER 7

Entrepreneurship in Publishing, Writing and Journalism

The publishing sector of the creative industries includes the publication of periodicals or non-periodicals. Non-periodical publishing includes 'the one-off printing and sale of such things as books and reports while periodicals include magazines and newspapers which appear at regular intervals' (McIntyre et al., 2019, p. 241). While many of them remain paper-based, 'increasingly there are now a number of digitally based publishing and self-publishing options that have threatened to disrupt the structure of this industry' (McIntyre et al., 2019, p. 241) as it undergoes radical changes in the twenty-first century. It is still in a state of dynamic flux. In a similar way to other creative industries sectors, it is becoming more reliant on precarious work and the gig economy (O'Donnell & Zion, 2019). Many of the professionals who make a living from writing, and all those in the field who support them such as literary agents, publishers, editors, art directors, designers and creative directors, photo editors, freelance photographers, marketers and salespeople, all work in tandem to promote, market, and distribute the work of writers:

> Writers are, of course, very important people in the publishing sector. They may come as freelancers who work to a brief or on spec for magazines, or as a staff writer who operates as a news journalist, a feature writer, a columnist, or they may be an author or blogger. Some writers may perform many or all of these functions. Their roles vary according to the title and position and

P. McIntyre et al., *Entrepreneurship in the Creative Industries*, https://doi.org/10.1007/978-3-031-19455-9_7

who they write for, but the main task is to produce engaging content. (McIntyre et al., 2019, p. 246)

Many of these 'professionals are being forced to wise up to new labour market realities and adjust their career expectations accordingly' (O'Donnell & Zion, 2019, p. 223). While traditional media organizations appear to be shedding enormous numbers of skilled workers, particularly in journalism, at the same time emerging technologies provide opportunities for practitioners in these areas to develop and deliver innovative content. In journalism, for example, Australian researchers discovered that around 3000 journalists had lost their jobs since 2011, with Australian media company Fairfax reportedly losing half its editorial staff by 2017 (Zion et al., 2018). The same study also recognized new players in the field such as *Junkee*, *The New Daily*, *The Saturday Paper*, and Australian versions of *The Guardian*, *The New York Times*, and *Huffington Post*. However, and as Craig notes, apart from those big, recognizable players, there is a 'vast global wave of online cultural producers fostering and blending old and new forms of media entrepreneurialism, management, creative labour, and user practices' (2019, p. 363). This 'vast wave' includes those working in the publishing sector such as writers and, among that broad category, journalists. These professionals are deeply embedded in an iterative, cyclical creative system in action consisting of a domain, field, and individual agent (McIntyre et al., 2016). While these practitioners have had to become even more innovative and entrepreneurial, it is pertinent to note that intrapreneurs are also a key feature of these professions. In this chapter, we present the work of award-winning journalist Stan Grant; multimedia journalist Isaac McIntyre; journalist, and writers festival founder and director, Rosemarie Milsom; publisher, and now full-time writer, Phillipa McGuiness; and fiction author Jaye Ford. These individual agents bring to the system their ability to internalize the domain structures and field requirements, as well as their own motivations, unique backgrounds, and personal attributes.

Janet Fulton's research into journalists and creativity found that while there were some similarities in 'personality, home and family environment, education and life experiences' (2016, p. 94) attributable to the respondents who took part in her study, there were also differences; the common denominator was the identification of a system of practice where the individual journalists operated effectively and creatively within the structures that afforded them the ability to take creative action. This idea can be applied to entrepreneurship in these industries. An examination of these structures, and how individual agents operate conditionally within them, is provided below, along with examples of how each of these practitioners has harnessed these understandings to operate entrepreneurially and intrapreneurially within the publishing sector as writers. One of the common elements in each of the case studies presented here is how each of them maintains strong networks and strong networking skills, as well as the transferability of skills across the domains they work within. Another common denominator is that they have learnt how to generate income streams rather than rely on steady employment.

Funding models in the publishing sector cover the gamut from the use of venture capital through to self-funding. Corporate sponsorship of events such as writers' festivals is common, as are private donations and government grants for individual writers. Advertising, while not as strongly income-generating in new media as it was in the traditional kind, is still included as a way to generate income with online ventures. In news media, major organizations can be owned by shareholders or private companies but, in the last decade, venture capitalism has made inroads into journalism, with publications such as *BuzzFeed*, *Vox Media*, and *Medium* raising significant funds to either start or continue operating (Usher, 2017). Philanthropy is also a form of support for journalists. Organizations such as the Knight Foundation in the United States and Australia's The Judith Neilson Institute for Journalism and Ideas provide funding to tell stories in different formats. Crowdfunding subscription models via platforms such as Patreon provide another option. Writers also charge appearance fees to take part in festivals and do corporate appearances and professional speaking gigs. To get started in his career, Australian author Matthew Reilly organized a bank loan for his first book and self-published 1000 copies before being noticed and signed by a commercial publisher (Cunningham, 2021). Royalties and copyright payments also now commonly form one part of a diverse income stream, as precarious work becomes increasingly insecure (O'Donnell & Zion, 2019). The writers we have selected for our case studies have generated income from sponsorship, advertising, grants, private and corporate donations, royalties and, at times, as waged employees for private and public companies.

Stan Grant is one example of not only a writer who has been able to forge a career across platforms, engaging in both entrepreneurial and intrapreneurial practices, but also one who, as a decision-making agent, brought to bear his idiosyncratic background, one that is unique to him but shared by many others, to his work within the creative system. Grant's television news and radio career as a journalist spans more than thirty years. He has worked for Australian Macquarie Radio Network, Australian television channels Seven, SBS, the ABC, and Sky News, and international television on CNN and Al Jazeera. In 2021, he was the International Affairs Editor for the Australian Broadcasting Corporation and worked with NITV and *The Guardian*. Outside of journalism, Grant has written a number of books and made a documentary, particularly focusing on his heritage as an Aboriginal man and the issues in Australia surrounding racism. His journalism, books, and documentary have won national and international awards. He claims it is his early life that shaped his approach to the world he inhabits.

He was born 'in Griffith in south-west New South Wales in 1963. His mother is from the Kamilaroi people and his father is of the Wiradjuri' (Celebrity Speakers, 2022). Grant lived in small communities across the state as his father, a sawmiller, moved the family to where the scarce work was. This itinerant life gave Grant 'a love of adventure and stories. He grew up listening to the tales of his grandfather and uncles and aunts. Despite poverty and an early sporadic education the security of his family and the larger Aboriginal community gave him a strong platform for life' (Celebrity Speakers, 2022).

It was the exhortations of academic and activist Marcia Langton that brought him to a university education. Among his many achievements across his career, and the life experiences these brought him, he became Professor of Global Affairs at Griffith University and Chair of Indigenous/Australian Belongings at Charles Sturt University:

> In 2016 Stan Grant was appointed as the special advisor to the then Prime Minister Malcolm Turnbull on Indigenous constitutional recognition. Stan has won many major awards including an Australian T.V Logie, a Columbia University Du-Pont Award (the broadcast equivalent of the Pulitzer Prize), and the prestigious U.S Peabody Award. He is a four-time winner of the highly prized Asia TV Awards including reporter of the year. (Celebrity Speakers, 2022)

In an essay for *Griffith Review*, Grant (2018) mused on his grandfather's life and the current political situation around the world. In it though, he also discussed what he has done in more than 30 years of journalism, nationally and internationally, and how he has been able to draw on his background, telling how these characteristics from across his life became key components in his success: 'All of this has shaped me' (Grant, 2018).

As Harper claims 'the future of journalism and media will be defined by people who can seamlessly mesh—and reconcile—solid journalism with business savvy, sustainable revenue models, technological innovation and inner hustle' (Harper in Evans, 2014, p. 142). Harper's prediction nicely encapsulates the experiences of Isaac McIntyre, a sports, entertainment, and electronic gaming journalist in Australia. One could claim he has entrepreneurial and intrapreneurial skills which he parlayed into a career as a journopreneur. He is a clear example of working among the precariat of journalism before gaining an income across a variety of endeavors. He is also an excellent case study in how to harness the skills, knowledge, and networks necessary to carving out a niche in the creative industries and generating that income.

Isaac McIntyre, taking whatever work experience was available to him throughout his university education, capitalized on each as he progressed his career in journalism. We will elucidate these more fully shortly, but given that multidisciplinary skills are required to work in post-industrial media, as O'Donnell and Zion (2019) argue, we can see this in action in McIntyre's work history, where he built up the necessary skills for each writing domain he entered into. Working across multiple platforms and various modes of gaining an income, his understanding of the domain knowledge for each is now quite significant. For example, when asked about the difference between print and digital journalism, having acquired domain knowledge in both areas, he noted that:

> The main difference for a journalist between print and digital is the time on the story. With online deadlines there is no time to sit on the story, write it, sub it and put a photo in. You've got more time in print. The dynamic of the story is different as well. Print needs all the info straight away. Online versions are more dynamic with more life to the story which can be added to and amended as the day goes by.
>
> Journalists are still writing an article. That skill set doesn't change. Same as print but going online. You work the same way. Essentially there's no difference in the copy. You just jazz it up for online. The structures are not necessarily different either. But print is copy focused with digital giving you a different way to tell the story and you can add links, images, links to the back story, snippets of audio. You sell more of the story online.

> As examples, The Herald's sports articles had no extra elements. They were old school with just photo and text. The ABC Rugby League coverage, which is only online, also highlights the technical aspects of the game with analysis like *The Herald.* But headlines and subheads are different, more images and gifs, sometimes audio with reasonable quality and 15sec videos, which is all designed to keep people on and give you a much better retention rate. They are richer articles. There's no value left in just print as it's not as optimal. (I. McIntyre, personal email communication, September 22, 2021)

Note the slightly different 'rules' for working online, where it is necessary to add elements such as images, soundbites, gifs, and links. These examples also align with Negus and Pickering's (2004) argument that to be creative one needs both tradition and innovation to be operative. McIntyre's description demonstrates this claim by pointing out that so-called traditional rules and structures, such as the skill set required to write a story, are still important in both online and print domains of journalism. McIntyre also exemplifies an understanding of the field when he mentions what is needed to keep an audience engaged in a story.

An agent working in this field brings their unique attributes, motivation, and personal background to the creative system, including education, background, and family circumstances, and, as discussed earlier, these attributes contribute to an entrepreneurial mindset. Isaac McIntyre's family is large, with five of the siblings employed in the creative industries. His parents' backgrounds are in music and journalism, with his father engaging in many entrepreneurial endeavors, including managing bands and running a music production service. McIntyre's education includes gaining a Bachelor of Communication, where he majored in journalism. During his stint at university, he took on internships and work experience opportunities at various organizations, where he initially honed his skills in sports reporting. *The Football Sack* runs an internship program for university students, where the students are given access to football teams around Australia and expected to cover them as professional journalists:

> They are a pretty fantastic company that gets university students into to do a season working covering A-League teams. You know, they're a pretty big A-League publication now in terms of the football scene in Australia. And they picked me up to do a year covering the Jets, A-League and W-League. (I. McIntyre, personal interview, May 11, 2020)

A further opportunity was with the Newcastle Jets Football Club, where he worked part-time as the marketing manager. He moved on to general news as an online radio reporter for the Australian Rural Communication Network, with an online audience of 1.6 million listeners each week. These opportunities during his education meant that the domain knowledge he was acquiring during his study was put into practice. A further advantage of these experiences was the ability to network or, to use Bourdieu's terminology, increase social capital and learn the 'preferences of the field' (Csikszentmihalyi, 1997, p. 47), to make himself more attractive in the marketplace.

It can even be said that McIntyre displayed intrapreneurial traits within the mainstream media organizations he worked for, by recognizing gaps in sports coverage and taking those ideas to management. For example, his initial full-time ongoing role in a newsroom was for the *Mudgee Guardian*, where he reported on general news, the council beat, and sports in the region. After transferring to the *Newcastle Herald*, he noticed the lack of women's sports reportage in the *Herald* and suggested that he cover women's sport:

> It's something that I had picked up in Mudgee as something that really hadn't been a coverage field for Mudgee, and it was garnering a lot of interest, putting up big numbers. I came back to Newcastle and floated the idea with the editors here. They kind of gave me free rein to start covering things. Like the netball was a big flagship one for that. And yeah, it was, I guess, something that exploded in popularity, something that hadn't been covered to the extent that maybe it could have been before. (I. McIntyre, personal interview, May 11, 2020)

This foray into women's sports at the Herald, and its subsequent demise when Fairfax started to 'trim the fat' (I. McIntyre, personal interview, May 11, 2020) in preparation for the Fairfax/Nine merger, is an example of Mazzarol and Reboud's assessment of the business culture required for successful innovation: 'For intrapreneurship to operate effectively in practice, the organisational climate must be right for the intrapreneur' (2020, p. 96).

However, it is McIntyre's later forays into the online space that demonstrate his entrepreneurial spirit and how he harnessed different forms of income to support himself. Part of this is because of his deep immersion in the domain and the cultural and social contexts. In 2015, while still working for the *Herald*, an opportunity arose that played into his love of esports and gaming: *Snowball Esports.*

> I realized there was this publication that was covering Australian esports, that was little more than a blog in terms of their writing experience. I stumbled across it, reached out to them, and said, look, I'm happy to edit your stuff, to help out to raise it a little bit, Australian esports is something like women's sport that I thought deserved to be covered. And yeah, eventually I moved up to an editor in chief role and the founding duo got me on board. The ownership has changed a little bit now, but yeah, basically picked up a percentage split. (I. McIntyre, personal interview, May 11, 2020)

McIntyre's professionalism in journalism, and his reputation, led to a team owner in the League of Legends competition urging the *Snowball Esports* owners to ensure McIntyre got 'a bigger role, more money and a bigger percentage of their company. They would instantly get the prestige of having me, who I guess had become the flagship writer for *Snowball* at this point, would get me as an editor, as a writer' (I. McIntyre, personal interview, May 11, 2020). And in return, McIntyre got a 25% share of the company. Here was another income stream, and a different form of income than that as a waged employee for the *Herald*. *Snowball Esports* is in the process of organizing sponsors to ensure the site stays viable, but there have also been approaches from investment firms to buy out the site.

In another startup in 2018, McIntyre took the lack of reporting on women's sport in the Hunter Region and developed *Hunter Women's Chronicle*, a site dedicated to reporting on women's sport in the Hunter, and focusing on the Hunter's women athletes nationally and internationally:

> When I came and worked in Newcastle for the year, I guess my contacts and the standing that I had in the community in terms of women's sports coverage kind of blossomed enough that I was able to build up a reputation where people would approach me for stories. When I contacted people, they would have already been reading my stuff. They knew kind of what I was doing. So when the women's sport got trimmed at ACM [the *Herald*], I had all these contacts. I had all these set up. I had this bank of photos. I had all these people still reaching out to me for articles and coverage. (I. McIntyre, personal interview, May 11, 2020)

The years of networking over several positions clearly paid off and the increased symbolic capital, in the form of a solid reputation, ensured the *Chronicle's* popularity. McIntyre won the Judy Dunbar Media Award for Community Media Excellence in 2019, a further example of symbolic capital at work. Furthermore, McIntyre provided opportunities for university students to network and hone their own skills, in a similar way to his experience with *The Football Sack*, by hiring the students as writers on the *Chronicle* site.

However, *Hunter Women's Chronicle* is not currently operating for several reasons. The COVID-19 pandemic meant that many of the leagues that were covered had stopped, and therefore there was little sport to cover. The university end-of-year break meant there were no contributors, which led to McIntyre taking on the bulk of the writing. In addition, and probably more importantly, the publication's business model was primarily based on sponsorship and COVID-19 led to a drop in sponsorship, meaning this online publication had to be suspended:

> A lot of the local sponsors that had been backing the *Chronicle*, fairly enough, realized that they kind of needed to consolidate their stuff. They pulled back a lot of their sponsorships that weren't I guess long term contracts. And that's fine, I completely understand that. But what it meant was that I was then doing the work completely for free, basically in my spare time. (I. McIntyre, personal interview, May 11, 2020)

While running the *Chronicle*, McIntyre discovered an opportunity in gaming to bolster his income and in 2019 founded the Australian branch of *Dexerto*, the largest international online gaming, esports, and social media influencer magazine, with teams working in Europe, the USA, and Australia. After applying for a position, his application was helped by the networking and previous experience in sports: 'they had already had my name wrapped around Australian gaming and esports already and had had me in the back of their mind as somebody they wanted to pick up' (I. McIntyre, personal interview, May 11, 2020). Working as the first Australian editor of Dexerto.com, he was then head hunted to write for dotesports.com, another esports and gaming site, this time based in Sydney. While there may be more to Isaac McIntyre's story to come, we can say at this juncture it is certainly the case that these many roles have drawn on his skills as a sports journalist, those skills that he had learnt systematically throughout his career both as an intrapreneur and an entrepreneur.

Rosemarie Milsom has also worked both intrapreneurially and entrepreneurially. Milsom, currently the Founding Director of Newcastle Writers Festival, also started her career at Fairfax as a cadet journalist at the *Newcastle Herald*. Her career at Fairfax lasted for almost 20 years. Her excellence as a journalist was recognized in 2012 when she won Journalist of the Year at the 45th Annual Northern NSW media awards and, in 2014, was awarded Best Feature (all media) at the NSW Regional Media Awards. Milsom's full-time position at Fairfax ended due to the disruption caused by the rapidly expanding digital world. She then set about rethinking her approach to gaining an income and determinedly decided to stay inside the world of writing. In 2013, Milsom founded the Newcastle Writers Festival, a not-for-profit community event. She has continued to develop and run this highly successful and rapidly expanding annual event since then. As the Festival Director she relies on a large team of volunteers who gift their time and service to the festival. The festival is also supported by corporate sponsorships, donations, and grants, with the latest a $200,000 Federal government grant from the 2021 Restart Investment to Sustain and Expand (RISE) fund, designed to help businesses affected by the COVID pandemic. During this time, Milsom supplemented her income as a radio broadcaster with the Australian Broadcasting Commission (ABC). Through all of this we can see that her domain acquisition and engagement with the field over many years of working as a journalist acted as a set of transferable skills enabling her to move into the book festival space.

Milsom started on the news desk at the *Herald*, where she learnt skills such as prioritizing information, stripping down facts to comply with hard news 'rules', and writing to a deadline. Working as a cadet, Milsom quickly learnt that skills important at university, such as writing an essay, were difficult to literally translate into the hard news space. However, two years into her career, she transferred to feature writing and found those essay writing skills played a more important part in this form of journalism:

> [I]t was almost like the years at Uni and the skills I'd learnt on the job in news melded, so I had more time, I could expand on thoughts, I could talk to different people which in a sense with a university essay you're looking at different sources, I could research. I mean with news, research is pretty much nonexistent, if you're on a job that happened that day it's quickly get out there, read the media release or quickly glance at some facts, but there's

> not that luxury of going into a subject necessarily very deeply. If you're going to investigations, yes of course, you can often spend weeks or months on a story…I really liked it, and I never went back. (R. Milsom, personal interview, September, 2015)

Milsom's individual background and personal traits, her idiosyncratic background, played an important part in her trajectory from a journalist to her becoming the director of a writers' festival. She was born in Bosnia and moved to Australia with her family when she was a baby. After growing up in Sydney, the family moved to Newcastle when she was 17 where she finished her schooling and went to the University of Newcastle and did an Arts degree. She then started work at the Newcastle Herald as a cadet (UON, 2015). Milsom's Arts degree included majors in English and Drama. She 'embraced English, essay writing … there's just something about writing that just comes naturally to me' (R. Milsom, personal interview, September, 2015). This love of writing, and competence in the skills it needed, played into her success as an award-winning journalist.

Milsom's engagement with the field when she was a journalist, those social networks so crucial to success, were also a key element in the establishment of the Newcastle Writers Festival. One role she had as a journalist was as the editor of the book review section of the *Sun Herald* and, in this role, she maintained a contact list of writers, editors, and publishers 'in Sydney in the publishing industry that are still in those jobs and have become friends of mine … one of my good friends is a publisher and I have good friends in marketing and PR and publishing, and I know lots of writers' (R. Milsom, personal interview, September, 2015). Some of those writers include other journalists, whose interviewing skills form part of the festival's panel sessions. Milsom's own skills as a journalist transferred successfully into the festival space where she has interviewed, on stage and online, such luminaries as former Australian Prime Minister Julia Gillard, musician and activist Peter Garrett, and actor/writer/director Richard Roxburgh.

While Milsom is steeped in books and publishing from a festival perspective, Phillipa McGuiness comes at publishing from a managerial perspective and, from 2020, as a full-time writer. In that process, McGuiness edited a collection of essays called *Copyfight*, which was published in 2015 by NewSouth and dealt with many of the themes highlighted in this current book. It is about:

> The connection between content, creativity and the internet. It is also about the future of creativity and the very different ideas, or even ideologies, about how we nurture and sustain writers, filmmakers, musical and digital artists. At one extreme, some people say copyright is an impediment to creativity in today's digital world. At the other end are people who say that copyright is as important as ever, that we need traditional modes of copyright protection that allow us to continue to make art that tells us who we are. The line—strong, faint, dotted and sometimes broken—that connect content, creativity and the internet is copyright. (McGuiness, 2015, p. 2)

This legal framework, one of the enabling and constraining structures we discussed earlier in this book, has been the subject of much debate as digitization, globalization, and neoliberalism interact:

> It seems the digital revolution that has brought us the wonders and transformation of the information economy has not delivered jobs in great numbers as well. Like most creative industries, while publishing has grown in all kinds of ways, we all have fewer full-time colleagues in-house than we would have had ten years ago. The Carnegies of the industrial age have been replaced by entrepreneurs who have highly valued companies with minimal staff. (McGuiness, 2015, p. 4)

Phillipa McGuiness's first sole-authored book was the non-fiction title, *The Year Everything Changed: 2001*, published in 2018. Her latest book, *Skin Deep: The Inside Story of Our Outer Selves* was published in 2022. *The Year Everything Changed: 2001*, written 'about the events of 2001 intertwined with a story of personal trauma' (Goodreads, 2022), was shortlisted for two literary awards—the 2018 Queensland Literary Awards and the 2020 Adelaide Festival Awards. She has also contributed her written work to publications such as *The Guardian*, *Sydney Morning Herald*, *Griffith Review*, *Inside Story* and *Meanjin* (McGuiness, 2021) and is the temporary editor of *Openbook*, the New South Wales Library quarterly magazine.

McGuiness worked for almost twenty years as a publisher with NewSouth/UNSW Press, where she was involved in the commission and publication of 'hundreds of books, particularly in Australian history, Asian studies, politics, art and culture, memoir and biography and popular science' (McGuiness, 2021). Prior to that she was a senior commissioning editor at Cambridge University Press. When asked about her personal pathway to publishing, McGuiness said:

> I was about to land a cadetship with *The Age* [newspaper], or so I thought. When I missed out, I applied for a job as a publishing assistant with Cambridge University Press. Before long I was working in CUP's Sydney office, a terrace in Surry Hills. Bits of crumbling wall would fall onto our desks, so manuscripts were often covered in sand. It has always been a glamorous industry, but one I'm very glad I fell into. (ABR, 2017)

McGuinness's long immersion in the domain of publishing has meant she acquired a useful understanding of the skills needed for her transition to being a writer: 'being a publisher for twenty years has definitely made me a better writer' (ABR, 2017). The insights her occupation provided were hard-won through years of experience: 'I think often along the way I surprised myself with how much knowledge I had about structure and tone and voice I had absorbed and tried to impart over the years' (Caro & Fox, 2019) and she also acquired a publisher's habitus, inculcated over a long period of time, which gave her 'the advantage of knowing what made a really good pitch' (Caro & Fox, 2019).

Jaye Ford has a different yet somewhat similar story. She is a successful full-time writer who worked across a gamut of media professions before having her first book published in 2011. This book, *Beyond Fear*, became 'the highest selling debut crime novel in Australia in 2011, won two Davitt Awards for Australian women crime writers (Best Debut, Readers' Choice) and was shortlisted for Best Adult Crime' (Ford, 2022a). Ford, under contract to Random House, has gone on to write six more thrillers, with her books being published in nine languages. She has also written two romance novels under the nom-de-plume Janette Paul: 'because sometimes a thriller writer needs a break from her dark side' (Ford, 2022b).

Ford grew up in Sydney in a family where there 'wasn't a lot of discussion about books or writing, just an understanding that reading was a part of life' (Smith, 2015). She received a Communication degree from the Mitchell College of Advanced Education in Bathurst, New South Wales (now Charles Sturt University). Her first job in the media was in radio, where she started as a cadet journalist but broadened her experience into news and sports journalism in print and on television. Ford 'became the first woman to host a live national sport show on Australian TV, fronting Sport Report on SBS. Later, she fronted Prime TV news in Newcastle' (Ford, 2022a). After working for 12 years in journalism, Ford moved to public relations where she ran her own consultancy firm until 2001, when she decided to give up her firm and started to write. Ford's long immersion in the domain of media provided the key skills required to become a fiction writer. However, it took 10 years to become a published author. In an interview, Ford noted the importance of risk-taking, persistence and resilience:

> not a small amount of that time was spent wondering if I was bravely determined or just stupid for persisting in the face of failure. I think you need to be both if you really want to get published! I'd also spent a lot of years before then starting stories that I gave up on—my first full manuscript was really an exercise in making myself actually finish something. (Wallace, 2014)

Ford has also noted how her work experience provided fodder for her books. In an interview with Verushka on pop.edit.lit, she discussed how working as a sports journalist provided inspiration for the women in her novels:

> Back in the 1980s, I was a sport journalist, a time when women's sport was invisible in the Australian media. I was fascinated by the stories behind sport and as the only woman on the sports desk, there were plenty of opportunities for me to interview female athletes. The women I met were competing at high levels with no recognition and no pay, training every day while holding down multiple jobs and sometimes raising families. They were strong, fearless, resilient and inspiring—and my memory of them still has an influence on my main characters. (Verushka, 2015)

Ford is also very cognizant of the interconnected field she works in. She is a keen networker and takes part in author panels, writers festivals, and other conferences, visits libraries, and takes part in workshops and writing classes. She also interviews other authors, thus drawing on key journalistic skills, and actively promotes her work through social network sites such as Facebook, Instagram, and Twitter, while also giving glimpses into her personal life. This skill in networking, and understanding how to network effectively, has meant that Ford has successfully carved a niche for herself in the publishing field, demonstrating at the same time that she, like her fellow writers, is part of a global wave of cultural producers 'fostering and blending old and new forms of media entrepreneurialism, management, creative labour, and user practices' (Craig, 2019, p. 363). We can find similar things occurring in the radio and music fields.

References

ABR. (2017). Publisher of the month with Phillipa McGuiness. *Australian Book Review*. Retrieved January 3, 2022, from https://www.australianbookreview.com.au/abr-online/archive/2017/207-may-2017-no-391/4081-publisher-of-the-month-with-phillipa-mcguinness

Caro, J., & Fox, C. (Hosts). (2019, June 8). Phillipa McGuinness [Audio podcast episode]. In *Women with clout*. PodcastOne https://podcasts.apple.com/us/podcast/phillipa-mcguinness/id1433876057?i=1000446281465

Celebrity Speakers. (2022). Stan Grant. *Celebrity speakers: Inspiring people*. Retrieved March 30, 2022, from https://www.celebrityspeakers.com.au/speakers/stan-grant/

Craig, D. (2019). Creator management in the social media entertainment industry. In M. Deuze & M. Prenger (Eds.), *Making media: Production, practices, and professions* (pp. 363–386). University of Amsterdam Press.

Csikszentmihalyi, M. (1997). *Creativity: Flow and the psychology of discovery and invention*. Harper Collins.

Cunningham, K. (2021, October 13). 'It was a lifesaver': Novelist Matthew Reilly on unpublished projects and unreliable trackpants. *The Guardian*. https://www.theguardian.com/lifeandstyle/2021/oct/13/it-was-a-lifesaver-novelist-matthew-reilly-on-unpublished-projects-and-unreliable-trackpants

Evans, M. (2014). Education and the new convergent journalist. In J. Potts (Ed.), *The future of writing* (pp. 135–148). Palgrave Macmillan. https://doi.org/10.1057/9781137440402_12

Ford, J. (2022a). About Jaye Ford. *Jaye Ford*. Retrieved January 14, 2022, from https://www.jayefordauthor.com/about-bio

Ford, J. (2022b). Writing as Janette Paul. *Jaye Ford*. Retrieved January 14, 2022, from https://www.jayefordauthor.com/writing-as-janette-paul

Fulton, J. (2016). Print journalism and the system of creativity. In P. McIntyre, J. Fulton, & E. Paton (Eds.), *The creative system in action: Understanding cultural production and practice* (pp. 87–99). Palgrave Macmillan.

Goodreads. (2022). *The year everything changed: 2001*. Retrieved March 30, 2022, from https://www.goodreads.com/en/book/show/40366421-the-year-everything-change

Grant, S. (2018). My grandfather's equality: Confronting the cosmopolitan frontier. *Griffith Review, 60*, 134–145.

Mazzarol, T., & Reboud, S. (2020). *Entrepreneurship and innovation: Theory, practice and context* (4th ed.). Springer.

McGuiness, P. (2015). *Copyfight*. NewSouth Publishing.

McGuiness, P. (2021). About me. *Phillip McGuiness*. Retrieved December 2, 2021, from https://www.phillipamcguinness.com/about

McIntyre, I. (2021, May 11). Personal communication [Personal interview].

McIntyre, P., Balnaves, M., Kerrigan, S., Williams, C., & King, E. (2019). *Creativity and cultural production in the Hunter: An applied ethnographic study of applied entrepreneurial systems in the creative industries: Final report, ARC Grant LP130100348*. University of Newcastle.

McIntyre, P., Fulton, J. M., & Paton, E. (2016). *The creative system in action: Understanding cultural production and practice*. Palgrave Macmillan.

Milsom, R. (2015, September). Personal communication [Personal interview].

Negus, K., & Pickering, M. (2004). *Creativity, communication and cultural value*. Sage Publications.

O'Donnell, P., & Zion, L. (2019). Precarity in media work. In M. Deuze & M. Prenger (Eds.), *Making media: Production, practices and professions* (pp. 223–234). Amsterdam University Press. https://doi.org/10.5117/9789462988118

Smith, A. (2015). *Q&A with Jaye Ford*. Australian Women Writers Challenge. Retrieved January 14, 2022, from https://australianwomenwriters.com/2015/08/qa-with-jaye-ford-author-of-already-dead/

UON. (2015). *Getting to know Rosemarie Milsom*. UON Engage. Retrieved May 16, 2016, from http://engage.newcastle.edu.au/getting-to-know-rosemarie-milsom/

Usher, N. (2017). Venture-backed news startups and the field of journalism. *Digital Journalism, 5*(9), 1116–1133. https://doi.org/10.1080/21670811.2016.1272064

Verushka. (2015, September 29). *Jaye Ford & her reluctant heroines*. Pop.edit.lit: Book Blogger and Editor. Retrieved January 14, 2022, from https://editingeverything.com/blog/2015/09/29/jaye-ford-her-reluctant-heroines/

Wallace, S. (2014, September 11). *Thrilling ride for Jaye Ford*. Sandi Wallace: Crime writer. Retrieved January 14, 2022, from https://www.sandiwallace.com/thrilling-ride-jaye-ford/

Zion, L., Sherwood, M., O'Donnell, P., Marjoribanks, T., Ricketson, M., Dodd, A., & Winarnita, M. (2018). *New beats report: Mass redundancies and career change in Australian journalism*. New Beats Project. Retrieved October 25, 2021, from http://www.newbeatsblog.com/wp-content/uploads/2016/12/New_Beats_Report.pdf

CHAPTER 8

Entrepreneurship in the Music and Radio Industries

Working in the music industry has always been a precarious process. Musicians in particular have rarely been employed full time, especially in the popular music field. For those working in the classical areas, in orchestras, theater, and operas, contractual arrangements have been closer to the norm. Radio, on the other hand, has had a much greater propensity to operate in a very structured way and tends to employ people on a full-time or contractual basis. While these two industries, music and radio, are treated separately, there are many synergies that have developed historically. Those relationships are still evolving as the twenty-first century continues to unfold. What is evident is that the music industry continues to be highly entrepreneurial while radio has had to continuously innovate in order to survive the disruptive forces it has faced. All of these characteristics can be sheeted home in the broadest sense to technological change, globalization, and the ongoing dominance of neoliberalism. We will start our discussion of this situation by treating each industry separately, while also looking at the interrelationships, and then exemplifying both of these situations with a variety of case studies.

For the music industry, there are a number of structural models available (e.g. Tschmuck, 2006; Wikstrom, 2020). While the recording industry is often conflated with the entire music industry, it can be seen that there is not one music industry *per se* but a 'set' of music industries (Williamson & Cloonan, 2007). Even with the changes wrought by the 'new' music industry, it remains the case that there are three major sectors within this industry,

P. McIntyre et al., *Entrepreneurship in the Creative Industries*,
https://doi.org/10.1007/978-3-031-19455-9_8

that is, publishing, recording, and live performance. There are, of course, ancillary sectors such as manufacture, retail, and media, both traditional and social (McIntyre, 2011), but we note these do overlap with other industry designations. There has been, as was predicted, 'the growth of a profitable and varied music services industry producing everything from remixes to music marketing strategies' Power, Dominic

(Power & Jansson, 2004, p. 425). As Power and Jansson foresaw, at the forefront of this new music industry were quite a number of firms 'attempting to combine in innovative ways music and ICT' (2004, p. 425). This eventually took a variety of forms, for example:

> selling and distributing music over the internet; web design and computerised advertising services tailored to music products; software design focused on multimedia products and virtual instruments; high-tech post-production and mixing services; and virtual centres and communities of music industry actors. (Power & Jansson, 2004, p. 425)

With the emergence of this post-industrial musical economy many of the traditional players, who were predicted to fall by the wayside in a period of exceptional disruption, have in fact survived and, in some cases, thrived. Despite the often naïve 'digital optimism', where 'simplified claims were made that musicians could now achieve success via the web without any assistance from the music industry' (Hesmondhalgh, 2019, p. 299):

> What happened eventually, after a period of uncertainty and chaos, was that a) the major record companies, even though they saw profits and revenues fall, retained their position as the organizations that signed, recorded and marketed the world's most popular, widely known music and artists, and b) firms from the IT industry came to play a significant role in circulating and mediating music to audiences, working with the major record companies. These IT intermediaries displaced the retail chains of record shops that briefly formed in the 1980s and 1990s, and joined broadcast media as the main institutions determining how audiences became aware of particular songs and artists. There was increasingly easy, ubiquitous access to a vast abundance of music for the wealthiest half of the planet, but few musicians were able to form sustainable careers from their music. (Hesmondhalgh, 2019, p. 295)

With recording incomes slowly diminishing for most musicians from 1999 onward, publishing revenues for songwriters saw a cumulative annual growth rate. But this was not to last. AM/FM radio had paid royalties to the songwriter and publishing houses through their collection agencies but for streaming services these firms paid on the mechanical royalties on recordings. This situation profited the recording companies, not songwriters (McIntyre, 2021). As one publisher explained to John Seabrook:

> Basically, the music corporations sold out their publishing companies in order to save their record labels. Universal Music Publishing took a terrible rate from streaming services like Spotify in order to help Universal Records. Which, in the end, means that the songwriters get screwed. (Quoted in Seabrook, 2015, p. 297)

This turn of events was coupled with a lack of growth in payments for live performance for the vast bulk of musicians, that is, professionals, semi-professionals, pro-ams (Martin, 2016), and the huge numbers of amateurs that underpin the music industry. These 'gig' payments did not even keep pace with the pressures of inflation over the last three decades. Consequently, it has become harder for musicians to secure reasonable income for their work, even though what they do is core to the rest of the industry. Most everybody else in the sector has profited at the expense of the precarity experienced by most songwriters and performers. Diversification and increased entrepreneurial activity seem to be the approaches most musicians have applied to survive.

As we can see from the above, this industry, in its entirety, is part of a broad system, whether it is called a business ecology, an innovation ecosystem, or, in our case, a creative system in action. Regardless of the designation, as we have argued, systems are central to the creation of novelty and value in the sort of changing marketplaces that now typify the creative industries.

Radio, as a cultural form related to music and as an economic concern interdependent on it, has continued to be resilient and adaptable inside this system. Like the domain of music, it has similarly strong rules, conventions, and traditions, which vary depending on the format applied with different genre expectations and formatting conventions. It must also adhere to the law of the land, with legislative measures and regulations set out for it to abide by. Terrestrial radio uses bandwidth licensed by the government and each sector has a set of advertised self-regulating ethical obligations it must follow. Radio is an important and mature sector within the creative industries sphere overall, having a long and deep history. In Australia, which has drawn on radio structures from both the USA and Britain, radio is populated by highly networked commercial businesses, government-funded stations with a strong terrestrial and online presence, a well-established community sector, and a set of independent operators working outside the prior categories. It seems counterintuitive but, despite increasing inroads from the digital world, in 2019 broadcast AM/FM radio was still a popular medium. This form of radio is still the leading audio platform with 61.3% of people listening to this medium, in comparison with streaming services like Spotify, Pandora, and Apple Music sitting at 15%, podcasting 7.3%, online music videos 4.4%, and TV music channels at 1.8% (CRA, 2022, online). Radio, in all its forms, remains one of the most steady and resilient types of media. Its personalities and its content, predominantly music, are drivers of this. Audio streaming has been readily taken up and established as a key to radio's continued survival. As a consequence, radio is now being talked about as a key player in the audio industry. Internet radio is maturing and music distribution services like Spotify, for example, are the natural extension of the automated processes networked radio has established. Podcasting straddles 'a position on both sides of the distribution divide between broadcasting radio and the online on-demand digital distribution systems' (Kerrigan et al., 2021, p. 3). It has become very popular very quickly and can be seen as a return to the types of formats that were present in radio's golden years (Baird, 1992; Ahern, 2020). The question is now how to monetize this most recent form, and is one which remains dominant for many advertisers and investors.

In terms of the interrelationship between radio in all its forms and music, some years ago Mike Byrne, former program director at NXFM and KOFM, both of which now belong to the Southern Cross Austereo (SCA) network, asserted that:

> Music is art and it is commerce and when the music industry treats itself like a business they sell more records. When what we are able to play intersects with what the music industry delivers to us, both industries benefit. When the music delivered by the popular music industry gets too arty or too unusual, as it does periodically, and moves away from the mainstream, the less we are able to play it and consequently the less the music industry sells. When the popular music industry, as a whole, delivers what mainstream radio can deliver to its audience and, make no mistake it's a large audience which is quite discerning in what it will and will not listen to, both the radio and music industries benefit. (M. Byrne, personal interview, 2003)

This is still the situation, as the first example of the creative and innovative approach taken by those involved in the independent radio sector demonstrates.

Sean Ison started Ison Live Radio (ILR) and operated it out of Newcastle, NSW, for some time. He began his career 25 years ago developing his initial cultural capital in the field of radio as a 'cart boy' working at various stations in the production side of commercial radio. He then moved to on-air positions on community radio and from there to narrowcast broadcasting. In the process he developed the habitus, the set of naturalized predispositions to action that are informed by a long-term way of being in the world, typical of a radio operative. He has also been immersed formally in the domain or knowledge system of radio as he has a BA (Comm. Stud.) from the University of Newcastle, where in 2004 he completed a media production major. He can demonstrate his symbolic capital by pointing to the title he now holds as the President of The Independent Australian Radio Broadcasters Association and has built a small media business that concentrates on successfully syndicating programming internationally, delivering content in narrowcast formats. He has also been developing streaming services and radio apps. As an active decision-making agent within this section of the radio business, he is now nominally the product manager for Australian Broadcasting Media, originally Ison Live Radio. Along with Israeli investors, members of the field in Csikszentmihalyi's terms, he owns half of that company. He oversees the music coming in from all online sources and the music going out. The songs he populates his programs with also constitute a significant portion of the domain of radio, and the musicians who send them to him also constitute a part of the field Ison deals with. In terms of the products and programs the company creates, both of which are part of the field of works, Ison asserts that 'every product that's created has to be saleable, it has to have a dollar value attached to it. It has to be something we can either fly with advertising or something we can sell as a package to other radio stations or TV stations' (S. Ison, personal interview, May 2015). It is worthwhile noting here that when Ison refers to 'we' he is indicating the partners he is working with rather than a set of employees, as this business is not structured in the traditional way. It has no traditional employees. In outlining ILR's operational methods, Ison claims that:

> [ILR] produces weekly radio programs for radio stations all around the world. In a range of formats our shows are heard by over a million free-to-air

> radio listeners each week. We also produce direct-to-radio programming from our studios 24 hours a day, 7 days a week. This is non-stop music programming in nine different formats, delivered via the Internet or via satellite straight through the mixing desks of Australian radio stations hooked up to our own ILR Media Server. (ILR, 2016, online)

ILR has thus used the affordances the internet provides to its own advantage. This wasn't always the case. Ison admits that initially 'I had no real use for the internet, no experience of it until I went back to university, and it opened up a whole world for me. And I was able to contact a lot of people and to make friends' (S. Ison, personal interview, May 2015). In developing this social capital, so important in operating freely in the field, Ison admits these social networks were heavily leveraged. Word of mouth proved to be the initial means of establishing success as far as the syndicated programs for ILR were concerned. The programs needed content, domain material, and they needed buyers, further members of the field, to buy the programs. As Ison explains 'our products, the actual specific shows, carried word of mouth with other stations. We also were working with a lot of musicians for the music to come in from the musicians, and a lot of them actually put us on to stations, believe it or not, which was pretty good' (S. Ison, personal interview, May 2015). Then in an able demonstration of the gift economy at work, Ison

> set up an industry website called ausradiosearch.com and offered all kinds of free services and content as a package [subscribers] could sign up to for free. This attracted a lot of Australian and overseas traffic from radio stations (about 800 visitors a day at its peak). We then hitched onto this and offered them shows. (S. Ison, personal interview, May 2015)

It was this free service, a gift to the community as it were, that demonstrated the value of reciprocity and which enabled the initial international contacts to be made. ILR was eventually delivering programs via the internet to stations across Asia, Oceania, Europe, and North and South America. Most of these were concentrated in Europe and North America. Additionally, as Ison indicates, 'although web casting is a somewhat minor concern with us, we also have a substantial share in online radio in Australia with our daily web casts reporting listeners from one end of the country to the other' (ILR, 2016, online). Furthermore, in a display of orthodox entrepreneurial behavior, focused on the use of financial capital, Ison diversified his interests by establishing Australian Broadcasting Media (A3M) along with a business partner:

> We went and got investors from Israel to set it up and we bought a stack of stations, they're all country music stations, they go down the Hume Highway, and there's a bunch of them go in towards the Riverina. That's basically where they're running. There's about 40 of them, I think. They're all what you call narrow casts; they're low power FM, although we don't run them quite at low power. But if you chain it together you end up with one big sort of radio station, and we bought those in 2005, sorry, 2008 we bought those and set them up. (S. Ison, personal interview, May 2015)

In this case, the business models Ison operates with are consistent with the notion of amplified hybridization set out by Lhermitte et al. (2015, p. 89). As Ison indicates, he now also runs a more traditional radio model along with his internet-based delivery, each feeding into the other.

> Our business is sort of two tiered now; we're still doing syndicated programming but we're also now able to put the same resources that we had coming into this syndicated side of things into actual radio stations of our own, and we play quite a lot of syndicated shows as well, we have a lot of syndicated shows coming in now. The way those [stations] are set up they go into independent mode where it's all computerised. They basically play, do their own thing at certain times of the day, because I decided it wasn't worth networking automation basically through the satellite link, it wasn't worth paying for it. And then at particular times we have a nationally syndicated morning show. That goes out, that's all in real time on that. I do an overnight show which is voice tracked most of the time, because I'm not usually creeping around at midnight anymore. And what else do we do? We have, oh, there's a drive time program. So, there's certain times of the day it's the same program going throughout the whole thing, covering the whole region, and then other times they're doing their own little thing, playing local advertising and stuff like that. (S. Ison, personal interview, May 2015)

In operating within the social, technological, economic, and political contexts of the field of radio, Ison also has to operate within a legal one. The main form of content he aggregates is music from the field of works, the accumulated cultural work completed up to this time in a particular field. This is for both his syndicated program and his narrowcast formats. As such, there is a legal requirement for these content providers, the musicians from the field who originate the content, to be remunerated. This is not done directly. ILR does not pay musicians for their content but is required to pay fees to the Australasian Performing Rights Association (APRA) incorporating the Phonographic Performance Company of Australia (PPCA), which remits the fees it collects to songwriters nationally. Significantly, APRA also has a remit to do the same with its partner organizations internationally via the Berne Convention. Ison states that his company, ABM, negotiated an arrangement with APRA. However, 'I mean of old we didn't worry about this, but we had to, especially once we started getting terrestrial radio stations, so we negotiated a special arrangement with them' (S. Ison, personal interview, May 2015).

Once he moved into streaming, a certain complexity moved into these practices. Given that 'measures of risk-taking behaviour have been found to correlate significantly with entrepreneurial orientation' (Mazzarol & Reboud, 2020, p. 49), and the fact that entrepreneurs like Ison tend to reinterpret situations of potential loss into situations of potential gain, we can claim here that there were commensurate forms of risk to be negotiated. As Ison explains, 'we started a thing called Radio Sydney which is 250-odd streams of internet radio, and we had to negotiate a special arrangement for that as well. I mean we've got a lawyer and we do play it close to the wind sometimes and interpret the law our way' (S. Ison, personal interview, May 2015).

Ison observes that 'the whole industry legally is in a state of flux' (S. Ison, personal interview, May 2015). Along with changing technology, the recent simulcasting court case tested the waters of what could be possible. As the Australian Copyright Council reported in 2015, Commercial Radio Australia (CRA) was unsuccessful in its Full Federal Court appeal. CRA had argued that an internet simulcast could not be seen as a broadcast, but they were unsuccessful and the judgment against them was upheld by the Federal Court. What was important about this decision was that radio broadcasters could no longer use their existing license with the PPCA to stream sound recordings over the internet. The Full Federal Court of Australia had previously concluded that:

> Online streams (simulcasts) of radio programs were not 'broadcasts'[1]. This was later affirmed by the High Court of Australia which rejected an application from the CRA to appeal. The decision meant that rather than having one PPCA licence covering both radio and internet broadcast, radio stations are obliged to have a second, separate PPCA licence to broadcast their programming online. (ACC, 2016, online)

For Ison, there were 'several concepts that were simply outdated that just didn't really apply' (S. Ison, personal interview, May 2015). He and his legal team, also seen here as players in the field of radio, argued in their negotiations with APRA that 'the wording of the legislation didn't cover what was being said, or it may have covered it, but it didn't cover it accurately' (S. Ison, personal interview, May, 2015). In those negotiations, ABM and APRA came to an arrangement that appears to have suited both parties:

> They're quite good, I will say, they're not quite the bogeyman I used to think they were. They're quite reasonable about negotiating things. But I mean fortunately APRA's open enough for example, for people like us to come along and say, 'Well, we want to do this. What will this cost? And what about 20% of this', and that sort of thing. And that's a situation that should exist, rather than arguing in the copyright tribunal, which is where it was going to end up, but I think we avoided that. (S. Ison, personal interview, May 2015)

Ison is continually scanning the horizon for further business opportunities. He knows that 'you have these different models overseas; I think we just need to catch up' (S. Ison, personal interview, May 2015). He also realizes this presents not only opportunities but also threats, but ones he is willing to confront. For him, it's a hostile situation because the technology is in flux and organizations like APRA, underpinned by copyright law, are asserting that current laws still apply. Noting the speed of change, Ison argues that these laws don't really apply. 'No one's actually clarified and sat down and defined [them], and I mean it's not just legally, the nature of things is changing' (S. Ison, personal interview, May 2015). For him:

> One of our major things that we get listeners from is podcasts, and the whole idea of on-demand entertainment where people, same as with television or whatever, people can choose what they want to hear when they want to hear it. That in itself is changing, yet APRA has a...podcasts are still a grey area. APRA says most podcasts are illegal, that everybody's doing the wrong thing because they're breaching the mechanical copyright of the musicians or whatnot. Others say that's not the case, so ultimately this will sort itself out when the technology gets to a stable point where it's not progressing. (S. Ison, personal interview, May 2015)

This may be a hopeful scenario, given the emphasis being placed on the ongoing nature of creative destruction and digital disruption where these are now seen as the new norm. Internet radio is often seen as a media where ‘anything goes’. Harry Criticos disputes this idea, however, arguing that internet radio, like all other cultural forms, sits ‘within a set of constraining and enabling factors that are in operation at one and the same time’. His claim is that ‘radio operatives are inevitably constrabled, that is, both constrained and enabled at exactly the same time, by the structures of Internet radio’ (Criticos, 2021, p. 3). He suggests that:

> The Internet in its current form supposedly provides an avenue for individuals to express themselves beyond the confines and filtered content of traditional media forms such as broadcast radio, television and print media. While Internet radio is not new, having been in existence since the 1990s, it can be argued that its increased uptake as a broadcast service, is due in part to the barriers of entry being far lower when compared to the setting-up of an analog radio service (Colapinto & Manzi, 2016). Added to a low barrier of entry, is the supposed sense of freedom that, when transferred to programming, readily engages the users of these platforms compared to the difficulties encountered when trying to use more traditional means of maintaining local voices and local content. (Criticos, 2021, pp. 1–2)

The specific local content he is talking about is that produced in 2018 by David Sayers and his team as they launched ‘internet radio station New2UW.com, narrowcasting via a streaming service locally from Newcastle, NSW, Australia’ (Criticos, 2021, p. 2). The internet radio space in Australia meant that 2UW did not ‘need to comply with Australian music content quotas, material of local significance and other local content regulations that exist within the BSA’ (Criticos, 2021, p. 7). In this case, many assumed it to be ‘free from broadcast regulation’ (Criticos, 2021, p. 2) which meant that there were negligible barriers to entry. Nonetheless, ‘there are rules that apply to Internet radio stations such as paying a license fee to play music (copyright and royalties) and compliance with laws such as defamation’ (Criticos, 2021, p. 2). Similarly, as Criticos points out, there are also operational procedures to be adhered to. In his study:

> It was found that in the overall operation of Internet radio, it maintained some, if not all, of the main structures of terrestrial radio. These structures include format clocks, music selection, program times, station IDs and

news. This study of the New2UW.com found that there was little discernible difference between it and terrestrial broadcasters in Newcastle, or for that matter, globally. (Criticos, 2021, p. 9)

Criticos argues that, 'regardless of whether regulatory or operational, the structures of the industry, Internet and state are as significant as individual agents, since neither agents nor structures operate in isolation from each other. We can see that this supports the idea of constrabling' (2021, p. 10). Criticos details this new term by explaining that:

'Constrabling' is a portmanteau word that combines the terms 'constraining' and 'enabling'. This term, constrabling, encompasses the idea that the structures in which practice take place, the habitus that assists practice, the agency that affects the way we practice, and the various forms of capital that help us engage in practice, do not in fact constrain us at one point and enable us at another. Rather, we as practitioners are constrained and enabled by these structures at exactly the same point in time. In other words, we are constrabled by these structures. (Criticos, 2021, p. 9)

Like David Sayers at 2UW and Sean Ison at ILR, Steven Pickett is also constrabled by his involvement in the structures of internet radio. His current venture, Newcastle Live Radio, is streamed via the internet or through an iPhone or Android app and his programs are also available as podcasts. The station is a self-described 'hyper-local online station' (NL, 2022) and is part of the broader Newcastle Live project Steven Pickett is involved in.

Newcastle Live (NL), started by Steven Pickett, claims to be 'the Hunter's premier online music, entertainment and lifestyle guide' (NL, 2017, online). It delivers a comprehensive online environment where those seeking what's going on in the valley 'keep up to date with the latest local entertainment and lifestyle news, reviews, features and giveaways' (NL, 2017, online). It has become an important media outlet for many regional performers and the touring acts which are promoted through the site. Pickett points out that, as a promoter and music agent:

I was in a situation where I was pushing local music to local radio stations and I actually had a program on New FM to start with, and NX FM…and 2NUR before that. But it was very hard to get support from the local paper, from the local radio stations, and virtually impossible from the local TV stations. It was hard. As the 21st Century dawned, the digital world came into being, and it occurred to me that I might be able to invest in the creation of

> something that could support local music without having to rely on those big media. We could become the media. And some quarter of a million dollars later Newcastle Live was born. (S. Pickett, personal interview, October 2015)

Before this venture, Pickett had dreamed of owning a recording studio. He was young, so he first went into teaching at the encouragement of his parents. After graduating from Newcastle College of Advanced Education, he was determined to see his dream come true. He worked during the day as a teacher and in the evening also worked part-time in a fast food outlet. Later that night he could then be found mixing live bands into the early hours of the morning. After five years of very little sleep he had saved the $120,000 he needed to open his own studio. He opened Eastern Acoustic Recording Studio in late 1988.

> We even started up our own distribution network, the Newcastle Music Network where we actually had bins made, and we took them around to all the local record stores. There were about 30 of them then. And Terry, who became my business partner, and I used to get in the van one day a month and travel around all the record stores and put local product in. We invested in a number of original music acts over a ten year period, and…we'd lost well over a million dollars over that period, that we'd invested in local musicians only to have them [fall apart at crucial moments]. Terry just came to me one day and said 'from a business point of view mate, we need to look at this' and virtually from the end of one year to the start of the next, EAO turned from being a recording studio, managing original artists, and supporting original artists financially, to becoming a cover agency. And financially it was the best thing we ever did. For the soul, I'm not sure. But I mean there was a lot of grief and we were worried about things. Terry and I were living on, we had the business running and we were going at, our only wage could be $98.00 a week because at $99.00 you had to pay tax and we couldn't afford it. So we'd get $98.00 a week from this business which was probably, I don't know, probably six/seven/eight years old by this point, and we're on $98.00 a week for a long time each. And he was going out and doing load ins at the Entertainment Centre or the Workers Club back in the day, and I was doing sound at the Castle. And that's how we made our money to live. (S. Pickett, personal interview, October, 2015)

As Rossiter et al. assert, 'there are many factors which motivate an entrepreneur' (2011, p. 10). They suggest that there is a standard motivation for many talented individuals working within the music industry and this is the line between passion and tangible results.

> Musical entrepreneurs have separate motivation for founding a business beyond control of socioeconomic factors...Musical entrepreneurship is a social service whose contributions change people's hearts, minds, and souls. They expound upon strategic entrepreneurship to discover new markets, new music, new inspiration, and competitive space seeking higher quality strategic actions within the entrepreneurial society. Music entrepreneurs combine their proactive behavioural resources with their capabilities to produce social capital. Friendships aid the formation of musical ventures through the concept of strategic creativity which lends itself to pursuing creativity and inspiration as well as achieving personal rewards. (Rossiter et al., 2011, p. 10)

Pickett now owns and operates, with a team of dedicated professionals, the Eastern Acoustic Organisation (EAO). He is also the Managing Director of EAO Entertainment and Marketing and he has developed marketing processes for a variety of venues and is working on 'media resources for radio, press, television and more' (S. Pickett, personal interview, October 2015). He has taken up the opportunities the digital world has presented by developing the Newcastle Live website and has begun to roll this franchise out across the country. He is also the director of advertising agency Brand Pool which came out of the marketing skills he developed for the bands he worked for but now taken a step further. Diversification across creative industries has been his byword as an entrepreneur working across radio and the music industry.

This has also been the case with Oxygen Music. Located in Geelong, Victoria, Oxygen Music has a number of arms to its enterprise. Oxygen Creative Arts College, for example, is a private provider offering vocational tertiary programs in music, photography, digital media, visual arts, film, and design. It is supported through the Victorian Government's Skills First program. Founded in 2006 by musician brothers Tony, Joe, and Dominic Monea, it grew out of a music school they started in 1986 as a way 'to supplement their performance income via regular teaching' (D. Monea, personal interview, June 17, 2019). The school continues with private instrument tuition for 100 students. While most of their students stay local, there are people 'doing international work', such as musicians Xavier Rudd and Evangeline, and Aboriginal artist Yirrmal. Geelong businesses have been supportive of the college's students in terms of offering internships and work experience for them—'There's no substitute for experience and getting in and getting your hands dirty'—and Geelong Workers Club is a strong promoter of local original music (D. Monea, personal interview, June 17, 2019). They've found dealing with local government 'a lot of red tape'. They employ a digital content specialist and a blogger to help tell their story. The internet has been vital to their business, especially teaching photography and graphic design, where applications such as Adobe are 'in the cloud', and they were fortunate that 'the street was picked up by network cable' nine years ago, prior to the NBN (D. Monea, personal interview, June 17, 2019). The brothers also run a recording studio which has affiliated rehearsal suites and live sound equipment for hire. They also started the music retailer Oxygen Music. This retail outlet sources instruments through wholesalers in Sydney, Brisbane, and Melbourne, from manufacturers in China and Japan, with some from the United States and Europe (H. Winiecki, personal interview, June 18, 2019). They have an in-house string instrument repairer and outsource bigger jobs as they come in (H. Winiecki, personal interview, June 18, 2019). They also run an online arm of the retail store, but most business is in-store, with promotion through social media and email (H. Winiecki, personal interview, June 18, 2019). They partner with local schools in 'battles of the bands' and provide 'sponsorship dollars' in prizes. For 10 years, they ran Drumania, a festival featuring student drummers, teachers, and touring professionals 'from all over the world', workshops, expos, and a family sausage sizzle (H. Winiecki, personal interview, June 18, 2019).

Musicians and music industry professionals like the Monea brothers work within a vast network of practitioners to produce, distribute, and perform their music. This music field consists of fellow musicians, songwriters, and performers, as well as artist managers, booking agents, promoters, publicity agents, touring crews, tour managers, front of house engineers, lighting operators, stage managers, monitor engineers, venue operators, A&R representatives, record producers, audio engineers, publishers, and all of the associated administration, legal, and accounting teams. Of course, without an audience none of these personnel would continue to subsist within the music industry. Some of these members of the field of music sustain economically viable careers focused specifically at songwriting and performance. Morgan Evans is one of these.

Morgan Evans is currently a successful recording and touring musician with a background in media and television presenting. He first worked at Foxtel after graduating from university and went on to become the face of Foxtel's Country Music Channel (CMC). He was also working as a performing musician who, after releasing two hit EPs that yielded three #1 singles, was named New Oz Artist of the Year at the CMC Music Awards. This was followed by four more trophies over the next two years, including Male Oz Artist of the Year which he won a number of times, all of which added to his steadily mounting symbolic capital in the field of country music.

Evans relocated to Nashville USA to record his debut album with an all-star group of A-list musicians and a Nashville-based producer. The album, released in March 2014, quickly went to #1 on the iTunes and ARIA Country Album Charts and debuted at #20 on the ARIA Mainstream Album Chart. The album produced three #1 singles and his first APRA nominations. His exposure in the US at the CMA Music Festival again and at the legendary Grand Ole Opry prompted William Morris Endeavor—the world's largest talent agency—to sign him up for international representation. This led to a recording contract with Warner Bros Records in the USA. Since then, 'Evans has proven time and again that taking the risk was well worth it' (Evans, 2020). For Evans, the skills he developed playing and writing in Newcastle, Australia, especially his live gigs, have been critical to his success in the USA. He feels he is totally comfortable whether he's playing in front of 50 people or 50,000: 'We've played weddings when the PA broke down and had to jump into the crowd and sing to people, you know, it's like what's the worst that can happen, it's already happened you know' (M. Evans, personal interview, April, 2016).

Evans now has over 450 million streams globally, his debut single in the US 'Kiss Somebody' topped the charts and the following single 'spent 25 weeks in the coveted No.1 spot in Australia' (Evans, 2020). The album achieved Best Country Album at the ARIA Music Awards in Australia in 2019 and he performed across 'eight countries with headlining shows sold out across three continents on his 2019 World Tour' (Evans, 2020). He is currently, in 2022, on a global tour. His career is a sterling example of not only an entrepreneurial and determined spirit but the necessary presence of a network of supportive actors redistributing creative and career responsibility across multiple networks. Not everybody has been this successful. Some are just beginning their journey down this road.

Kirsty Lee Akers is also a country artist. Like Morgan Evans, she is willing to find out how the game is played and capitalize on any opportunities that present themselves. She recorded her first EP at the age of 16, funding that recording with the money she made busking in Australia's country music capital Tamworth. She went on to study at and graduate from the CMAA Academy of Country Music and she is the only artist to have won the 'holy trinity' of Australian Country Music awards. Between 2006 and 2008 she won the Telstra Road to Discovery (2006), Toyota Star Maker (2007), and a Golden Guitar (2008). In 2010 Akers began recording her first self-funded independent album 'Naked' which, on its release, went on to receive three Golden Guitar nominations. She is 'proud of her indigenous heritage as a woman of the Wonnarua people (Hunter Valley—Australia), she has embraced a global musical culture and now spends her time between Australia and the USA' (Akers, 2018).

The idea of a global music culture points to the evident complexity individual agents now face as they make decisions within the structures of both the music and radio industries. While radio is increasingly becoming networked, forcing out smaller and medium enterprises, often family-run stations, and automation becomes the norm, large corporations like Clear Channel have come to dominate the global airwaves. These broadcasting companies also operate television channels, SVOD content supply, music apps, and a host of other diversified processes. Despite the growing success of podcasting, the largest share of money being made now also resides predominantly with large corporates like Apple Podcasts/iTunes, Spotify, Google Podcasts, and Amazon/Audible. Similarly, as Dayan Thussu points out, the global music industry is still 'dominated by a few Western and Eastern conglomerates, which control 80 per cent of the world market' (2019, p. 179). Far from digital optimism producing a democratization of music making where all artists would be 'able to market and sell their products directly to audiences via the web without the need for multinational corporations, and where lowly professionals and even amateurs would be able to reach appreciative listeners' (Hesmondhalgh, 2019, p. 296) the majors have proved to be surprisingly resilient. As they undertook a form of vertical disintegration by selling off their manufacturing and distribution sections, and seeing distribution taken up by ICT companies, the traditional record companies consolidated their power over marketing and promotion. The approach they have adopted over the latter is 'global in scope and yet local in execution' (Thussu, 2019, p 180). While some performers did adopt a DIY approach, they soon learnt that 'while the individual action of uploading tracks or videos to streaming sites is relatively easy, the "new DIY" world enable by digital technologies is in many respects even more complex than the old industry' (Hesmondhalgh, 2019, p. 296). As Powers attests, 'as cultural entrepreneurialism returns a great deal of intermediating back to the musicians, their responsibilities often grow so immense that few musicians are willing or able to do the work themselves' (in Hesmondhalgh, 2019, p. 302). As well as maintaining their live work and songwriting they have also been taking on recording, promotion, and distribution, but also 'use many aspect of the old business, including publicity firms, booking agents, lawyers, accountants, designers and manufacturers' (Power in Hesmondhalgh, 2019, p. 302). Many projects require massive investment of time, energy, and money and often rely on the gift economy and much unpaid labor. As we noted at the beginning of this chapter, those working in the music industry have had to continue to be or become highly entrepreneurial in order to gain an income, while radio still has to continuously innovate so it can survive the growing disruptive forces it faces. The complexity of these processes continues to evolve across a creative system that both enables and constrains, constrabling the daily actions of its creative practitioners.

References

ACC. (2016). Navigating the content streams. Australian Copyright Council. Retrieved June 25, 2017, from https://www.copyright.org.au/acc_prod/ACC/News_items/2016/WINv9_-_PPCA.aspx

Ahern, S. (2020). *Making radio: A practical guide to working in radio in the digital age*. Milton Park.

Akers, K. (2018). *Bio & media*. Kirsty Lee Akers. Retrieved August 24, 2018, from http://www.kirstyleeakers.com/bio-media/

Baird, L. (1992). *Guide to radio production*. AFTRS.

Byrne, M. (2003). Personal communication [Personal interview].

CRA. (2022). *Share of audio 2019*. Radio Alive. Retrieved April 21, 2022, from http://www.radioalive.com.au/Research-Insights/Share-of-Audio/2019/Share-of-Audio-2019

Criticos, H. (2021). The constrabling effect of internet radio. *Journal of Radio & Audio Media*, (online), 1–12. https://doi.org/10.1080/19376529.2021.1937629

Evans, M. (2016, June). Personal communication [Personal interview].

Evans, M. (2020). News. Morgan Evans. Retrieved April 21, 2022, from https://www.morganevansmusic.com/news/morgan-evans-speaks-his-truth-new-docuseries-highway-1-sessions-8126

Hesmondhalgh, D. (2019). *The cultural industries* (4th ed.).
ILR. (2016). *Home*. Ison Live Radio. Retrieved July 19, 2016, from http://www.isonliveradio.com/index.html
Ison, S. (2015, May). Personal communication [Personal interview].
Kerrigan, S., Criticos, H., Kerrigan, V., & Ritchie, S. (2021). Podcasting as a creative practice and the spirit of radio: Local histories of Maitland. *Journal of Radio & Audio Media,* (online), 1–20. https://doi.org/10.1080/19376529.2021.1897986
Lhermitte, M., Blanc, S., & Perrin, B. (2015). *Cultural times: The first global map of cultural and creative industries.* EYGM Ltd.
Martin, B. (2016). *An ethnographic analysis of pro-am audio production within the systems model of creativity.* Unpublished honours thesis, University of Newcastle.
Mazzarol, T., & Reboud, S. (2020). *Entrepreneurship and innovation: Theory, practice and context* (4th ed.). Springer.
McIntyre, P. (2011). Rethinking the creative process: The systems model of creativity applied to popular music songwriting. *Journal of Music Technology and Education, 4*(1), 77–90.
McIntyre, P. (2021). Songwriting practice and production: The past, present and future. *Journal of Songwriting Studies, 1*, 5–26.
Monea, D. (2019, June 17). Personal communication [Personal interview].
NL. (2017). *About.* Newcastle Live. Retrieved June 12, 2017, from http://newcastlelive.com.au/about/
NL. (2022). *Newcastle live radio.* Newcastle Live. Retrieved April 21, 2022, from https://newcastlelive.com.au/radio/
Pickett, S. (2015, May). Personal communication [Personal interview].
Power, D., & Jansson, R. (2004). The emergence of a post-industrial music economy? Music and ICT synergies in Stockholm, Sweden. *Geoforum, 35*(4), 425–439.
Rossiter, N., Goodrich, P., & Shaw, J. (2011). Social capital and music entrepreneurship. *Journal of Management and Marketing Research, 7*, 1–12.
Seabrook, J. (2015). *The song machine: Inside the hit factory.* W.W. Norton & Co.
Thussu, D. (2019). *International communication: Continuity and change* (3rd ed.). Hodder Arnold.
Tschmuck, P. (2006). *Creativity and innovation in the music industry.* Springer.
Wikstrom, P. (2020). *The music industry: Music in the cloud* (3rd ed.). Polity Press.
Williamson, J., & Cloonan, M. (2007). Rethinking the music industry. *Popular Music, 26*(2), 305–322.
Winiecki, H. (2019, June 18). Personal communication [Personal interview].

CHAPTER 9

Entrepreneurship in Film and Screen

The screen industries, which for our purposes include film and television, have been operating globally for some time. The film sector of the screen industries has been in production for more than a century (Dawson & Holmes, 2012), while the television sector has been operating for three-quarters of that time. More recently, this latter sector has experienced exponential global growth due to innovations occurring in streaming and distribution platforms (Lotz, 2014). Interestingly, these highly creative sectors rarely use the term entrepreneur to describe what successful film-makers and television makers do, even though many of the entrepreneurial and intrapreneurial processes and characteristics we discussed earlier occur for most professionals gaining an income from these industries. Creative agents, decision-making entities such as screenwriters, directors, and producers, constantly pitch new screen ideas as films and television series, which are then developed and created through a highly procedural business sector. To illustrate this point, this chapter will present case studies of film and television professionals who operate as intrapreneurs and entrepreneurs, like freelance television story editor and screenwriter Vanessa Alexander. Another film, television, and theater actor, writer, producer, and director Leah Purcell is recognized for her intrapreneurial and entrepreneurial traits, while feature film producers from the Dendy Icon Group Bruce Davey and Mel Gibson provide a global entrepreneurial case study.

As cited earlier, Mazzarol and Reboud attest that entrepreneurs pursue 'the generation of value through the creation or expansion of economic

P. McIntyre et al., *Entrepreneurship in the Creative Industries*, https://doi.org/10.1007/978-3-031-19455-9_9

activity by identifying and exploiting new products, processes or markets' (2020, p. 15). As far as new products go, for these case studies a television show or film falls into this category. A production company executes the filmmaking processes, often innovative to cover the exigencies of the novel script, while the marketing of a film or show occurs through screen-based distribution, and exhibition companies also employ innovative approaches to these tasks.

As mentioned, we use the term screen industries to combine cinema and television activities. In line with this conflation, we also use the term film to refer to either a cinematic feature film or a television show, which allows us to use the term filmmaker to refer to a wide variety of activities undertaken by either a feature filmmaker or a television practitioner. This consolidation of terms permits us to mount a general argument identifying the existence of entrepreneurial and intrapreneurial processes inside the global screen industries, where new films are pitched, developed, created, and distributed by filmmakers. The entrepreneurial and intrapreneurial filmmakers involved in these activities typically own or are employed by a production company or create a company for the specific project they are involved in. While these film production companies are generally formed to make films (Lee & Gillen, 2011), they do hire in creative specialists and subcontract creative services at different points across the development, planning, production, post-production, and distribution of a film. These creative and collaborative screen production actions are often highly industrialized, technologically and digitally demanding activities that, once funded, enable the 'financial means to employ highly skilled creative team members to complete the production tasks' (Kerrigan, 2019, p. 355). As part of the broader creative industries, they operate using 'a combination of *individual creativity* and the *mass-production of symbolic cultural goods*' [italics in original] (Davies & Sigthorsson, 2013, p. 4). As McIntyre and Kerrigan argue, 'every experienced filmmaker knows, there is just as much art in gaining the finances from the field so that they can proceed, as there is in making the movie itself' (2014, p. 146). Once finance is gained, the work begins on ensuring the success of the work. Once these works are in play in the marketplace, the profits are usually measured as 'return on investment' (ROI). This is the global profit that a film returns from box office sales (Velikovsky, 2016). Research reveals successful films, based on box office returns, are rare, with 70% of films failing to "break even" or recoup their production budget in cinema release (Velikovsky, 2016, p. xv). This means the selection of viable screen ideas is complex and potentially, financially risk laden. Business structures inside the television industries tend to be less focused on the specifics of ROI but, instead, tend to be focused on low-cost production practices and selling television formats and shows globally (Lotz, 2014), including selling shows to streaming services. This situation does, however, allow for the profits, the ROI, to be maximized. In this case, we assert that the commercial imperatives at play are as essential to filmmaking as they are to ensuring that the screen idea (Macdonald, 2012) has cultural currency. It is thus highly evident that a very real 'combination of creativity and commerce is a crucial enabler in the field of creative screen industries' (McIntyre & Kerrigan, 2014, p. 146). These systemic relationships can also be scaled up, as they still require the action of state structures in the form of government policies and legal frameworks, which help support enterprise development programs that also enable film businesses to prosper (Olsberg SPI, 2012, p. 8).

The complex set of global screen businesses, agencies, studios, production houses, and networks gives audiences access to films, while supporting a myriad of filmmaking professionals who earn incomes through leveraging entrepreneurial and intrapreneurial activities. Of all the specialist roles in the screen industries it is the film producer who is most likely to be called an entrepreneur, since film producers more obviously pitch novel ideas to film and television executives from government funding agencies, studios or broadcasting networks in order to have their projects 'green-lit'. The executives from these agencies, studios, or networks hold a great deal of power, as these are the ones who commission films and decide what screen ideas will be funded, where those productions will be made, and by whom. These gatekeepers are considered to be highly creative as well, as they have been able to 'internalise the rules of the domain and the opinions of the field, so that [they] can choose the most promising ideas to work on, and do so in a way that will be acceptable to one's peers' (Csikszentmihalyi, 1999, p. 332).

The film producers themselves will typically own and run a film production company, which shoulders the majority of the risk involved in developing, financing, producing, and exhibiting a film (Lee & Gillen, 2011). In *The Producer's Business Handbook*, Lee and Gillen describe the business practices used by producers to mitigate or reduce the risk of a feature film failing. They describe how production houses can be set up as a suite of businesses, operating across the discrete stages of film production, in order to diversify revenue streams and reduce the risk/return parameters

(Olsberg SPI, 2012). A global example of this mode of operation can be found with the Dendy Icon Group, which is Australia's leading independent entertainment company, owned by Australian actor and producer Mel Gibson and feature film producer Bruce Davey. Dendy Icon is made up of four companies that services multiple aspects of the cinema industry (Icon Movies, 2021).

Icon Productions was Davey and Gibson's first company, founded in 1989 as a film production company. It has produced award-winning films such as *Braveheart* (1995), *What Women Want* (2000), and *The Passion of the Christ* (2004). Within this group of companies there are two that focus on distribution and exhibition, Icon Film Distribution and Dendy Cinemas. The film distribution arm began in 2002 and offers script analysis and development services, as well as sourcing cinematic work from international film markets and festivals. Icon Film is described as an '"all rights" business that distributes content throughout theatrical, home entertainment, ancillary, pay per view, digital and television' (Icon Movies, 2021, online). The exhibition company is Dendy Cinemas, which was acquired in 2008 and is one of Australia's oldest independent cinema chains, being established in 1940. Dendy has 40 screens across three Australian states and also exhibits opera, ballet, and theater productions from the Royal Shakespeare Company. The newest company is Icon Film Finance, which provides financing for Australian film and television productions. Introduced in 2020 to the Dendy Icon Group, it aims to provide an 'end-to-end facilitation of production financing, distribution, and exhibition' (Icon Movies, 2021, online). These four companies form the Dendy Icon Group which are focused on creating quality features and screen content for Australian and New Zealand markets.

The Dendy Icon Group showcases a text-book business structure (Lee & Gillen, 2011, p. 158), where the relationships between these companies are underpinned by three aims pursued by the producer: create the film, sell it to audiences, and return a profit (Lee & Gillen, 2011, p. 11). These film companies are structured in a way that enables a film producer to finance a film and attract a team of highly skilled filmmakers to make the film, which is then distributed to a global audience. It is in the distribution and exhibition of a film where the profit is typically made, as consumers paying to see a film, either in a cinema or through a subscription service, allow the producer to 'recoup production costs and receive a fair participation in the film's future earnings' (Lee & Gillen, 2011, p. 11). This arrangement of businesses and business objectives highlights one aspect of the entrepreneurial processes that a film producer engages with in order to sell a screen idea, make the film, and return a profit through marketing it. Some film producers operate at a high-risk level, as they may become, for any number of reasons pertinent to maintaining their cultural capital, too focused on 'the creative purity of the vision they have for each picture' (Lee & Gillen, 2011, p. 10). The protection of their creative vision, while suitable for the maintenance of their own cultural and symbolic capital, may lead to the producer making decisions that are expensive and risky, consequently blowing out production budgets, which may result in films never earning enough income to cover production costs. In this case, getting the balance right between cultural, symbolic, and economic capital—that is, servicing the needs of a creative vision within the production budget—is complex and fraught with risk, which requires a mature and sophisticated understanding of suitable financial strategies.

The film producer has a range of ways to finance the production of the film, and they will often exhaust all options to ensure it has an appropriate budget. The size of the production budget will determine the creative production options. The budget is used to assemble creative individuals and groups, including securing high-profile actors and key creative crew to help ensure that the film to be made will be 'unique and novel' (Kerrigan & Batty, 2016, p. 355), and, from there, profitable. In this case we can assert that the production budget will both constrain and enable the aesthetic and production choices (Kerrigan, 2019). Typically these budgets are described as either 'big budget', with hundreds of millions of dollars at the production's disposal; 'moderate budget', with tens of millions of dollars; 'low budget', with less than 10 million; or a 'ultra-low budget', where films are made for less than US$300,000 (Screen Actors Guild—American Federation of Television and Radio Artists, 2022). Film producers will initially draw on formal structures built around government funding and contracting the screen idea to film studios and television networks. They will also draw on informal financial structures like self-funding, labor sharing by drawing on amateurs or volunteers as cast and crew, and/or use the gift economy to reduce cost of equipment and facilities. When the budget is determined, the film producers will exploit the parameters of the budget based around actors, key creative roles, length of the film shoot, post-production schedule, marketing, and distribution of the film.

In this process we can see that an entrepreneurial film producer's business carries most of the perceived risk, both financial and creative, of the production and distribution of the film. They need to be motivated to take on these entrepreneurial processes as they 'identify an opportunity and pursue it to economic success regardless of the resources that are under their control' (Mazzarol & Reboud, 2020, p. 13). The strategies that a motivated film producer adopts to manage some of the perceived risks associated with making and selling films include implementing a detailed planning process 'demonstrating that conditions associated with the market, financials and management of the business have been considered' (Mazzarol & Reboud, 2020, p. 230), as well as drawing up a production and distribution budget to allow for the hire of a suitably appropriate film crew. This film crew is a creative team that is contracted to work on the production in a freelance capacity across a range of specialist roles: screenwriter, producer, director, cinematographer, art director, editor, color grader, VFX supervisor, sound designer, actors, musicians, recordists, and audio mixers are some of the roles. Many of these creatives are employed as freelancers and their own survival relies on highly developed networks and relationships. The navigation of these networks could be described as both entrepreneurial and intrapreneurial (Mazzarol & Reboud, 2020). Securing work in the 'gig' economy, as Richard Caves argues, is becoming increasingly entrepreneurial where '[t]hese collaborations rest on deals and contracts—perhaps of the "handshake" variety, perhaps elaborately drawn' (2000, p. 1). These formal and informal structures enable daily collaborations between highly skilled creative specialists who 'see themselves in some measure as artists (along with teamsters and accountants, who likely do not)' (Caves, 2000, p. 1). The deals and contracts on offer allow these specialists to 'choose the most promising ideas to work on, and do so in a way that will be acceptable to one's peers' (Csikszentmihalyi, 1999, p. 332). This process of choosing work, identifying and exploiting cinematic and narrative opportunities by marshaling resources and satisfying a professional need they perceive exists, provides these creative filmmakers with the opportunity to become entrepreneurial.

Other key creative roles in filmmaking like showrunner, screenwriter, or director also exhibit many entrepreneurial traits, which may also be described as intrapreneurial since they are engaged at times in implementing new ideas within an established organization (Mazzarol & Reboud, 2020, p. 96). An intrapreneur, just as readily as an entrepreneur, makes things happen; they 'learn from their mistakes and have a reasonable tolerance of failure as a normal process of learning' (Mazzarol & Reboud, 2020, p. 97). We place these intrapreneurs inside the project-based scenario, the 'gig' economy, of the screen industries, since they secure a contract with a production company that then offers them the right organizational climate, allowing that individual to be 'given the freedom to create and market their own ideas' (Mazzarol & Reboud, 2020, p. 97). It is expected by the production company that the showrunner, screenwriter, or director will bring their own unique and creative processes to this contracted form of employment, and at the same time the production company must provide the right working environment to 'foster creativity and innovation, tolerate failure and encourage enterprising behaviour' (Mazzarol & Reboud, 2020, p. 96). An example of how these intrapreneurial processes are manifest in screenwriting and directing is seen here in the career of Vanessa Alexander.

Vanessa Alexander is an award-winning television showrunner, screenwriter, and director. In 2020 she wrote for the Netflix series *Vikings: Valhalla* and was story editor of *The Great*, a comedy drama series available on the Stan subscription service. As a screenwriter, Alexander is positioned 'both literally and theoretically, as an embedded and conditioned agent inside a cultural production and creative system, practically known as a screen production and distribution system' (Kerrigan & Batty, 2016, p. 134). Out of these processes, Alexander has learnt:

> Writing is a blueprint for something else that doesn't exist yet. So you create this blueprint as the first part of your job for which you don't need that much money…but then you need this very large sum of money to build the house. So, you end up drawing lots of pictures of houses which are never going to be lived in. That is essentially the job of a writer, and you go, 'Oh that would have been a nice house! I'm glad someone paid me to draw it'. (V. Alexander, personal interview, August 24, 2015)

Beginning her journey as a screenwriter, Alexander immersed herself in both the domain and field of screenwriting by completing multiple internships with global businesses that were engaged in script development. In the early 2000s, she was an intern with the UK production house *Working Title* and did a director's internship on US television series *Murder One* and *NYPD Blue* with Steven Bochco Productions. She also completed workshops with the *Royal Shakespeare Company* in the UK and in Europe participated in the screenwriting lab eQuinoxe to develop a screenplay she was working on.

Alexander had a global upbringing. She was schooled in both the US and New Zealand. Currently she is living in Newcastle, Australia. She obtained a formal education with an Arts degree in English, literature, and drama from an NZ University. She has a Graduate Diploma from The Victorian College of the Arts and a PhD from an Australian university. Alexander also taught filmmaking at The University of Auckland and became the Director of Screen Production for three years, reinforcing the idea that a tertiary education is one way for a filmmaker to acquire foundational knowledge of a creative domain, immersing themselves in it while also drawing on 'their own personal experiences' (Kerrigan & McIntyre, 2010, p. 121). In terms of her own idiosyncratic background, Alexander has raised six children and frequently draws inspiration for her writing from her personal life. Her career began with writing for the stage where she won an international playwriting contest in the 1990s. Her first feature *Magik and Rose* screened at the Cannes Film Festival and won a number of awards. This low-budget movie was funded by a New Zealand Film Commission scheme and her first television job was in New Zealand on the teenage series *Being Eve*, where she was employed as a director and writer from 2002–2005. Alexander accepted the job on *Being Eve* because she needed paid work. She was invited to re-make the pilot episode because Nickelodeon, based in the US, disliked how the original New Zealand production team approached the content:

> I re-made it—same script, but the show is completely different because they'd hired these fifty-five-year-old men to make it. They knew nothing about being a teenage girl, and what they made was just diabolically awful and dull and a bit patronizing in tone. And Nickelodeon were not happy [with] how their money had been spent—they wanted a fresh innovative show. (V. Alexander, personal interview, August 24, 2015)

Alexander was then hired by South Pacific Pictures as the producer for *Being Eve* and her intrapreneurial and innovative approach proved successful. She hired filmmakers who had only worked on shorts and used a steadi-cam instead of adopting the studio cameras. Alexander admits she was naïve and didn't really understand the impact this novel approach would have:

> …so I blew the budget and the schedule every single day for six weeks. But Nickelodeon was happy with our rushes—and the show went on to be nominated for an International Emmy and won a bunch of awards including a Gold Medal at the New York festival. So I think everyone forgave me. (V. Alexander, personal interview, August 24, 2015)

Being Eve was Alexander's first paid job in the global film and TV industry. Her innovative work on the re-filming of the pilot episode showed that she was capable of presenting new ideas within an established format. It impressed Nickelodeon, and the consequent action of them employing her to carry it forward gave her the freedom to alter and adjust the production approaches to realize her screen ideas. Nickelodeon's investment in Alexander was recognized when the series was nominated for an International Emmy Award. She also received a Gold and Silver medal at the New York Festival and the Grand Prix at the Danube Television Festival for her roles as producer/director on this innovative program.

Then in 2013, Alexander co-created, wrote, and directed the TVNZ highly rated comedy series *Agent Anna* (2013). This production, which received an NZ Writers Award for Best Comedy, has given her further symbolic capital in the field of television production. Her skills, experience, and access to networks, situated as cultural, social, and symbolic capital, all necessary for the creation of television fictional series, are extensive. Her work in multiple roles on a television series is quite unique. As she attests in regard to bringing her directorial skills into the writers' rooms in Australia:

> The thing that I have that is different to a lot of other TV writer/directors is a dual experience in both roles. It's common in film but not in TV. In fact, I'm yet to meet a person on a TV writers table who has any directing background. So that's a unique thing, and it's surprisingly useful, especially once you get down to beating out episode storylines. (V. Alexander, personal interview, August 24, 2015)

Since 2015, Alexander has focused her career on writing, so she can balance her family commitments with earning an income. For her, and most like her, accessing the field requires tenacity coupled with a determination to immerse herself in the necessary writing skills to enable her to be employed on global television shows. Alexander relies on a formal network; she is represented by a literary agent based in Sydney who helps secure freelance film and television writing 'gigs'. She operates as a sole trader and her agent charges a commission on any work that is secured. It means Alexander doesn't have to cold call people herself, and as her literary agent is highly connected to the field, in other words, she is highly networked, her literary agent can also see what new projects are on the horizon. Alexander feels that her literary agent is necessary to helping her secure work as she lives in a regional city:

> I mean it's not a guarantee that you're going to get work but that support structure enables it and enables me to live in Newcastle. I think it would be quite hard for me to be here and not have an agent. (V. Alexander, personal interview, August 24, 2015)

As a freelance screenwriter, Vanessa Alexander also has had to establish her own personal and less formal networks, and one aspect of this has been by meeting with other film producers:

> I remember working out what the point of the meeting was. You know cause when you first go and have a meeting, you think 'Well are they going to offer me work?' Then eventually you realize that the meeting is an interview for some imaginary thing that might happen in the future. It's really just about do you like each other, and you know because it's such a collaborative industry nobody wants to work with people that they don't have any connection with. And just navigating that is a minefield, if you can become relaxed with that it is easier. Whereas I know people who get very tense in those environments and it might unfairly disadvantage them. (V. Alexander, personal interview, August 24, 2015)

Alexander's networking ability, her access to the field of Australian commercial television production, has been successful in resulting in her writing for a number of television series including *Love Child* (Channel 9), *The Wrong Girl* (Network 10) as well as *The Secret Daughter* (ABC).

In 2015, Alexander predicted the impact that streaming services like Netflix and Stan would have on Australia's film and television screen sector. She recognized that 'current and future markets are poised on the brink of the most enormous change in television and I really hope that it crushes the dull crap that we've been forced to suffer through from broadcasters for so many years' (V. Alexander, personal interview, August 24, 2015). What these streaming platforms offered was the ability to create content that would bypass local content laws and offer freelance writers like Alexander access to global screen industry opportunities. This is exactly what happened with scripted television in Australia, as it was being completely overhauled (Lotz & Sanson, 2021). We can argue in this case that her own intrapreneurial skills and the structures she engaged with were advantageous to her gaining international work as a screenwriter and showrunner.

During the COVID pandemic in 2020, Alexander worked remotely as a screenwriter from her home in Newcastle using electronic means, and accounting for time differences, she synchronized her work activity with the Irish production team of *Vikings: Valhalla*, the historical action-fiction drama that is a spin-off of the highly successful series *Vikings*. *Vikings* was written for the History Channel in Canada and later distributed on the Netflix streaming service. While the production was stalled because of COVID, Alexander delivered two scripts without ever setting foot in the production office. She was also a staff writer on the first season of *The Great*, the comedy-drama series streamed on Hulu, and was story editor for the second season, which was nominated for two awards, the Writers Guild of America and the Primetime Emmy Awards.

At this point Alexander's career is on an upward trajectory. Her next freelance writing gig is as lead writer on the television series *Artemisia*, about the Italian artist Artemisia Gentileshi, which is being produced by ViacomCBS International. It is highly likely that she will soon be credited as a 'showrunner', that is, a writer-producer who manages the writers' room and the range of options available to the production. This work entails an entwining of Alexander's creative agency and the constrabling effects of the structures that surround her, as a showrunner, 'often celebrated as a singular author is in fact notoriously buffeted by conflicting obligations to his/her own creative compass and to the many corporate players involved in maintaining the commercial engine and bureaucratic constraints of the network television industry as a whole' (Mann, 2009, p. 103). Achieving the status of lead screenwriter—a showrunner—on an international television series showcases her as someone who, like all entrepreneurs, takes risks and has a tolerance of failure. Alexander learns from her mistakes and, when given opportunities within the commercial structures that enable this activity, is able to manifest the novel ideas she comes up with as screenplays, which are brought into being—that is, created—and is then recognized by her industry peers—that is, the field of television production. She carries significant symbolic capital, with her experience in this game being recognized through the many awards she has won. The corporation she gains her income from, ViacomCBS International, is itself an entrepreneurial global media and entertainment structure. It creates experiences and content for worldwide audiences, streaming services and live events, and markets affiliated merchandise to consumers. Media and entertainment corporations like ViacomCBS operate in a global marketplace that upscales traditional television business methods and reorganizes them through industrial structures. This situation allows them to behave in an entrepreneurial way by commissioning the mass production and distribution of film and television shows (Lotz, 2014; Lotz & Sanson, 2021). Western cinema and television industries have been dominated by these sorts of businesses as they engage with production companies, legal firms, regulators, funding agencies, hire companies, distributors, streaming services, and highly skilled intrapreneurial and entrepreneurial creative filmmakers. Highly experienced intrapreneurial and entrepreneurial film and television crews gain their income through what seems to be interchangeable work across multiple screen projects. Working this way affords them the possibility of behaving creatively. They are, like all creatives, conditioned agents who have immersed themselves in the conventions of the filmmaking domain and internalized the ways the field of film and television entrepreneurs behave (Kerrigan, 2019, p. 355).

Leah Purcell fits well within this schema. She is an actor, writer, director, and producer who has received prizes and obtained commercial success in those roles in theater, film, television, and literature (Oombarra Production, 2019). Purcell is a First Nations woman of Goa-Gunggari-Wakka Wakka Murri descent. She owns Oombarra Productions with her business partner Bain Stewart. They are agents of change who convert the many opportunities they encounter by creating new ventures. In short, the way they approach their content creation business aligns with most entrepreneurial behavior (Mazzarol & Reboud, 2020, p. 13). Their business is focused on producing stories for multiple media platforms in film, television, theater, and literature (Oombarra Production, 2019).

Purcell's intrapreneurial skills started to develop as a stage actor, performing the lead role in *Bran Nue Dae*, a coming-of-age comedy-musical about a First Nations teenager. The musical toured nationally in 1993 and it allowed Purcell to learn the ropes. A few years later, she presented the world premiere of her one woman show *Box the Pony* at Sydney's Opera House, a play based on Purcell's life in the rural Queensland town of Murgon. It deals with violence and racism and explains her personal struggle to break the cycle that has constrained generations of women in her family (Rankin & Purcell, 1999). The play was commissioned for the 1997 Festival of Dreaming and was co-written by Purcell and Scott Rankin. The play toured nationally, including at the Adelaide Festival and internationally at the Barbican Centre BITE: Arts Fest London as well as the Edinburgh Festival. The published play received the 1999 NSW Premier's Literary Award and the 2000 Queensland Premier's Literary Award for Best Play. The touring of the play nationally and internationally demonstrated the commercial viability of the play, while the awards provided the complementary way for the artistic quality of Purcell's work to be symbolically recognized.

Purcell's career began to expand. She started to gain an income for her work as a screen actor throughout the nineties and the naughties, working with some of Australia's finest stage directors such as Neil Armfield and Wesley Enoch. She also began to direct and write more work for the stage. She created *Black Chicks Talking* (2003) and *Don't Take Your Love to Town* (2012). This risk-taking capacity was then manifest in Purcell's creation and collaboration on multiple innovative stage shows, highlighting her as 'a person who historically has brought new ideas or products to market with the ability to create wealth and employment' (Mazzarol & Reboud, 2020, p. 13).

Over the next twenty years, Purcell continued to develop her intrapreneurial and entrepreneurial skills as a screen actor, contracted to appear in leading roles in television series such as *Janet King, Police Rescue* and *Wentworth*. She also appeared in the feature films *Lantana*, *Jindabyne*, *The Proposition*, and *Last Cab to Darwin*. At the same time she developed a profile as a screenwriter, obtaining television credits with the acclaimed First Nations series *Redfern Now* (ABC). She was also employed as the Indigenous story consultant for *Love Child* (Nine/Playmaker) and directed episodes of the highly acclaimed series *Cleverman* (Goalpost/ABC). She also directed episodes of *My Life is Murder* (Network Ten/CJZ) (Oombarra Production, 2019). She is now recognized in the field as a First Nations cultural storyteller, as she has exploited her creative talents in multiple roles across the structures of both stage and screen. Her cultural capital affords her the possibility of being able to create new ventures as an entrepreneur (Mazzarol & Reboud, 2020, p. 13).

She has also adapted and re-told Henry Lawson's 1892 short story *The Drover's Wife* as a play, a novel, and a feature film and was able to perform in the lead role of the stage play *The Drover's Wife* (2016) and in the feature *The Drover's Wife: The Legend of Molly Johnson* (2021) (Oombarra Production, 2019). Drawing on her experience as a playwright, Purcell adapted *The Drover's Wife* for the stage in 2016. The play has won multiple literary awards and prizes, which shows that her peers take her work seriously while also recognizing her creative and novel contribution to the cultural domain of Australian storytelling. In an interview from 2019, Purcell explains that she always 'felt close to the Lawson story, despite its failure to portray the Indigenous frontier experience' (Daley, 2019, online). Purcell's mother read the short story to her as a child, and she goes on to explain that:

> I wanted to find a new way of telling an old story, one that appreciates who we are as Australians, and one that is looking at our Indigenous Australian historical experience…They [contemporaries] said it was 'brave—cheeky—but good on you'. And I said, 'We'll see what happens. I don't know the rules yet. And people have loved it. (Daley, 2019, online)

Purcell secured a book deal with Penguin Random House in 2018 and focused the novel on the isolated wife of the absent drover. Purcell explains how she was writing the novel and the feature film script between stepping onto set to act in her scenes on *Wentworth*.

> And what was exciting was, when I was writing the screenplay I'd go, 'Oh I've got to remember to put that in the novel'—and then when I was writing the novel I'd come across this backstory and I'd say, 'Hang on a minute, that's a bit of backstory for the character breakdown for the screenplay'…then I went back and re-read Henry Lawson's story, I went back to the play and said, 'I can't forget that line'. So, I borrowed and stole from each. (Daley, 2019, online).

This brief account of Purcell's career, and the development of her most recent work, illustrates her creativity. It was through a confluence of storytelling pathways; her immersion in the domains of performance, writing, and directing; and her continued commitment to First Nations storytelling that enabled her to master multiple sets of rules, conventions, and practices to become an entrepreneurial storyteller. Purcell's position as a First Nations creative has given her license to re-frame Lawson's original story to authentically reflect the multiple stories of First Nations survival, and her understanding and immersion in Australian culture have enabled her to recognize and value an iconic Australian literary work, to retell a classic story from a First Nations perspective, as she went on to 'produce a novel variation in the content of the domain' (Csikszentmihalyi, 1999, p. 315). The symbolic recognition that Purcell achieved throughout her career as an actor, writer, director, and producer enabled her to achieve the status of an entrepreneur. While her career choices may be seen as diverse, moving between roles in front of the camera and behind it, it is her ability to convert 'opportunities into marketable ideas, often assuming risks, implementing the idea and realizing any rewards' (Mazzarol & Reboud, 2020, p. 13) that marks her out as entrepreneurial.

In recap, the Dendy Icon Group owners Gibson and Davey were enabled to create work and find market niches for them through exploiting entrepreneurial business structures, as they continue to operate within a global film ecosystem. The entrepreneurial characteristics displayed by the careers of Gibson and Davey also emphasize the financial risk they carry as film producers, which is mitigated across a suite of companies that allow for innovative strategic practices to be implemented. Both Alexander and Purcell's careers illustrate how their ability to take creative action has been fostered through the screen industries. They learnt to be resilient, exhibiting a tolerance for failure as they became innovative and enterprising. While screenwriter Alexander's story is primarily one of being intrapreneurial, it is Purcell's career that demonstrates how it is possible to be both an intrapreneur and an entrepreneur, as she developed as a First Nations storyteller. This analysis of their careers shows how they leveraged their growing skill and experience to enable them create and market increasingly novel screen ideas, which, in turn, helped create employment and wealth for them and others in the entrepreneurial and intrapreneurial ecosystems they exist within.

References

Alexander, V. (2015, August 24). Personal communication [Personal interview].

Caves, R. (2000). *Creative industries: Contracts between art and commerce*. Harvard University Press.

Csikszentmihalyi, M. (1999). Implications of a systems perspective for the study of creativity. In R. Sternberg (Ed.), *Handbook of creativity* (pp. 313–335). Cambridge University Press.

Da_ey, P. (2019, December 22). Leah Purcell on reinventing The Drover's Wife three times: 'I borrowed and stole from each'. *The Guardian*. Retrieved September 12, 2021, from https://www.theguardian.com/books/2019/dec/22/leah-purcell-on-reinventing-the-drovers-wife-three-times-i-borrowed-and-stole-from-each

Davies, R., & Sigthorsson, G. (2013). *Introducing the creative Industries: From theory to practice* (1st ed.).

Dawson, A., & Holmes, S. (2012). *Working in the global film and television industries: Creativity, systems, space, patronage*. Bloomsbury Academic.

Icon Movies. (2021, January 1). *About Icon Film*. Icon Film Distribution. Retrieved November 2, 2021, from https://www.iconmovies.com.au/about.aspx

Kerrigan, S. (2019). Innovation in the arts: Collaborative and creative filmmaking processes. In P. B. Paulus & B. A. Nijstad (Eds.), *The Oxford handbook of group creativity and innovation* (pp. 335–352). Oxford University Press. https://doi.org/10.1093/oxfordhb/9780190648077.013.20

Kerrigan, S., & Batty, C. (2016). Re-conceptualising screenwriting for the academy: the social, cultural and creative practice of developing a screenplay. *New Writing, 13*, 130–144. https://doi.org/10.1080/14790726.2015.1134580

Kerrigan, S., & McIntyre, P. (2010). The 'creative treatment of actuality': Rationalizing and reconceptualizing the notion of creativity for documentary practice. *Journal of Media Practice, 11*(2), 111–130.

Lee, J., & Gillen, A. M. (2011). *The producer's business handbook: The roadmap for the balanced film producer*. Focal Press.

Lotz, A. (2014). *The television will be revolutionized* (2nd ed.). New York University Press.

Lotz, A., & Sanson, K. (2021). Foreign ownership of production companies as a new mechanism of internationalizating television: The case of Australian scripted television. *Television and New Media*, 1–20.

Macdonald, I. (2012). *Screenwriting poetics and the screen idea*. Palgrave Macmillan.

Mann, D. (2009). It's not TV, it's brand management TV: The collective authors(s) of the lost franchise. In V. Mayer, M. Banks, & J. Caldwell (Eds.), *Production studies: Cultural studies of media industries* (pp. 99–113). Routledge.

Mazzarol, T., & Reboud, S. (2020). *Entrepreneurship and innovation: Theory, practice and context*. Springer Singapore.

McIntyre, P., & Kerrigan, S. (2014). Pursuing extreme romance: Change and continuity in the creative screen industries in the Hunter Valley. *Studies in Australasian Cinema, 8*(2–3), 133–149. https://doi.org/10.1080/17503175.2014.960680

Olsberg SPI. (2012, June 1). *Building sustainable film businesses: The challenge for industry and government*. Film Institute. Retrieved October 11, 2021, from https://www.filminstitutet.se/globalassets/2.-fa-kunskap-om-film/analys-och-statistik/publications/other-publications/building-sustainable-film-businesses%2D%2D-the-challenges-for-industry.pdf

Oombarra Production. (2019). *Profile Leah Purcell*. Oombarra Productions. Retrieved October 12, 2021, from https://oombarra.com/

Rankin, S., & Purcell, L. (1999). *Box the pony*. Hodder Headline.

Screen Actors Guild – American Federation of Television and Radio Artists. (2022, January 1). *Ultra low budget projects*. SAG Production Centre. Retrieved January 18, 2022, from https://www.sagaftra.org/production-center/contract/819/agreement/document

Velikovsky, J. (2016). *Communication, creativity and consilience in cinema: A comparative study of the Top 20 return-on-investment (RoI) movies and the doxa of screenwriting*. Doctoral dissertation, University of Newcastle, NOVA.

CHAPTER 10

Entrepreneurship in Visual and Performing Arts

Talking about 'Art' in a book on entrepreneurship and the creative industries could be seen as a contentious proposition. For those deep inside their art world (Becker, 1982) it probably is. But as Pierre Bourdieu argued in relation to the fraught interaction between Art and money, between creativity and commerce, it is the case that the doxa of Art, 'the common beliefs and unquestioned truths peculiar to that field…the taken-for-granted internal logic of the world of art' (McIntyre, 2015, p. 4) reveals that artists must see themselves, and insist others must see them, as autonomous from the impositions of finance. This doxa has been the means 'through which artists free themselves from bourgeois demand by refusing to recognize any master except their art [which] produces the effect of making the market disappear' (Bourdieu, 1996, p. 81). However:

> Although myths of marginality, alienation, 'outsider' status and creative freedom remain potent and have a strong hold on artists themselves, the reality of marketplace requirements currently dictates a different set of demands…In the 21st century artists are required to be experimental and innovative, and to push the frontiers of art while capitalizing upon the development of a distinctive and marketable individuality. In this market-savvy entrepreneurial role, artists are encouraged to exaggerate and exploit their individuality and to feed into popular myths to reinforce their occupational authenticity. Thus many contemporary artists have consciously or unconsciously sought to preserve their symbolic marginalization (social, economic or cultural) and their mythologized alienation. (Bain, 2005, p. 29)

P. McIntyre et al., *Entrepreneurship in the Creative Industries*,
https://doi.org/10.1007/978-3-031-19455-9_10

But, given the evidence to the contrary, we will be putting the doxa of art aside. As Ellen Dissanayake argued, '"Art" as a concept seems to have been born of and continues to be sustained by a commercial society, is therefore only roughly two centuries old, and hence is relative, even discardable' (1995, p. 41). We also argue from the point of view of Janet Wolff (1993), Mihaly Csikszentmihalyi (1988, 1997, 1999), and Raymond Williams (1981) that all art practice relies on some form of patronage or another. In all the cases outlined by Williams (1981, pp. 41–47), a system of gaining an income has to be a fundamental part of the creative process, that is, in order to continue to afford to make art, an income of some sort is necessary for art practitioners to sustain themselves. Many have become 'artpreneurs' to secure that income.

'Artpreneurs' can be found right across the history of art in the West. For example, Marilena Vecco provides 'several examples of entrepreneurial marketing practice drawn from the Italian Renaissance and from modern art history' (2019, p. 96):

> 'Artpreneurs' combine artistic qualities with business sense: they have a deep knowledge and feeling of art, creativity, and a strong inclination and proactiveness in recognising and taking opportunities and risks in the cultural business environment (Klamer, 2011; Rentschler, 2007). Compared to managers in the art sectors, artpreneurs are more proactive and may potentially fully (it depends of course on the scale of the business) manage their value chain process. They developed specific skills and capabilities which allow them to survive and adapt themselves to an unstable environment. (Vecco, 2019, p. 99)

Artists enter their enterprises through varied routes. Overall, they face less well-structured industry and support systems, work in markets that depend on changes in technology and aesthetic fashion, and are subject to intense competition for discretionary expenditure. Visual artists generally seek representation through a gallery to exhibit work with a commission paid on sales of 40–50%. Gallerists help manage artists' careers, supporting them but also exerting some control, usually restricting their artists' freedom to show elsewhere, and sharing in prize money. Artists, on the other hand, may reduce those costs and avoid commissions by selling direct to the public through 'open studio' events and showing in artist-run spaces where costs are less. One driver of this move to greater control on the artists' part is rising commission costs, which have accompanied a declining market. Artwork prices have fallen as much as 40% since the 1990s and again post-GFC, which represent a challenge to artists' incomes (McIntyre et al., 2019, p. 321). This situation is reflective of the contribution visual and performing arts make to the creative industries as a whole.

While the most recent analysis undertaken estimates the contribution to GDP of Australia's cultural and creative activity at $111.7 billion, 'the creative arts, being a small sub-sector of the broader creative economy, was valued at much less' (Trembath & Fielding, 2020, p. 34). Visual arts and crafts contributed just 2.9% and performing arts contributed 2.1% to this total figure. Regardless of how much money is being made, and who is making it, it is still the fact that for artists working in the visual and performing arts sector of the creative industries, gaining an income has always been a precarious pursuit for the vast majority of artists. Visual artists, in particular, have rarely been employed full time and generally their incomes are much lower than other professions.

Some of the professions listed by the Australian Bureau of Statistics (ABS) in the visual arts sector include that of painter, illustrator, sculptor, visual arts and crafts professionals, potter or ceramic artist, gallery or museum curator, and jewelry designer (McIntyre et al., 2019, p. 141). Many of these are included in our discussion below on how an artist might gain an income. We showcase Australian landscape artist John Bradley, gallery curator Trevor Richards, art hub owner and manager Stewart Guthrie, bespoke knifemaker Tobi Bockholt, and ceramic artist Chela Edmunds. The performing arts sector includes theater, musical theater, dance, music, opera, comedy, circus, mime, and much more. It is a diverse sector covering many aspects of artistic expression which involves people using their bodies and/or voices, or extensions of those, to communicate with an audience. Professions in this sector include actors, dancers, clowns, playwrights, dramaturgs, producers and directors, lighting designers, sound technicians, set designers, make-up artists, and many more. This sector is represented here by Carl Caulfield, a playwright, actor, and dramaturg, as well as the Geelong company Back to Back Theatre.

John Bradley is a prominent artist who he has been painting for 40 years and is known internationally for his Australian landscapes. Art investors have been paying up to $20,000 (AUD) for an original of his artwork. Bradley's originals are for sale through three Australian art galleries and from his own website, John Bradley Studio (John Bradley Studio, 2022). As an independent artist Bradley will paint by commission from clients too, creating a painting of a particular scene and dealing directly with that client. He used to participate in traveling art exhibitions, where a group of artists would tour with their collections and sell artwork directly to the public. This type of fine art touring exhibition helped promote his work and helped build his reputation as a fine artist (McIntyre et al., 2019, p. 332). Around 2010, in line with the pragmatic actions of neoliberalism, which has decimated the middle in all industrial sectors, creating the whales and plankton phenomenon (Davies & Sigthorsson, 2013, pp. 49–50), Bradley noticed subtle changes in the market for original art, with the mid-range buyers disappearing:

> We used to have the bulk of our sales…$2,000 to $5000 bracket. What we're finding now is that they were getting back down into the $1000–$1500 and then they jumped to the investors. We are still selling $10,000 and $20,000 pieces but not a lot. The middle ground is gone…It's very volatile. (J. Bradley, personal interview, September, 2015)

Bradley also felt at this time that for him Art had become a disposable decoration, with Chinese prints being sold for $100. These had become his main competition. The volatility appearing in the art market at this time continued, and Bradley had to re-invent his portfolio to maintain his sales. He adjusted the size of his paintings, started painting verticals instead of horizontals, and changed the palette, choosing monochrome and painting nightscapes in order to make his artworks more attractive for the first-time buyer (J. Bradley, personal interview, September, 2015).

For Bradley, understanding how the art market functions is a necessary skill for a fine artist, as his income is derived from creating and selling these original artworks. Bradley's intuition regarding the preferences of a buyer's market began during his previous career as a national marketing manager for a large Sydney company (McIntyre et al., 2019, p. 332). He explains that Australian artists do not receive any commission when their art is re-sold (J. Bradley, personal interview, September, 2015), and this situation means artists have to generate an income from selling the originals or from reproductions and publications of their original works that they themselves control. He also suggests that diversifying income streams is extremely important for artists wanting to earn an income from their art. Typically reproductions give an added income stream, and prints of his artwork are now part of his income management. Bradley creates limited edition prints which are signed and numbered so that they hold their value. Purchasing these allows new buyers to enter the market at a lower price point, with the hope that these buyers will eventually return to purchase an original. Bradley explains the value of an artist's signature on an artwork:

> In signing the work we're saying it's finished. The signature on it makes it worth a lot more obviously. An unsigned painting might be worth $500 and with a signature it might be worth $8000. So, it does have a value of some sort as a collector's item or an investment item…Once it's signed I'm saying I'm happy with it, and then you can do prints from it. So, you multiple it, you leverage it and then of course you hand sign every print and put a number on them if they form part of a limited edition. (J. Bradley, personal interview, September, 2015)

Another way to create an income stream through reproduction is for the artist to license copies of the original to a printing company for publication. The printing company will typically on-sell the publishable rights to other companies, though sometimes the artist deals directly with a company who makes a product, for example, 'John Bradley has jigsaw puzzles, then every quarter there is a cheque that comes in from Modern Brands for the royalties from the jigsaw puzzles' (T. Richards, personal interview, September, 2015). Bradley also earns a passive income from licensed publication of his artwork to a North American printing company. As an intermediary, they on-sell the reproduction rights of Bradley's artwork to the US, Russia, England, and Hong Kong. Bradley explains:

> They've licensed over 140 images, to the biggest print company in the world and just recently they have sold another 120 to the largest curated printing company in the world. They reproduce them, mainly as wall hangings, canvases, prints, tray prints et cetera. Some of them go into jigsaws and stuff like that. One of the companies supplies three-quarters of America's prints. So, it's a big company. (J. Bradley, personal interview, September, 2015)

While this sounds like an impressive example of globalization, Bradley points out that the returns are small:

> They are only licensed for a year with an option to renew at the end of it. You always keep the IP on it—that's pretty much how I think most of them work. There is not a lot of money, but the publicity is fantastic, and they split the commission between them and me. So, as passive income, there is a few thousand a year in it. (J. Bradley, personal interview, September, 2015)

As a highly experienced artist, Bradley has found a diverse range of ways to create an income. This includes self-publishing artwork in books or as a calendar, as Bradley has done. He has created two books of his works. Finally, another way for an artist to create an income is to show others how to replicate these processes and make an income from their skills. For 15 years Bradley has been teaching 'how to paint' landscapes classes to budding artists. He also offers services in framing, printing, and photographing artworks, a skill he developed to create his limited-edition prints. He also uses his website and Facebook pages to promote his work, but he also realizes that his relationship with the curator of the gallery where his work is on sale is paramount. Bradley originals are for sale at Morpeth Art Gallery in the Hunter Valley in NSW, along with fifteen other artists (Morpeth Gallery, 2022).

Morpeth Investment Art Gallery has an international reputation for its collection of original Australian landscapes and wildlife art. Exhibiting over 300 original artworks, many sold as investments, some will fetch up to $50,000 (AUD). This gallery represents Australia's most renowned wildlife artist William T. Cooper, who was hailed by Sir David Attenborough as 'Australia's greatest living scientific painter of birds; he is possibly the best in the world'. Cooper's last exhibition was held in Morpeth in 2013, and in 11 minutes all 31 artworks were sold for a net worth over $200,000 (T. Richards, personal interview, September, 2015).

The gallery is owned by art curator and entrepreneur Trevor Richards, who runs the gallery in conjunction with Campbells Store Craft Centre Complex, employing about 30 retail and gallery workers. The complex opened in 1991 and since then Richards has built a reputation as an investment art gallery. As well as William T. Cooper's work, it holds the largest collection of Gordon Hanley's work as a metalpoint artist:

> Gordon Hanley, has been given the status of "Living Master" by the US Art Renewal Centre (ARC). Hanley is Australia's only "Living Master". He resides in Queensland and draws with a special 18 carat gold pen. His work includes ballerinas and Australia wildlife and he is the most published print artist in Australia over the last 20 years. (T. Richards, personal interview, September, 2015)

All of the artists on sale at Morpeth are published artists. This fact permits Richards' gallery to sell the art products and artwork reproductions, for example, as domestic tableware products, books, jigsaws, and calendars. Australian artist Frederick McCubbin's work has been published on greeting cards and it even appeared in a Kit-Kat advertisement. Richards believes it is important for artists to have their work published, as the published products raise the profile of the artists, which, in his opinion, helps to increase the value of the original artworks. It also allows the artist to receive a passive income paid as a royalty, with the works under license from the artist. Trevor Richards explains that wildlife artist Gary Fleming earns

> a quarter of a $1 million a year in passive income from these products. Every quarter Natalie Jane Parker gets a cheque from Ashdene for the royalties on the coffee mugs, plates and trays and they are selling hundreds of thousands of those worldwide. Some artists can receive more than $60,000 a year in royalties from one company without lifting a brush. (T. Richards, personal interview, September, 2015)

Richards emphasizes that only a very small percentage of fine artists are able to earn a primary income from their art; however, there are other examples of visual artists who have found a way to earn an income from their art, using some of the strategies discussed above, as well as employing online methods to promote and sell artworks.

Many artists will now market themselves through establishing websites and online catalogs, use social media like Facebook and Instagram to promote exhibitions, sell at weekend market stalls, as well as also showing in a gallery. To assist that process they need to establish themselves using whatever symbolic capital they can. Building a visual artist's reputation and business through prizes, grants, awards, and residencies has become *de rigueur* in this process. Such structural mechanisms provide opportunities for artists to be critically acclaimed from within an art world (Becker, 1982) and such recognition in turn contributes to their social and cultural capital, often leading to private, public, and corporate commissions. One such example is that of visual artist knifemaker and bladesmith Tobi Bockholt, whose business is Metal Monkey Knives. Bockholt custom makes bespoke knives in a prepared blacksmiths forge (Metal Monkey Knives, 2022) and has received awards like Best Knife in Australia 2018, and 2nd in Best Chef Knife in Australia 2019. He takes commissions and sells his knives internationally with a reputation in the USA and Europe (Kerrigan et al., 2020, p. 27). Similarly, visual artist and potter Chela Edmunds owns and runs her business Takeawei Ceramics (2022). Her tableware is made from a handmade design which is focused on both craftsmanship and functionality. Her business uses food-safe glazes with each piece being fired in very hot kilns of 1280 degree Celsius. This small arts business employs four staff and has retail and wholesale outlets in Melbourne and Sydney (Kerrigan et al., 2020, p. 27). Both these visual arts businesses are located at Ashmore Arts on Victoria's Surf Coast.

Ashmore Arts is a thriving rural artistic hotspot, operating as a hub where 30 arts and crafts businesses operate (Kerrigan et al., 2020, p. 27). It is home to a huge range of artistic expertise covering fine art, large art (such as murals), illustration, animation, photography, graphic design, weaving, leather book binding, calligraphy, furniture making (wood), furniture making (concrete), blacksmithing, sculpting in wood and stone, pottery, knife making, picture framing, home interior décor design, and music production (Kerrigan et al., 2020, p. 27). The hub offers large and small studio spaces in shipping containers, sheds, and where required, outdoor purpose-built facilities for making artworks like a blacksmithing forge, kilns, and sawmills for large wooden sculptures. Ashmore Arts is owned by Stewart Guthrie, who is also an artist, and he rents these spaces to arts businesses. There are huge benefits for visual artist to gather together communally in hubs like these. While this might seem like a new trend, it is something that has been happening for hundreds of years, with its origins in the artists' guilds of the Renaissance era.

As populations grew in Europe and societies stabilized, guilds developed which regulated the conditions of work for its members. Overseeing both quality and price, the guilds set wages and hours and prescribed what were acceptable tools and techniques for their members to use: 'In this way, they functioned to preserve traditions; but beyond that, they also carried a certain mystique that may have contributed to the developing status of the artist' (Haynes, 1997, p. 76). Once these collectivist city-based enterprises gave way to private patronage around the fourteenth and fifteenth century a distinction began to be made between exceptionally skilled artists who could set their own prices and afford to ignore the guilds. Many of these became stars, as it were, and a number began to see 'their work not in terms of economic gain (or loss) but as a calling. Thus the artist qua artist began to emerge' (Haynes, 1997, p. 104).

While it is not member run the communal project taking place at Ashmore Arts employs twelve people in a range of jobs to assist the visual artists collected there in their primary endeavor, that is, in creating art.

> These artists are 'rock stars', and with that comes personal business branding, the development of their social persona (on a biz level) is something they are and should be very protective about. Online sales means no shop front costs, no gallery fees and a far wider and more specific audience. (S. Guthrie, personal interview, June 29, 2020)

The owner of the facility, Stewart Guthrie, estimated a total turnover in 2006 of nearly $3 million dollars (S. Guthrie, personal interview, June 29, 2020). This estimate was based on discussion with residents, truck movements, and staffing. Of course since 2006 the number of residents has grown, indicating that the combined income today would be far greater. Its financial acumen with significant returns for the artists means Ashmore Arts has a waiting list for studio/workshop space, and Guthrie is planning to further develop his site to double capacity (S. Guthrie, personal interview, June 29, 2020).

While there are occasional success stories like these in the visual arts, earning an income from the performing arts sector has become increasingly challenging. For example, the closing of the Australian Major Performing Arts Group (AMPAG), which represents twenty-nine companies, occurred in 2020, and this one act signifies the impact of the economic issues facing this sector. It affects the theater, circus, dance, opera, and symphony orchestras that have relied on AMPAG's advocacy across this sector (Watts, 2020, online).

Having conducted research into the theater industry, focusing on Newcastle NSW, Bransdon found that the industry was stagnant. While the city 'has had professional theatre companies operating in the past, the research was unable to identify any fully professional theatre companies currently operating' (Bransdon, 2021, p. 267). While the city and the surrounding areas have a population of more than 365,000 (McIntyre et al., 2019, p. 137), Bransdon's research found that the economic value of the theatrical sector was surprisingly low, with 'approximately $3.1 million in ticket sales and $1.8 million in production expenditure over the 12-month research period' (Bransdon, 2021, p. 266). Most companies used a pro-am business model, with two companies operating on a profit share arrangement. Bransdon argues that a 'few key people are paid a fee to create the production while most contributors volunteer' (2021, p. 267). This research indicates that the traditional business models used in the sector are struggling to be competitive in the digital age. One theater company that has been operating for more than twenty-five years is the

Stray Dogs Theatre Company (Stray Dogs, 2014) in Newcastle, Australia. Co-artistic directors are Carl Caulfield and Felicity Biggins. They have run this company since 1996 and annually stage new plays written by Caulfield. The company was established through an NSW Ministry of the Arts grant, and Performing Arts Newcastle (PAN) provides insurance coverage for the company (McIntyre et al., 2019, pp. 379–380).

Their first play *Angel of Mercy* was written by Caulfield. He is a playwright, director, actor, dramaturg (script consultant), and educator, while Biggins, his partner, is a theater director, journalist, radio presenter, and educator. Caulfield was born in the United Kingdom. After an early passion for soccer, he followed his interest in writing and performing, completing a Bachelor of Arts in English and Drama at Leeds University where he met his wife, Felicity Biggins. He has also completed a Master's in Creative Arts at University of New South Wales, where he also taught, and completed a PhD at University of Technology Sydney.

Most of Caulfield's plays are performed in Newcastle, often as part of the city's Civic Theatre subscription season, but he has written, staged, and performed in a significant number of works across his career:

> His works include *Seems Like Old Times*, *Dante's Dream*, *Human Resources*, *Shakespeare's Fools*, *The Anatomy of Buzz*, *Where Late the Songbird* and *Hecuba Reimagined*. *Being Sellers*, Carl's award-winning, one-man play about British Goon Peter Sellers, was first produced in 1998 at the Playhouse in Newcastle, before transferring to the Edinburgh Festival and then to London at the Man in the Moon Theatre, Kings Road. *Being Sellers* was recently reprised at the Waterloo East Theatre in London with David Boyle as Sellers and then went on to the 59E59 Theatre in New York. His most recent play, *Mark of Cain*, explores the impact of PTSD (post-traumatic stress disorder) on a group of returning soldiers. Carl has just written, directed and co-produced his first short film, *Chloe Comes Through*. (NWF, 2017, online)

Caulfield feels that writing for the stage is different from other jobs:

> The playwright's job is to kind of get inside there and get the audience thinking and feeling again…play-writing [sic] has always been in my view a humane project, it's a humanitarian project, there's no doubt about it. And you may spend your time trying to get inside the mind of a monster, you may be trying to evoke a character who is repellent, you may be doing any

number of things but ultimately it is a project that I trust as being a humane project. (C. Caulfield, personal interview, May 29, 2015)

As an experienced playwright, Caulfield understands that his work is constrained by the limited budgets theater companies have. He comments that:

> Theatre companies won't look at your work if you're writing for more than seven actors anyway…nobody is putting on these large-scale plays unless you're the National Theatre…I mean it's great to have the chamber pieces, but we also want to see the large-scale work that deals with big social issues, you know, or the movements of history. (C. Caulfield, personal interview, May 29, 2015)

Caulfield is acutely aware of the decline occurring in the theater sector and is sanguine about it:

> I mean, the theatre has always been dying, yeah, there's nothing new about that! And, all of these technologies that people mention and the bright new things…nothing is going to replace live performance, and I think ultimately people will come back to it, just as they come back to reading the novel. (C. Caulfield, personal interview, May 29, 2015)

When asked about the state of theater in Newcastle, Caulfield responded:

> there is this strong tradition here of doing good theatre. It's been around a hell of a long time, and it's one of the best things about this city, to me. I mean, I think it's very easy to get projects up here…but on another level, I have to be frank with you and say, it's as depressing as it ever was. And the lack of support is just as it ever was, if not getting worse, in a way…I think we're moving into a kind of brutal, corporate kind of mindset. (C. Caulfield, personal interview, May 29, 2015)

Back to Back Theatre is another regional theater company, this time based in Geelong, Victoria. Back to Back were established thirty years ago and Executive Producer Alice Nash and Artistic Director Bruce Galdwin have both occupied their roles for more than twenty years. Together they have grown the organization and created an internationally recognized theater company (A. Harvey, personal interview, June 18, 2019). They use a presenter model to gain income. The use of this model means they create original works and market those shows directly to the presenters of local, national, or international festivals. With this model, as the company's Director of Marketing and Development, Katherine Branch explains, 'we don't hold the ticket sale responsibility because we sell our shows to presenters' (K. Branch, personal interview, June 18, 2019).

Senior Producer, Ally Harvey, explains their company creates unique performances because they employ an 'ensemble of artists with intellectual disabilities. And the company exists because of those artists, not for those artists' (A. Harvey, personal interview, June 18, 2019). These six artists produce the work which is 'written by them through a process of improvisation, conversation and research and then eventually scripted and performed. So that work comes from their current interests, their current experiences of the world from their perspective' (A. Harvey, personal interview, June 18, 2019). Their work has been performed all over the world and has received international recognition (Kerrigan et al., 2020) including the Ibsen Award, an international, biennial award that 'honours artists who have brought new dimensions to the world of drama or theatre' (Cooper, 2022). *The New York Times* described their 2019 work *The Shadow Whose Prey the Hunter Becomes* as an 'extraordinary play' (Back to Back Theatre, 2020). The work was co-commissioned by Arts Centre Melbourne, Geelong Performing Arts, and Melbourne International Arts Festival. Sponsorship to develop the work was received from Sydney Carriageworks and some North American presenters: the Public Theater as part of Under the Radar Festival and also Arts Emerson in Boston. Additional funding was also received from the Costa Foundation in Geelong and from Thyne Reid who are based in New South Wales (A. Harvey, personal interview, June 18, 2019).

As a company, Back to Back seeks sponsorship from a variety of areas, but it is also funded by government agencies, from the federal level by Australia Council for the Arts, at state level through Creative Victoria, and locally through the City of Greater Geelong council (A. Harvey, personal interview, June 18, 2019). The company also raises additional income through private investments, something they have been doing since 2014 (Back to Back Theatre, 2014, p. 30). A Creative Industries report on Geelong breaks down the income streams for Back to Back as follows:

> The largest source of income is performances (36%) followed by operational grants (31%). In terms of expenses, artists' wages are highest (29%) followed by core employee wages (26%) and production costs (19%). (Kerrigan et al., 2020, p. 22)

There is a very experienced creative team behind Back to Back's success, and the decision to use the presenter business model demonstrates a mature understanding of how to develop value from their intellectual property. Back to Back's programming and activities were temporarily suspended due to the COVID-19 outbreak in 2020 (Back to Back Theatre, 2020).

It is interesting to note that the majority of theater companies operate with meager budgets and performers are rarely paid for most of them. Some companies use profit-share mechanisms, a few companies are supported by grants, but all rely heavily on the gift economy to survive with only a few principals deriving a wage from their artistic activity. As in many other sectors, the main paid work for those in the performing arts sector comes not directly but often from teaching, employment with councils, and precarious, usually 'one-off' engagements. Digitization is also now increasingly a part of marketing and production, as well as providing a forum for interactive participation (Towse, 2013). Ruth Towse argues from the available evidence that box office functions and promotion in particular have been affected by digitization. Websites are now ubiquitous in the performing arts, as is the use of social media, giving audio-visual previews, histories of the show, stories about the cast, and so on, all of which are linked to ticketing. These websites also encourage new audiences, providing insights through forums for learning about the art forms with virtual backstage tours of theaters, video of rehearsals, and interviews with performers. In terms of production, digitally controlled scenery changes and lighting have reduced the need for a number of backstage staff, while streamed live performances done in real time via satellite to HD cinemas are becoming increasingly common. While smaller companies and individuals, however, are increasingly using low-cost methods for promotion—mobile phone footage posted to social media platforms—this audio-visual material usually comes with its own production costs, extra crew, and necessarily intense coordination with the theatrical event itself. There are, as a matter of course, multiple rights to be negotiated, whether the audio-visual material is embedded in social media or sold on DVD at the event site (Towse, 2013, pp. 311–321).

In combining artistic qualities with business sense many of the artpreneurs we've described above have exploited their deep knowledge of creative practice as artists and been highly proactive in taking opportunities and absorbing the risks they face in what are often uncertain business environments, mitigating those risk with a variety of adaptive ways of gaining incomes. As Vecco (2019, p. 19) indicated, these artpreneurs have managed to exploit the value chain process at various points and, in the process, developed resilient skills and capabilities which have allowed them to survive and adapt as they continue to persist in making what they love.

References

Back to Back Theatre. (2014). *2014 year in review*. Retrieved April 30, 2022, from https://backtobacktheatre.com/cms/wp-content/uploads/2015/05/2014-B2B_YIR-40pp_med-res-FINAL.pdf

Back to Back Theatre. (2020). *Home*. Retrieved April 30, 2022, from http://backtobacktheatre.com/

Bain, A. (2005). Constructing an artistic identity. *Work, Employment and Society, 19*(1), 25–46.

Becker, H. (1982). *Art worlds*. University of California Press.

Bourdieu, P. (1996). *The rules of art: Genesis and structure of the literary field*. Polity Press.

Bradley, J. (2015, September). Personal communication [Personal interview].

Branch, K. (2019, June 18). Personal communication [Personal interview].

Bransdon, S. (2021). *Valuing Newcastle's theatrical performing arts Industries: A systemic approach to unpacking the economic, structural and social challenges faced by the Newcastle theatre industry*. Doctoral dissertation, University of Newcastle, NOVA.

Caulfield, C. (2015, May 29). Personal communication [Personal interview].

Cooper, E. (2022, March 21). Back to Back Theatre in Geelong wins $300,000 International Ibsen Award. *ABC News*. https://www.abc.net.au/news/2022-03-21/australian-back-to-back-theatre-group-wins-ibsen-award/100924732

Csikszentmihalyi, M. (1988). Society, culture and person: A systems view of creativity. In R. Sternberg (Ed.), *The nature of creativity: Contemporary psychological perspectives* (pp. 325–329). Cambridge University Press.

Csikszentmihalyi, M. (1997). *Creativity: Flow and the psychology of discovery and invention*. Harper Collins.

Csikszentmihalyi, M. (1999). Implications of a systems perspective for the study of creativity. In R. Sternberg (Ed.), *Handbook of creativity* (pp. 313–335). Cambridge University Press.

Davies, R., & Sigthorsson, G. (2013). *Introducing the creative industries: From theory to practice*. Sage.

Dissanayake, E. (1995). *Homo aestheticus: Where art comes from and why*. University of Washington Press.

Guthrie, S. (2020, June 29). Personal communication [Personal interview].

Harvey, A. (2019, June 18). Personal communication [Personal interview].
Haynes, D. (1997). *The vocation of the artist*. Cambridge University Press.
John Bradley Studio. (2022, January 1). *Home*. John Bradley Studio. Retrieved April 30, 2022, from https://johnbradleyart.com
Kerrigan, S., McIntyre, P., McCutcheon, M., & Cunningham, S. (2020). *Australian cultural and creative activity: A population and hotspot analysis: Geelong and Surf Coast*. Digital Media Research Centre. https://research.qut.edu.au/creativehotspots/
McIntyre, P. (2015). Creative industries and identity: From older conceptions to new models of creativity. In D. Paterno, M. Bourk, & D. Matheson (Eds.), *Refereed proceedings of 2015 ANZCA Conference: Rethinking Communication, Space and Identity* (pp. 1–13), University of Canterbury, Queenstown, New Zealand, July 8–10, 2015.
McIntyre, P., Balnaves, M., Kerrigan, S., Williams, C., & King, E. (2019). *Creativity and cultural production in the Hunter: An applied ethnographic study of applied entrepreneurial systems in the creative industries: Final report, ARC Grant LP130100348*. University of Newcastle.
Metal Monkey Knives. (2022). *About us*. Metal Monkey Knives. Retrieved April 30, 2022, from https://www.metalmonkeyknives.com.au
Morpeth Gallery. (2022). *Home*. Morpeth Art Gallery Retrieved April 30, 2022, from https://www.morpethgallery.com/
NWF. (2017). *Carl Caulfield – biography*. Newcastle Writers Festival. Retrieved January 24, 2018, from http://www.newcastlewritersfestival.org.au/speaker/carl-caulfield/
Stray Dogs. (2014). *Home*. Stray Dogs. Retrieved April 30, 2022, from https://www.carlcaulfieldstraydogs.com/stray-dogs
Takeawei (2022). *Home*. Takeawei. Retrieved April 30, 2022, from https://takeawei.com
Towse, R. (2013). Performing arts. In R. Towse & C. Handke (Eds.), *Handbook on the digital creative economy* (pp. 311–321). Edward Elgar.
Trembath, J., & Fielding, K. (2020). *Pre-release extract, Australia's cultural and creative economy: A 21st century guide*. Produced by A New Approach think tank with lead delivery partner the Australian Academy of the Humanities, Canberra.
Vecco, M. (2019). The "Artpreneur", between traditional and cultural entrepreneurship. A Historical Perspective. In J. B. William & A. Brkić (Eds.), *The Routledge Companion to Arts Management* (pp. 85–103). Taylor & Francis Group.
Watts, R., (2020, July 28). *AMPAG to close after 21 years*. Arts Hub and Screen Hub. Retrieved April 30, 2022, from https://www.artshub.com.au/news/news/ampag-to-close-after-21-years-260803-2368014/
Williams, R. (1981). *Culture*. Fontana Press.
Wolff, J. (1993). *The social production of art* (2nd ed.). Macmillan.

CHAPTER 11

Entrepreneurship in Advertising and Public Relations

Traditionally, media enterprises have been focused on creating products for audiences, with advertising being a central force that sustains commercial endeavors (Sinclair in Cunningham & Turnbull, 2014, p. 209). But things have changed. Legacy media business models in advertising, marketing, and public relations have been transforming across recent decades as a result of digitization, globalization, and the interconnected implementation of neoliberal market policies. These structural forces have impacted those professions and practices associated with advertising, marketing, and public relations (Villi & Picard, 2019).

> Globalizing, particularly in the past two decades, has had a profound impact on the advertising, marketing, and public relations industries…those who offer advertising and public relations services worldwide have had to begin paying closer attention to different media landscapes, consumer preferences, various regulations, and economic and cultural factors if they want to maintain successful businesses. (Vujnovic & Kruckeberg, 2020, pp. 338–339)

The convergence of practices in advertising, design, and PR agencies has led to these being described simply as an 'agency'. A typical agency will offer a full range of advertising, promotional, marketing, and design services to provide clients with all they 'need for the entire advertising function' (Solomon et al., 2009, p. 43). These expanded agencies use an entrepreneurial mindset aimed at exploiting new products and new

P. McIntyre et al., *Entrepreneurship in the Creative Industries*,
https://doi.org/10.1007/978-3-031-19455-9_11

markets, achieved through an 'expansion of economic activity' (Mazzarol & Reboud, 2020, p. 15).

The relationships between consumers and media enterprises are continuously evolving. The emergence of digital media technologies has resulted in media enterprises creating new products and processes and finding innovative ways to present the digital content that evolves from them (Villi & Picard, 2019, p. 121). Villi and Picard, in describing how media business models are transforming, argue that contemporary models 'are not just about revenue, but increasingly about relationships with consumers, value creation and continual product and service improvements' (2019, p. 129). In pursuing that value creation, advertising and public relations agencies foster highly innovative and unique approaches to producing new forms of advertising and new advertising products. This type of '[i]nnovation must contain a degree of novelty, and the type of innovation can be new to the firm, to the market or to the world' (Mazzarol & Reboud, 2020, p. 21), but each creation of novel symbolic cultural messages requires practitioners in these fields to work innovatively and cooperatively within dense entrepreneurial networks of agents, decision-making entities, and stakeholders who have a part to play in each respective field of production.

Full-service agencies provide a one-stop shop for their local, national, and global clients, offering a complete range of services including 'planning, creating, producing, and placing the ads, as well as research before the campaign and evaluation after it to assess the campaign's effectiveness' (Solomon et al., 2009, p. 43). Expansion of these services has been critical to successfully operate at scale with services like public relations, event planning, media buying, and design having now been included in the range of services offered. More recently these agencies have expanded to include the use of emerging digital technologies in-house (Mills, 2013, online). For example, app development and boutique website coding for online sales are some of the newer services that an advertising entrepreneur will acquire for their agency. This typically means larger agencies eventually expand as they diversify, acquiring smaller boutique businesses that offer just one service, to ensure that a full service can be offered to the customer from the one business source (McIntyre et al., 2019, p. 276). The aim is to 'marshal the specialist skills and knowledge of others and to configure resources for commercial benefit' (Mazzarol & Reboud, 2020, p. 14). The merging or take-over of enterprising startups generally occurs rapidly. The case for this form of integration allegedly results in improved and higher quality products being created, changes to the methods of their production, and the eventual opening up of new markets.

This change in services being offered through advertising means its purpose inside the media landscape is being updated and redefined (Rosengren, 2019). It has been argued that this evolution occurs as a result of new technologies and new platforms becoming available, along with an emphasis on changing consumer behaviors caused by co-creation and engagement opportunities (Dahlen & Rosengren, 2016; Rosengren, 2019, p. 392), and this can be traced historically, back to the early 1920s when advertising was described as 'selling in print' (Rosengren, 2019, p. 391). Rosengren argues that 'advertising has evolved from flyers and magazine ads in print media via radio and tv commercials in broadcast media, to contemporary content marketing and social media campaigns targeting specific individuals and audiences through digital media' (Rosengren, 2019, p. 389). These changes can be traced in the history of Victorian-based advertising agency Pace, described as 'Australia's longest-serving advertising agency established in 1964' (Pace, 2019, online).

Pace is owned by Nicholas Heath. His father established the business in Geelong in regional Victoria, with its 60-year evolution illustrative of how the changes in media have affected the services offered by advertising agencies, and, as a result, affected the types of practices, skills, and professions needed to keep up with changes in media technologies and consumer behaviors. Pace emerged from the car industry. It was initially the in-house advertising department that was part of the Ford dealership group, itself also based in Geelong (N. Heath, personal interview, June 17, 2019). During the 1960s, Pace employed copywriters and artists in their art department to create the artwork for a quarter page advertisement for the Melbourne newspaper *The Age*. The 'ad' would be driven from Geelong up to the Melbourne newspaper's publishing premises for a 2 a.m. deadline (N. Heath, personal interview, June 17, 2019). The 2 a.m. drive to Melbourne was replaced by facsimile machines in the 1980s, and eventually a digital pipeline was established that eliminated the need to physically deliver the artwork to the printing press. During the 1970s and 1980s Pace also began making television commercials and employed freelance writers and cinematographers (N. Heath, personal interview, June 17, 2019). During this time they changed from employing specialist staff in-house to hiring expertly skilled specialists on a project-by-project basis. As their business and its relationship to the media industries they worked with were evolving, so were the services offered by Pace. They changed with the times, solidifying an entrepreneurial approach that include 'initiative, strong persuasive powers, moderate risk taking, flexibility, creativity, autonomy, problem-solving ability, need for achievement, imagination, leadership and hard work' (Mazzarol & Reboud, 2020, p. 16).

Pace now exemplifies an agency where advertising, marketing, and public relations have converged, with its employee talent pool changing dramatically over the last thirty years. The first thing to notice is that there is no longer an art department. Instead, today it employs fifteen people in diverse roles, looking to university graduates who are designers and coders to help provide the skills for the full-service agency. They still offer traditional advertising, but along with marketing and various ancillary digital strategies including the production of websites, apps, and digital content. They also offer services in monitoring, analyzing, and optimizing clients' online activity using web stats and insights to plan digital strategies for those clients. They also operate an integrated media delivery system and their 'comprehensive reporting and tolls allow detailed analysis of media performance and cost-benefit analysis' (Pace, 2019, online). The types of digital marketing offered at Pace include optimizing search engine marketing (SEM), search engine optimization (SEO), and social media marketing (SMM), while their digital production services include 'writing blog content and EDM development to YouTube video production' (Pace, 2019, online). In doing so they have clearly challenged the original perspective of what an advertising agency is. They are now seen, in scholarly terms at least, as being involved in 'brand-initiated communication intent on impacting people' (Dahlen & Rosengren, 2016, p. 334). This description draws together the broad areas of advertising, marketing, design, social media, coding, and public relations, where professional and business practices are driven by 'an increased interest among companies to use advertising to do more than affect customers and sales' (Rosengren, 2019, p. 390).

Pace's owner, Nicholas Heath, has had to be highly entrepreneurial to help maintain the company's position as a market leader. In 2019 Pace acquired an app development agency called Choc Chip that employs six full-time coders and app developers. Pace has been enmeshed in local, state, and national marketing for almost three decades and has consulted throughout Australia and overseas on a hugely diverse range of matters. Heath attributes the longevity of Pace to what he calls his insurance strategy, ensuring that Pace has diversified accounts 'across multi-sectors…we need to have some government clients, some private clients, some retail clients'. While he admits they'd be better off financially with three big clients, that strategy would leave them too financially exposed. He attests that he has 'seen it before. When agencies lose two or three big customers, it gets pretty dark pretty quickly' (N. Heath, personal interview, June 17, 2019). Pace not only has Melbourne and regional Victorian clients but, because they are based in a regional location, they have lower overheads and can be 'a little bit more price oriented than some of the Melbourne companies' (N. Heath, personal interview, June 17, 2019).

Heath's entrepreneurial inclinations developed across his whole career, where his 'behaviour combines social, political and education attributes which values entrepreneurship' (Mazzarol & Reboud, 2020, p. 40). Heath worked in advertising in the US and Australia and joined his father at Pace in Geelong in 1995, where he worked closely with him, allowing Heath to develop the habitus of an 'ad man'. Habitus, as discussed prior, is 'a map that allows a person to understand the territory in which he [sic] exists' (St Clair et al., 2005, p. 146). It is a term that 'emerges from Bourdieu's early work where it frames the ways in which the everyday world of social practice is constructed and learned...habitus is a way of knowing the world, a set of divisions of space and time, of people and things, which structure social practice' (Hiller & Rooksby, 2005, p. 284). It 'produces "dispositions"—the sense of how to behave and what to expect in life' (Kahn-Harris, 2007, p. 70). As Johnson explains it, habitus is:

> ...a 'feel for the game', a 'practical sense' (*sens pratique*) that inclines agents to act and react in specific situations in a manner that is not always calculated and that is not simply a question of conscious obedience to rules. Rather it is a set of dispositions which generates practices and perceptions. The habitus is the result of a long process of inculcation, beginning in early childhood, which becomes a 'second sense' or a second nature. (Johnson in Bourdieu, 1993, p. 5)

Adding to his informal inculcation into the world of advertising, Nicholas Heath was formally educated through an Economics degree and post-graduate studies at Deakin University in Melbourne, and at the Royal Melbourne Institute of Technology (RMIT) in marketing. He also took on some postgraduate research in applied IT at Monash University. Heath majored in Internet and Ecommerce, wrote a minor thesis on Web Interface Interaction, and did research work on web design, software selection, and digital security. He is now a highly sought-after consultant, an active board member, and an advertising entrepreneur.

Entrepreneurs like Nicholas Heath, and the services offered by their businesses, are also managed and populated by intrapreneurs, hired to focus on client services, creative services, marketing, and financial management (Solomon et al., 2009, p. 44). For example, an advertising director 'typically runs the in-house agency' (Solomon et al., 2009, p. 45). They make the decisions as to which creative services are to be bought in and which are to be performed in-house, such as creating an advertisement for print, television, or social media, while development of an app for the client might be subcontracted to a specialized agency. The Advertising Director works to the specifics outlined in a creative brief for a client, which:

> outlines the information and objectives to inspire the creative idea. Creative briefs may take different forms and include a variety of elements, including describing what the advertising is trying to achieve, identifying the main idea to be communicated, and outlining the target audience for that idea. (Solomon et al., 2009, p. 248)

The creative brief proposes the big ideas that the client is wanting to achieve by engaging the advertising agency. It is specifically created for a client by the agency, where both parties must agree on the approach and works proposed in the creative brief. Creative briefs are usually 'written by account planners collaboratively with input from the client, account team, and the creative director' (Solomon et al., 2009, p. 248) and each creative director must have a deep understanding of the modes of communication at their disposal so they can design a strategy and use tactics to honor and implement the creative brief. Highly skilled creative directors conceptualize ideas that address the needs of the clients, which can then be delivered through a campaign that is pitched, approved, created, and delivered within the agency. As they do this, they tailor these into an advertising campaign, which is executed through a range of advertising collateral, delivered via media in precise digital markets. In this process they have to understand the roles of the writers, art directors, designers, planners, strategic communication, researchers, public relations, public affairs, and digital content creators. This understanding allows them to pull together a highly creative team to execute that client brief (Solomon et al., 2009, p. 257). For a creative director, an organizational climate that can foster 'creativity and innovation, tolerate failure and encourage enterprising behaviour' (Mazzarol & Reboud, 2020, p. 96) is ideal, with many advertising agencies known because of their creative directors.

Out of the Square Media (OOTS), a design agency in Newcastle, Australia, employs the services of creative director Jamie Lewis, who has had a highly successful career in advertising. For more than a decade he has gained an income as a creative director, working with national and international clients ranging from financial institutions to telcos, as well as hospitality, education, and social movements. Lewis' description of his work in advertising pinpoints how creative work is carried out for commercial means, demonstrating how commercial imperatives have become essential within the creative industries, enabling those involved to gain an income. These commercial imperatives may seem to be constraints but they also, at the same time, enable creative practice, with Jamie Lewis being a good example of a creative director who delivers novel media collateral while delivering on client needs. His work exemplifies the entwining of creativity and commerce.

Jamie Lewis grew up in Toronto, a suburb of Newcastle, NSW, and attended the University of Newcastle, initially enrolling in a Commerce degree:

> I was very interested in HR and industrial relations, for some reason, I'm not sure why but I always love writing...I wanted to create, write and produce...And so I jumped over into Communication. And physically began to play with incredibly clunky media production machinery. (J. Lewis, personal interview, 2019)

During his studies, Lewis joined the Footlice Theatre Company, who produced original plays for local and school-aged audiences. He also began work at the Media Communications unit at the University in Newcastle and graduated in 1996 with a Bachelor of Arts (Communication Studies). His advertising career started as a junior copywriter/production assistant with a local advertising company:

> A job came up at a local advertising agency, which was kind of a perfect combination of writing/junior production assistant. And I was, like, that's everything I'd done at Uni. So...I wrote a joke letter by simply saying I knew at that point in time, advertising fills the myth about long lunches and all that sort of stuff so I wrote a letter about being in person, I would basically clean them up after they were off their chops. And I would do all the work for them, while they are off getting drunk...They said come on in for an interview based on this, but I honed it, I spent two days reading this paragraph and a half that was super concise, because it was about copywriting and making this one really tight little intriguing paragraph. So they

> invited me in and then gave me a proper advertising brief, along with three others who were shortlisted, and said 'come back in a week with your ideas'. And I wrote two very normal ideas, but then I went for two really out there ideas and end up getting the job, and that was the start of my career in advertising. (J. Lewis, personal interview, 2019)

Lewis' early years in advertising were with the advertising agency Enigma Communications (2003–2012), where he began to seriously develop the necessary habitus, taking on a range of advertising jobs including corporate branding, logo design, digital strategy, and many forms of visual communication such as copywriting, art direction, graphic design, website layout, and shooting and editing television commercials. All of the advertising collateral was created to comply with the client's brief, and the creation of the campaign was focused on delivering clear and precise messages:

In Newcastle, we often have many hats and I do a lot of copywriting as well as directing commercials, corporate videos and different forms of content as well as presenting to clients. That is kind of my role in a nutshell as a creative director. (J. Lewis, personal interview, May 11, 2015)

As a junior copywriter, Lewis explains how he was mentored by highly seasoned creative directors. His advertising copy, written as a script, was frequently returned with red lines all through it:

> They were just teaching me how to be so succinct and in advertising every word is a tiny bit of real estate that you've got to get right in the way you put them all together to make them work in some intriguing way and they were the masters of that, but then also sitting alongside these are directors and other creative directors and seeing how they just create a visual language and made images and text work together and how to construct a 30 second micro story. (J. Lewis, personal interview, 2019)

Lewis explains how each Creative Director he worked with taught him a different way to approach the process of making advertising. Some, for example, liked to work in a very linear way:

> We worked with another Creative Director who has always been about the ending, and we had to perfect the end of the commercial first. Because that's what everyone will remember. It doesn't matter if you have 20 seconds of shit, as long as your last 10 seconds is good. (J. Lewis, personal interview, 2019)

It's clear that Lewis' understanding of advertising, his habitus, his feel for the game, the practical sense of how things worked developed through 'on-the-job' training, where he was exposed to a range of different styles that were used by the field of experts that he worked under. Lewis describes how valuable it was to be exposed to this range of advertising approaches and techniques and to learn as if by osmosis:

> You'll pick up so much by just absorbing what other people are doing and by being around other advertising professionals. I was able to pick up on the why, by letting myself be imbued in it all, you know immersed. (J. Lewis, personal interview, 2019)

Being immersed in the world of advertising means that Lewis had to constantly come up with ideas—ways to address a client's brief in a clever and unique way. Here he reflects on arriving at a great concept for a client's message:

> When you have conceived something and 'Ahhh' that is so on the brief that is required, and it is so correct for that client or business now. In another two years it may not be but at this point it is…So, they are things that motivate me, when the clincher moment happens and whether that is for myself or for the team and when it pops into the ether and you get it, it's like 'Ahhhh—that's really good'. (J. Lewis, personal interview, May 11, 2015)

Arriving at the 'Ah-ha!' moment, the moment of insight Graeme Wallas has called 'illumination' in his staged creative process model (Wallas, 1976; Kerrigan, 2019, p. 340) is the point at which the creative process yields a solution to satisfy the client's brief. Lewis acknowledges that not only has his informal inculcation into the field and domain of advertising, largely acquired through an informal process, allowed him to succeed, but it has also enabled him to recognize failure (Kerrigan et al., 2020) and how to be resilient in the face of that failure:

> To admit something is horribly wrong, it just doesn't work, that's okay! So let's scrap it and move on, but often you'll find something from that horrible mistake that will become wonderful or work a bit later…But the whole term failure is weird to me because it may not work, I look at it that way, and then you reconstruct it to make it work better or abandon it and start again. One of the great things I learned from someone is the difference between a

> bad producer or a good producer is a good producer knows what mistakes to leave in. (J. Lewis, personal interview, 2019)

Throughout his advertising career Lewis has also worked as a filmmaker. He has taken on the multiple roles of screenwriting, producing, directing, acting, and editing. By drawing on his cultural and social capital, the foundations of his habitus derived from his education and career immersion, Lewis was able to make the feature film *Mikey's Extreme Romance*, which combined multiple components of his past practice and also brought together 'his former acting friends, his friends in the various production crews that he employed and those he engaged as a result of his eccentric humor and dedicated professionalism' (McIntyre & Kerrigan, 2014, p. 143). This feature film was successful. *Mikey's Extreme Romance* was part of the official selection at the 2011 Chicago Comedy Film Festival. It was also the winner of the Los Angeles Comedy Festival award for 'Kick Ass Original Filmmaker'. These awards are a form of symbolic recognition bestowed on, in this case, a feature film, and that symbolic capital is transferred to Lewis as the film's creator because he wrote, directed, acted, edited, and co-produced the romantic comedy with its own slant on the world: 'I just love creating fantasy stories in terms of anything that has a twist on reality. I love to take something that is quite normal and put a spin on it in some way' (J. Lewis, personal interview, May 11, 2015). Lewis explains that there is 'never a shortage of ideas' for creative projects, it's finishing them that is much harder:

> Creatives are good at coming up with ideas, but they need someone to make it finish because their brain isn't exercised in the art of finishing and completion. So, it's like, 'OK you want an idea and you reward me, as a brain, because you're happy with an idea, good! So, I'll just keep giving you ideas'. (J. Lewis, personal interview, May 11, 2015)

Lewis' boss at OOTS, Marty Adnum, is an entrepreneur who has developed several innovative companies. He is the founder and Managing Director of Out of The Square Media and started his working career as a television camera person before deciding to go out on his own. As well as their commercial work, Adnum and his team also donate their time and resources to promote their hometown of Newcastle, producing an award-winning campaign called *Feel Inspired*. Adnum also co-founded

TheatreNewcastle and a talent agency, and developed The Baby Diaries, an app produced to enable new parents to track their babies' activities. OOTS itself, while starting off as an advertising agency, is now a full-service agency that employs a full cohort of creative practitioners—film-makers, graphic designers, sound engineers, actors, and many, many more. It offers media placement and buying services, audio and video production, copywriting, graphic design, photography, app development, web design, event management, and brand strategy (OOTS, 2022, online), as it merges advertising, marketing, and public relations functions.

While it is clear that the professions of advertising and public relations are converging, there are similarities in how 'both groups perceive their own roles and organizations' significance' (Supa, 2019, p. 407). As a profession, public relations has had a long-integrated history with advertising and media industries. However, scholarship in this area tends to focus on the differences between advertising and public relations, which can be seen in the levels 'of territorialism with regard to specific tasks within the organizational communication matrix' (Supa, 2019, p. 407). These territorial claims can be better understood by looking at the original definition of PR from the 1990s. In this period, PR was defined as 'a management function that establishes and maintains mutually beneficial relationships between an organization and the publics on whom its success or failure depends' (Cutlip et al., 1994, p. 1). It had a focus on relationship building and maintaining positive communication between organizations and audiences, also called publics, so that 'the audiences perceive that their voices are heard and trust is engendered' (Supa, 2019, p. 400). In many ways this is still how most PR practitioners see themselves.

To understand what a public relations practitioner does, we'll turn to AJ, short for Alexandra Joy, who now calls herself a minimalist leader and cultural healer. She is a highly sought-after international company culture coach, a property investor, motivational speaker, philanthropist, humanist, author of several books, podcaster, and leadership advocate. Her businesses offer services that are delivered online or in person, through retreats, keynotes, and a short online program called 'The 10 Degree Shift' (Alexandra Joy, 2021). AJ attracts many clients, including high-profile CEOs and politicians, and she is hired for her skills as a professional communicator and business coach. She doesn't publicize who she is working with; she says her clients come to her through her networks and discretion is extremely important.

> People hire me because I'm a vault, because I won't share who my clients are unless it's a public thing. So they are hard in that way because they don't want anyone else to know. I'm working with someone to increase their participation in the game, and particularly with a lot of them, I work with them on their body language because often they're super smart, they're really experienced. They know this stuff, but they're letting themselves down because of the way they communicate their messages. (A. Joy, personal interview, October, 2019)

The type of work that AJ does is in line with the public relations literature, which explains that, for the digital age, professional communicators have been forced to 'rethink their approach with regard to audience relationships' (Supa, 2019, p. 407) in order to succeed. In this case, PR practitioners are now required to 'have a strong understanding of how different message platforms and strategies impact audiences' (Supa, 2019, p. 407). AJ's career through public relations, public affairs, business coaching, property development, and philanthropic work presents a lived experience of how to behave as a PR entrepreneur.

Alexandra Joy (AJ), previously known as Heidi Alexandra Pollard, built a suite of enterprises that focus on harnessing business power. She founded two companies, Leading Value and UQ Power, where she styled herself as the Chief Empowerment Officer. The main services provided by these businesses were aimed at future-proofing businesses and empowering and leveraging business leadership by targeting HR professionals, CEOs, and event planners. The transition from UQ Power to Alexandra Joy occurred between 2016 and 2018, which also mirrored a personal transition.

In 2016, AJ participated in a leadership retreat program run by Richard Branson called Business Chicks and Virgin Unite. She attests that 'it was a hugely inspiring and energising experience. The theme was about when bold minds and big thinkers come together' (A. Joy, personal interview, May, 2016). It was around this time that AJ's personal life and business direction changed. She re-branded herself and her companies and built and moved into a tiny house. By 2018, AJ had let go of 75% of her possessions and began selling her services and enthusiasm for life through two businesses: 'The Joy Box', which was an online shop; and 'Alexandra Joy the meeting of two' (Alexandra Joy, 2021), which offers coaching and business services.

AJ has always had a strong work ethic. At 14 she had three jobs, which continued through her university education. Post-university she stepped into a salaried position as PR manager with a large regional hospital.

However, she soon realized she 'wasn't going to be able to change the world with a day job' (A. Joy, personal interview, October, 2019), which was when she began investing in property to build her personal wealth and understanding of business enterprises. She established the property management business First Firm and bought land and cottages every year from the age of twenty-two. Her immersion in buying and selling properties was reinforcing and growing her business understanding:

> it actually added a lot to what I was doing professionally, because it taught me to negotiate. It taught me to have influence, to communicate with people, because while you're going through property purchases and things like that, there's loads of ways that can go. (A. Joy, personal interview, October, 2019)

Her salaried position as the PR manager at Newcastle's John Hunter Hospital was the beginning of her career. She had a car accident on her first day of work:

> So I actually arrived via an ambulance to the emergency department. I had to ring my brand new boss and said, I'm going to be a little bit late and I'm going to be coming in via Emergency. Maybe it was first day nerves, but I actually remember saying about three months into the job that I've learned more in the three months than I felt I'd learned in three years of my degree. (A. Joy, personal interview, October, 2019)

AJ had completed a Bachelor's in Communication, majoring in Public Relations. She also has a Graduate Diploma and Master's in Professional Communication. It wasn't until she was about three years into her career that she really began to see how her formal education helped her with managing strategies and running campaigns. This knowledge, applied to this high-intensity position, also allowed her to be resilient, team focused, and intrapreneurial. Her leadership skills blossomed:

> But in the first probably three to six months of my career, it was more just learning office politics, how to work with an executive, how to deal with the media when you get 15 calls within ten minutes from different media outlets in your life. I wasn't really prepared for this. I used to spend a whole day to write a media release. Now I have to punch something out in 10 seconds and get it approved by an executive and a minister and get it out to the media. (A. Joy, personal interview, October, 2019)

AJ moved on from her role as PR manager at the hospital to a further education institution, Hunter TAFE, where she became the manager for Marketing and Public Affairs. Then she went on to work for a large state agency as Director of Communications at Workcover NSW.

> I found that I'd had staff that had worked for me at John Hunter, who'd followed me to TAFE, then followed me to WorkCover. So people would keep saying, I want to work with you. I actually love the human side of what we do, connecting people and developing connections. (A. Joy, personal interview, October, 2019)

Her skill as a networker helped her establish the Professional Communicators Network in 2003. Its purpose was to bring together like-minded communication professionals to discuss PR and communication and campaign issues. The network is registered as a charity and is now in its 18th year, with its membership including PR students and professionals.

Around 2006, AJ began building credentials as a business coach. She did a coaching course and built her profile by offering pro bono business coaching, while working four days a week with Workcover. This led to her setting up her business coaching practice (A. Joy, personal interview, October, 2019) out of which grew a keener interest in entrepreneurial groups and networking. In 2006 she joined an entrepreneur's group in Los Angeles:

> I couldn't find people here in Australia to hang out with…And so for four years, I went five times a year to the states just to go and be with this network. And the very first time I walked in, I realized I found my people. They were entrepreneurs. The group had people from Spain, England, Sweden and Canada. (A. Joy, personal interview, October, 2019)

AJ acknowledges that she has invested time and money in building up her entrepreneurial profile. Being part of the entrepreneurial group in LA meant she had to invest in herself. She says 'you pay to play' (A. Joy, personal interview, October, 2019). AJ also offers opportunities to mentor women, and in 2010 she set up a program called 'Leading Ladies International', offering a 12-week program through a mix of online and in-person training aimed at 'women who have been in startup mode for at least a year. So they've established their brand. They know what they want to be and what their product is' (A. Joy, personal interview, October, 2019). AJ is noted for giving back to her communities by setting up and managing charities. Working with a friend she set up 'Got Your Back Sister', which hosts fundraisers and enlists volunteers to support women who have fled from domestic violence. The charity is also approached to support refugees in the Hunter: 'what we do is support them and their children to start their life again. Whether that's household items, clothing, groceries, helping them with getting their first lease and rent and those sorts of things' (A. Joy, personal interview, October, 2019). Setting up charities in this way pushes AJ toward being a social entrepreneur, which is a category of entrepreneurs driven to achieve outcomes that are both socially and economically focused. Social entrepreneurs are not 'characterised by profit-seeking and profit-maximising, social entrepreneurship is concerned with enhancing the welfare and betterment of others' (Mazzarol & Reboud, 2020, p. 472), which is what AJ does in this part of her life as an entrepreneur.

This enterprising activity is typical in the advertising and public relations sectors. The advertising agencies of Pace and Out of the Square Media, which are managed by entrepreneurs Heath Nicholas and Marty Adnum respectively, operate with entrepreneurial business structures that are well placed to exploit the convergence of advertising, design, and PR agency functions, together with recent growth in digital forms of advertising and changing media structures. Jamie Lewis, on the other hand, adopts an intrapreneurial mode in his role as Creative Director with Out of the Square Media. Finally, we can see that AJ's career demonstrates she has been entrepreneurially motivated before refocusing her attentions on being a social entrepreneur.

References

Alexandra Joy. (2021, January). *Home*. https://www.alexandrajoy.com.au

Bourdieu, P. (1993). *Field of cultural production*. Columbia University Press.

Cunningham, S., & Turnbull, S. (2014). *The media and communications in Australia* (4th ed.). Allen & Unwin.

Cutlip, S., Centre, A., & Broom, G. (1994). *Effective public relations*. Prentice Hall.

Dahlen, M., & Rosengren, S. (2016). If advertising won't die, what will It be? Toward a working definition of advertising. *Journal of Advertising, 45*(3), 334–345. https://doi.org/10.1080/00913367.2016.1172387

Heath, N. (2019, June 17). Personal communication [Personal interview].

Hiller, J., & Rooksby, E. (2005). *Habitus: A sense of place*. Ashgate Publishing.

Joy, A. (2016, May). Personal communication [Personal interview].

Joy, A. (2019, October). Personal communication [Personal interview].

Kahn-Harris, K. (2007). *Extreme metal: Music and culture on the edge*. Berg.

Kerrigan, S. (2019). Innovation in the arts – Collaborative and creative filmmaking processes. In P. B. Paulus & B. A. Nijstad (Eds.), *The Oxford handbook of group creativity and innovation* (pp. 335–352). Oxford University Press.

Kerrigan, S., McIntyre, P., Fulton, J., & Meany, M. (2020). The systemic relationship between creative failure and creative success in the creative industries. *Creative Industries Journal, 13*, 2–16.

Lewis, J. (2015, May 11). Personal communication [Personal interview].

Lewis, J. (2019). Personal communication [Personal interview].

Mazzarol, T., & Reboud, S. (2020). *Entrepreneurship and innovation: Theory, practice and context* (4th ed.). Springer.

McIntyre, P., & Kerrigan, S. (2014). Pursuing extreme romance: Change and continuity in the creative screen industries in the Hunter Valley. *Studies in Australasian Cinema, 8*(2–3), 133–149. https://doi.org/10.1080/17503175.2014.960680

McIntyre, P., Balnaves, M., Kerrigan, S., King, E., & Williams, C. (2019). *Hunter Creative Industries Final Report*. University of Newcastle.

Mills, H. (2013, July 29). *The structure of advertising agencies*. Slideshare. Retrieved December 13, 2021, from https://www.slideshare.net/heleenmills/hoofstuk-22-ad-agencies-slide-share

OOTS. (2022). Services. *Out of the square media*. Retrieved April 23, 2022, from https://outofthesquare.com/services/

Pace. (2019). *Home*. http://www.pace.com.au/

Rosengren, S. (2019). Redefining advertising in a changing media landscape. In M. Deuze & M. Prenger (Eds.), *Making media: Production, practices and professions* (pp. 389–398). Amsterdam University Press. https://doi.org/10.5117/9789462988118

Solomon, M. R., Duke Cornell, L., & Nizan, A. (2009). *Launch! Advertising and promotion in real time*. Flatworld Knowledge.

St Clair, R., Nelson, C., & Rodriguez, W. (2005). Habitus and communication theory. *Intercultural Communication Studies, 13*(4), 142–156.

Supa, D. (2019). Perceptions and realities of the integration of advertising and public relations. In *Making media – Production, practices and professions* (pp. 399–409). Amsterdam University Press. https://doi.org/10.5117/9789462988118

Villi, M., & Picard, R. (2019). Transformation and innovation of media business models. In M. Deuze & M. Prenger (Eds.), *Making media – Production, practices and professions* (1st ed., pp. 121–132). Amsterdam University Press. https://doi.org/10.5117/9789462988118

Vujnovic, M., & Kruckeberg, D. (2020). Global advertising and public relations. In Y. H. Kamalipour (Ed.), *Global communication: A multicultural perspective* (3rd ed., pp. 325–343). Rowan and Littlefield.

Wallas, G. (1976). Stages in the creative process. In A. Rothenberg & C. R. Hausman (Eds.), *The creativity question* (pp. 69–73). Duke University Press.

CHAPTER 12

Entrepreneurship in Design, Fashion, and Architecture

Design appears to have become an omni-category for the creative industries. For example, the ANA Report *Australia's cultural and creative economy: A 21st century guide* (2020) claimed that 'the largest and fastest growing of the creative industry domains is Design' (Trembath & Fielding, 2020, p. 14). For them, 'Design activity includes architectural services, commercial art services, fashion design, graphic design, interior design, jewellery design, signwriting, textile design, ticket writing, advertising services, computer system design, and exhibition and display design' (Trembath & Fielding, 2020, p. 14). While this list constitutes a statistically unwieldy category, it does give us the basis for presenting case studies of creative entrepreneurs who work in the fields of interior design, graphic design, fashion, and architecture. In many ways these sectors have become deeply entangled and are emblematic of the changes that have occurred within the creative industries. For example, industrial design and architecture both have 'a long history of interdependence, collaboration and overlap' (Kelly & Jamieson, 2020, p. 2), converging in the 1950s and 1960s when there was a rising interest in the mass production of industrial and consumer-oriented goods. This situation contributed to the idea that it could be possible to conflate designing buildings, as architects do, with designing consumer products. Kelly and Jamieson suggest that:

P. McIntyre et al., *Entrepreneurship in the Creative Industries*,
https://doi.org/10.1007/978-3-031-19455-9_12

> If buildings could be thought of in the same way as cornflake packets and architects in the same way as commercial design teams, then the lines between studying the history of architecture and the history of design could be redrawn. (2020, p. 4)

The unifying idea is that designing objects and designing buildings use similar design processes so as to create bespoke products for clients. Unfortunately, the relationship between these disciplines is not quite that simple, even though good design in both sectors seamlessly incorporates aesthetics and function. While both disciplines are rooted in art, there are divergences that reveal 'distinct disciplinary identities, priorities and practices' (Kelly & Jamieson, 2020, p. 2). There are then, as in most things, similarities and differences between categories, but here it is very much the case that many related businesses now exist that prioritize and identify with design processes (Naiman, 2017). While the tools and techniques of design production have changed over recent decades, they have also enabled, for example, the growth of a unique design sector that emerged between publishing and advertising (Young, 2015, p. 230). The nomenclature of the sub-sector descriptors has also been largely abandoned. No longer are there overt 'advertising', 'marketing', 'PR', or 'design' agencies, but simply 'agencies which herald both digital creative services and an adoption of a greater entrepreneurial approach' (Nizan et al., 2009, p. 43). As Mazzarol and Reboud point out, entrepreneurial approaches exhibit 'a degree of novelty, and the type of innovation can be new to the firm, to the market or to the world' (2020, p. 21). All of the businesses that adopt this approach engage in 'innovative strategic practices' (Mazzarol & Reboud, 2020, p. 18), as they work with their clients to develop and deliver a creative design brief (Nizan et al., 2009, p. 248).

Over many decades, the exact nature of this design work has changed significantly, greatly influenced by the introduction of new technologies that permitted smaller companies to offer specialized, typographic, layout, and graphic design services. With the introduction of computer technologies, these agencies tended to favor 'a more educated, artistically sensitive individual, working, often independently, with image and typography in layouts for production' (Young, 2015, p. 229). Over decades these technologically savvy and artistically sensitive creators worked as freelancers, sometimes developing design studios and agencies that now offer a wide variety of in-house creative services to deliver a uniquely designed product for a client brief. The types of services offered by design studios and agencies include writing copy, branding and strategy, graphic design, website and app development, media buying, building social media channels, and screen-based production of television and radio commercials. It is no surprise then that intrapreneurial activities built around people who can make things happen were given priority, allowing for the implementation of 'new ideas within the established organisation' (Mazzarol & Reboud, 2020, p. 96). The intrapreneurial roles associated with making media products, for example, include copywriters, illustrators, artists, designers, filmmakers, photographers, voiceover artists, coding, and website developers. Each of the people who occupy these roles are not only intrapreneurial but are also resilient and adaptable professionals who 'learn from their mistakes and have a reasonable tolerance of failure as a normal process of learning' (Mazzarol & Reboud, 2020, p. 97).

Many agencies subcontract to sole operators to hire in specialized services. This shift, presaged by the adoption of a neoliberal ideology by many states around the globe, has been occurring for some years. We have witnessed, in essence, a shift to a temporary workforce, 'making it easier for companies to fire employees, expanding the various ways in which a company can subcontract and outsource labor, as well as providing incentives to workers to become self-supporting free agents (or "entrepreneurs")' (Gershon & Deuze, 2019, p. 300). Other scholars have noted that slightly larger businesses tend to become bigger by acquiring smaller specialist and boutique businesses, allowing them to provide a complete range of in-house services for their clients (Nizan et al., 2009, p. 45). Whether a business is subcontracting services or buying smaller businesses outright, they must focus in some way on improving 'relationships with consumers, value creation and continual product and service improvements' (Villi & Pickard, 2019, p. 129).

With this as brief background and emphasizing the design process as the central structuring element, the case studies discussed below feature two agencies, RAAK and Mass Motion, and an entrepreneurial designer in Donna Burrell who is the owner of Hunter Design School. We also exemplify the design of clothing and apparel, using the case of specialist designers from the fashion industry, High Tea with Mrs Woo. These will be featured alongside fashion stylist Lara Lupish. Large architectural firms like DWP/Suters that design commercial buildings will be given some attention in relation to smaller entrepreneurial operations such as that run by Debra McKendry, who owns and manages McKendry Hunt Architects.

Donna Burrell is a design entrepreneur. She is the Creative Director of Hunter Design School (HDS) and the owner of Liquid Colour, an interior design studio, which offers the services of a team of professional colorists and interior designers. She herself is a builder, a painter, and an interior designer and has over thirty years' experience with interior design for homes and workspaces. Burrell collaborates with Mezzanine, a brand leadership design consultancy agency based in Newcastle, NSW, for her interior design work, and passes on her skill for a fee in her other business. The Hunter Design School opened in 2010. It is a private college, offering training qualifications to the diploma level for Interior Design and Graphic Design. Graduates frequently go on to start their own business as a sole operator, while others also join established businesses. Burrell says there are a good range of career choices for HDS graduates as graphic design is part of a fast-growing industry. She explains that designers' skills are sought after across the broader economy:

> It could be desktop publishing in an accountancy firm, web designers, they need back ends on their webs—the interface, people are needing brochures, they are needing advertisements, they are needing design-thinking in their companies. (Burrell, personal interview, April 5, 2016)

HDS offers vocational training with local industry placements, which helps establish networks for students, occurring with Australian agencies like Mezzanine Media, Headjam, and White Magazine.

To illustrate the convergences currently occurring within and across design, we can introduce you to RAAK Creative, which is a design agency from Victoria. It exemplifies this process. It is co-owned by Peter Lodewijks and specializes in brand identity, digital design, and digital development. RAAK is focused primarily on graphic design but its digitally delivered branding delivers about 85% of their work, where they produce coded websites to streamline online sales for their clients' businesses (Lodewijks, personal interview, June 25, 2019). RAAK currently has seven employees, previously they had nine, and this number changes as circumstances change. In line with the larger structural realignments that occur within the STEEPLE factors we discussed earlier, in this case the economic, these are reflected in the business as well: 'there's ups and downs in a business of this size, the challenge is the fluctuating demand' (Lodewijks, personal interview, June 25, 2019).

The work RAAK undertakes, as they cope with the social, technological, economic, environmental, legal, and ethical constraints they operate within, is managed by a Design Director, a Digital Director, and an entrepreneurially focused Business Development Director. Their subscription-based web-design service also has a philanthropic component, called *zimpul.com*. Subscribers hire the web-design services and 10% of their fee goes to a charity they nominate, with the target market being business owners who need a website but don't have time to engage in a range of design decisions. RAAK's emphasis on back-end coding of websites for online sales moves them further away from the idea of the traditional graphic design studio and closer to the designing of information architecture that creates a structural framework for simple user navigation. This mode of operation ensures that the aesthetics and function of the design are as seamless as possible for its end user operation.

Mass Motion, based in regional Victoria, has a slightly different focus. While it identifies as a design studio, owned by graphic designer and videographer Luke Keys, it offers a range of multi-disciplinary design services for Melbourne-based and regional clients. Mass Motion is retained by their clients on a project-by-project basis, offering creative services in strategic branding, advertising, film, and animation. The studio employs five full-time creative specialists and contracts a number of freelancers when the projects demand it (J. Walsh, personal interview, 27 June, 2019). The multidisciplinary nature of the company means the intrapreneurial roles are fluid. They employ 'younger people who are looking to really further their career' (J. Walsh, personal interview, 27 June, 2019) who enjoy a variety of design work. They might 'be on the set filming one day and the next day you'll be doing a bit of graphic design, the next day…you might manage the whole animation job' (J. Walsh, personal interview, 27 June, 2019).

Mass Motion is defined as a small to medium enterprise (SME) (Mazzarol & Reboud, 2020, p. 140). Their smaller clients usually spend between $6000 to $10,000 (AUD) on a design rebranding campaign that would include 'new logo, new website, the suite of graphic design material, illustrations, strategy [and] copywriting' rather than film (J. Walsh, personal interview, 27 June, 2019). Their bigger clients will also commission television commercials and spend up to $80,000 (AUD) in a year. 'You tend to have one or two bank-rollers, and then all the other jobs sort of fill in the gaps' (Walsh, personal interview, June 27, 2019).

Designers also work in highly specialized fields like fashion. This sector of the creative industries is often seen as an industry in its own right, but it is one that relies on the designing of garments and apparel for consumers. It is also tightly bound up with the advertising, marketing, and graphic design sectors, as fashion labels are dependent on those services in order to sell garments and apparel. While many high-end fashion designers can be called entrepreneurs, so too can those fashion stylists who are intermediaries working between fashion designers and advertising markets. Fashion stylists usually work freelance, project to project. They are hired to create advertising content for fashion labels as they sell through global retailers. Their key role is to style for private clients, promote a new range for fashion designers, design an advertising campaign for them that will sell the client's latest designs through the media (traditional and social), and they also style for retail outlets. Current fashion is promoted digitally, through blogs, Instagram, and social media channels, with this type of fashion publishing originating out of the traditional print-based magazine and newspaper industries, demonstrating the truth that all creative work comes out of a set of antecedent conditions. These antecedent conditions, the traditions that reside there, provide opportunities for entrepreneurial innovation in fashion.

Lara Lupish is a fashion stylist and an entrepreneur. She has worked internationally as a stylist and as an elite fashion editor. Describing herself as a 'Style Director', she focuses on celebrity styling and advertising with an editorial role and works closely with various Australian designers by directing their fashion shows (Lupish, 2019). Typically, a stylist like Lupish might work in many different areas 'from fashion editing in-house for magazines, to freelance magazine work, to red carpet, TV, costume design for film and music videos' (Liebenberg, 2017). She has styled for many celebrities including Dannii Minogue, Michael Hutchence, Delta Goodrem, Heath Ledger, and Mel B, with high-end fashion label Giorgio Armani choosing to work with her (Lupish, 2011).

After decades of working freelance as a stylist, Lupish started her own business, *Styling by Lara Lupish*, in 2015. This evolved to include *Façon*, a glossy magazine that creates world-class advertising imagery and is considered a high-end fashion publication (Lupish, 2019). *Façon* was originally published as a hard-copy magazine, with a print run of 5000 distributed in Australia, Hong Kong, Dubai, Malaysia, and Singapore. It is now available as a digital version, but Lupish has extended that remit. The *Façon* brand has now been developed as a group of businesses including *Façon*

Creative, a creative agency, and *Façon Workshops and Runways* (Lupish, 2019). Social media is a very important tool for the *Façon* group of businesses, with 2039 followers on Facebook (as at 21 December 2021) and over 12K Instagram followers (as at 21 December 2021). The *Façon* brand is well established, with other brands requesting their styling services: 'they ask us to create their imagery for their campaigns or their advertising or their social media to help them develop a brand strategy around imagery' (Lupish, personal interview, October 27, 2016). This ability to drive a brand strategy aligns with the work done in the broader agency sector. Lupish explains, 'It's all about creating the image and having people feel like they could be in Sydney or London or New York or wherever' (Lupish, personal interview, October 27, 2016).

The work that Lupish does as a fashion stylist relies heavily on the relationships she has with fashion labels. Her networking skills in the field of fashion, her array of social capital, are exemplary. Her global career began in Canada as a wardrobe stylist in the film industry in Vancouver, styling music videos and television commercials; however, at university she studied Psychology. Lupish says she 'stumbled into styling, starting with a photoshoot with one of the top rock photographers in the country' (Liebenberg, 2017). She progressed to feature film costume design, working with high-profile actors in North America and the UK such as Naomi Watts, Sir Ian McKellen, Laura Dern, and Mark Ruffalo. She was mentored by prominent film industry personalities and worked with leading US advertising agencies where she learnt to sell herself (Liebenberg, 2017). Lupish returned to Australia in 2004 and established herself in Sydney before moving to the regional city of Newcastle, New South Wales.

As an entrepreneur and owner-manager of a small business, Lupish's unique skills, the idiosyncratic agency she brings to the system, are critical to the survival of the business. During the early years of establishing *Façon* it was financially risky. Lupish explained she has had to supplement her income 'by working in Sydney because the *Façon* brand took some time to make money' (Lupish, personal interview, October 27, 2016). In addition, Lupish presents as typical of many entrepreneurs in that her business adopts 'a culture that is reflective of the personality of the founder' (Mazzarol & Reboud, 2020, p. 141). She is a driving force in the business, typically shouldering the majority of the responsibility, working 'with limited resources and high levels of uncertainty' (Mazzarol & Reboud, 2020, p. 140). Founders like her 'are often forced to depend on others external to their firm for assistance due to the absence of sufficient resources to bring such capacity 'in-house' (Mazzarol & Reboud, 2020, p. 140). On the positive side, as the owner-manager of a small firm, she is 'very close to customers and has the ability to see the venture in a holistic manner, encompassing all aspects of its activities' (Mazzarol & Reboud, 2020, p. 140). Lupish's drive as an entrepreneur is underpinned by her desire to produce high-quality work and to share highly professional fashion industry processes, her crucial domain and field knowledge, with the next generation, while also 'working with local brands and local people' (Lupish, personal interview, October 27, 2016). Lupish demands an international standard from her team, with an emphasis on detail 'and how important it is to styling' (Liebenberg, 2017).

Most fashion designers, as opposed to stylists, who establish their own fashion label are by necessity entrepreneurial as they build a reputation for designing high-end garments which sell globally. They are, of course, one necessary but not sufficient factor working within a broader and more complex fashion ecosystem, itself located within the textiles, clothing, and footwear (TCF) sectors. Fashion designers create new designs from fabrics or textiles. The textiles industry includes raw material suppliers who weave, knit, dye, and design fabrics. The mass production of these into fashion garments occurs in the clothing manufacturing sector, who manage the making, buying, and distribution of the garments globally. As wholesalers, their customers include retail outlets like department stores, other designer labels, and specialty stores. Most of these businesses are involved in some way in the design processes, though not all. The story of High Tea with Mrs Woo provides us with another example of entrepreneurial activity located within this broad system.

High Tea with Mrs Woo is a highly successful fashion label, deeply concerned with ensuring they are using sustainable practices in their business operation. Run by the Foong sisters, Rowena, Angela, and Juliana, their business designs and manufactures a range of clothing that has a distinctive shape. They specialize in flatteringly fitted culottes, tops with cowl necklines and scooped sleeves, and classically designed dresses and skirts, all made with very high-quality cotton fabrics (High Tea with Mrs Woo, 2021). The garments are created in a suburban studio factory in Newcastle, New South Wales. Using traditional tailoring techniques, the three business owners do most things themselves: making patterns, grading fabric, cutting and sewing, ordering fabrics, running the retail shop and online sales (High Tea with Mrs Woo, 2021). Two sisters, Rowena and Juliana, have qualifications in graphic design and visual communication. The other sister Angela previously worked for Deloitte in San Francisco and draws on her economics and commerce background as she manages the finances and legal matters. The graphics and marketing for the website and corporate identity are done by Rowena, and Juliana manages the retail outlet and does most of the pattern-making. All of them work in the retail outlet 'because that's the best way you can interact with your customer' (A. Foong and R. Foong, personal interview, March 31, 2016). They all collaborate on design and manufacturing. The sisters make all their business decisions together, combining their various skills in design, marketing, and business acumen to create their unique styles and approach to sales. They say that 'the unit of three is actually the power of one' (A. Foong and R. Foong, personal interview, March 31, 2016).

The three sisters are self-motivated, drawing on their Malaysian family history of running a small business selling hand-crafted products. Their grandparents ran a 100-year-old goldsmithing and watch shop, which was also the family home, before their parents migrated to Australia in 1988. The sisters established High Tea with Mrs Woo in 2004 as a startup. They gained three TCF (Textile, Clothing, and Footwear) grants, totaling close to $90,000, with the largest paying for a full retail/manufacturing point-of-sale system to manage the manufacturing, fabric, and sales. The sisters also won the Mercedes Benz Start-Up award at Australian Fashion Week in 2005 and threw themselves into the national and international fashion show circuit.

The Foong sisters operated globally, selling through an Italian retail outlet in Treviso and sourcing fabrics overseas. At their peak, High Tea with Mrs Woo had up to 35 retailers selling their garments and they showed at Sydney Fashion Week. For five years they had a retail store in Paddington in Sydney where they employed ten staff and had a turnover of $700,000 pa. At this time, High Tea with Mrs Woo was creating up to 30 garments across the fashion business cycle, providing a designed range to fill three buying and selling seasons annually. Then the Global Financial Crisis (GFC) occurred, and with it their business model had to change. During the GFC, Sydney rents were increasing and many of retailers in this large metropolitan hub had to close their stores.

Looking back on that time, they acknowledge how hard they worked designing clothes for the fashion industry over many years: 'It was ridiculous. Like we didn't sleep, we couldn't keep up with it, it was so stressful...And it's not that sustainable' (A. Foong and R. Foong, personal interview, March 31, 2016). They were also cautious of the excessive waste in the fashion industry, with big fashion labels typically designing 30 pieces in a collection but 'a retailer might buy five garments out of 30 and there's all this waste' (A. Foong and R. Foong, personal interview, March 31, 2016). This process did not sit well with their ethical values, representative of a growing concern for this generation. The legal element of the way the industry works was also a factor in the way they approached their business. At one point they experienced a copyright design breach first-hand and took legal action to stop a manufacturer copying their designs. They found out that protecting copyright on fashion designs is difficult. As the Foong sisters explain, pointing to one of their designs, 'like if this top had a pocket on it, it wouldn't be the same. Someone could just take that exact design, tweak it by 2% or something and that wouldn't be considered a copyright breach' (A. Foong and R. Foong, personal interview, March 31, 2016). While it might be possible for big fashion labels like Prada or Gucci, with legal teams often on retainer, to protect their copyright, the Foong sisters feel that they'd 'rather put money into awesome fabrics than IP' (A. Foong and R. Foong, personal interview, March 31, 2016). This array of STEEPLE factors at play in their world led them to make some big changes in the way they operated.

In 2016, as the Foong sisters were recovering from the effects of the GFC (A. Foong and R. Foong, personal interview, March 31, 2016), they realized their turnover was now less than half their peak income, pre-GFC. To survive they had to completely change their business model. Demonstrating that entrepreneurial agents can be 'highly flexible in the face of external environmental challenges or opportunities' (Mazzarol & Reboud, 2020, p. 138), by scaling the business right back the Foong sisters have been able to continue to sell their exclusive fashion lines through their retail outlet in Newcastle, and also by moving sales online and attending various design markets. The determination of the Foong sisters to ensure that their fashion label survives is testament to their hard-won entrepreneurial skills. They realize being located in a regional city has allowed them to live 'on the minimum wage…we wouldn't earn enough to live in Sydney' (A. Foong and R. Foong, personal interview, March 31, 2016). The benefits of scaling back have included finding more time to raise their young families, as they have been rebuilding a sustainable business (A. Foong and R. Foong, personal interview, March 31, 2016).

Having chosen simplicity and 'lifestyle' over money and status, their business operations are more environmentally sustainable. They do not manufacture overseas and at the same time have ensured high-quality garment production:

> We don't want to go and spend three quarters of the year or whatever managing production overseas. The quality that comes back can be terrible…We are not interested in spending half our life in China chasing issues…That means you are producing more than you actually need and all of that excess ends up going on sale…and anything that doesn't get sold gets dumped. We don't want to be part of that process. (R. Foong, personal interview, March 31, 2016)

As Rowena stresses, 'we aren't in this business to be millionaires' (R. Foong, personal interview, March 2016). However, there are some downsides to pursuing sustainable production goals:

> It's more expensive to do everything less but it means we are not adding to this madness of excess production, excess fabric…Sustainability is for us not just how we work or move through the world but what we are as people. We try our very best in the way that we manage our waste and source our fabrics and for the sustainability of our business, all of it has to work in together. (R. Foong, personal interview, March 31, 2016)

When they scaled back to just one retail outlet in Newcastle, they weren't interested in online shopping and hoped that customers would come in and 'feel the fabrics and wear the clothes' (A. Foong and R. Foong, personal interview, March 31, 2016). However, they have had to adapt to online sales as they felt they were missing out on certain types of consumers, and with that change of thinking their internet shop has 'gone gangbusters' (A. Foong and R. Foong, personal interview, March 31, 2016). Approximately 5% of their online business is European and American sales, while the majority of their online customers are Australian. They realize the growth in their online market is the future for them and they have employed a local business to revamp their online store and profile. 'We are going to aim to get that online section 20% or more of our sales' (A. Foong and R. Foong, personal interview, March 31, 2016).

Like fashion, architecture is a profession which prioritizes design. It is unusual for practitioners and entrepreneurs to move between the areas of design and architecture, even though generic designing skills are common to both. Both processes begin by determining a client's needs and creating a brief, and most designers now use digital technologies and software to create their products (Young, 2015). Many engage in some form of user testing to ensure that the product meets with the client's brief, design specifications, and function. There is, however, significant divergence between architecture and design, which occurs during the latter phases of product, or building, creation. This phase may lead to the mass production of a designed product, the realization of a uniquely digital bespoke product, or the erection of a building that complies with construction codes and regulations.

The work of the best architects dominates the skylines of global cities. High-profile architects, so-called starchitects, are hired for their reputations, built into their symbolic capital, to design contemporary, modern, and striking structures. For example, Antoni Gaudi designed the Spanish cathedral La Sagrada Familia in the Baroque, Gothic Moorish style in 1883. His designs are striking and have themselves deeply influenced architectural designs globally, just as he drew on what came before him. Similarly, Frank Lloyd Wright, famous for his twentieth-century designs of residential and commercial buildings, has also had a global influence.

Despite the elevation of architects to the level of 'artists', they must work to their client's brief, with the design of a building being part of the commissioning process, as clients approve the interior layout and exterior design. The structural design has to comply with building codes and regulations, and there are layers of approval secured before the construction phase begins. It is the architect who oversees all these stages of design, compliance, and construction with the documentation and pre-design phase constituting around two-thirds of the architectural businesses. The architectural client base is generally divided between commercial/industrial and residential buildings, followed by public works and non-building work with less than 10% of residential homes being architecturally designed (AACA, 2016, p. 6).

Architectural business models vary enormously, with structures ranging from boutique sole operators to large global firms working internationally in risk-averse economies on complex projects with long-timelines. DWP/Suters is a good example of the latter. They were originally two businesses. DWP was an internationally focused firm and Suters Architects was an Australian architectural business. The merger of these two occurred as a result of their collaborations during 2013. The collaborative venture was so successful that in 2017 Suters was fully acquired by the Bangkok-based DWP (Bleby, 2017, online) and became DWP/Suters. The intention was for them to 'operate together as a fully integrated design solution'

(Architecture and Design, 2013, p. 1). The merger allowed for a larger range of services to be offered to local and international clients, with 'a greatly expanded resource network right across Australia, Asia and the Middle East. Their focus is on hospitality, residential and corporate design delivered through local teams' (Architecture and Design, 2013, p. 1).

As a global firm, they now employ 170 staff across five offices located in Sydney, Melbourne, Brisbane, and Cairns (Architects of Australia, 2017). This type of business merger is common between national corporations and global companies. The usual benefits exist, in terms of maximizing skilled staff and software across more projects, but there are also possible concerns specific to architecture such as the offshoring of local jobs, reduced quality of work due to different countries construction codes and language barriers (McIntyre et al., 2019, p. 476). At the same time these larger architectural operations require many specialists to handle a range of contingencies with many architects also moving into major engineering and project management companies so they can focus on delivering the whole project at the lowest cost where design-related factors may not be the top priority (AACA, 2016, p. 7). This situation is seen as a threat to the architectural profession, as during the approval stages a client may bring in a project manager to oversee the construction. While having their own project manager on the job can certainly be cost effective for the client, it may mean that the architectural design is eroded as low-cost options are preferred to the more expensive custom designed ones (McKendry Hunt, personal interview, May 25, 2015).

These issues emphasize the key role of an architect which is to design structures for specific sites and local building codes. Buildings are designed for geographical and environmental specifications as well as complying with a client's brief. Mark Lawler, an architect with over 30 years' experience designing residential and large-scale commercial and office buildings for Australian capital cities, describes his design process:

> Architectural design is a process of creative problem solving. This requires analytical skills to firstly define the problems to be solved. Then we use our design skills to propose creative solutions to address the identified problems. The design process is open-ended and is a path of discovery for all involved. (Lawler, 2017, p. 1)

As a boutique sole operator, McKendry-Hunt Architects is owned and operated by Debra McKendry-Hunt, who has over 25 years' experience working as a practicing architect. Small entrepreneurial SMEs like McKendry-Hunt Architects are 'dependent to a much greater degree on their entrepreneurial leaders' (Mazzarol & Reboud, 2020, p. 138). McKendry-Hunt's career path shows the depth of her skills, which reflects that range of architectural designs she can undertake. McKendry-Hunt was Chair of the regional division of the Australian Institute of Architects and she has worked as a Senior Architect and Associate Director for two large local architectural practices, DWP/Suters and EJE Architects. She is now the Principal Architect in her own firm, McKendry-Hunt Architects in Newcastle. She explains the importance of the client's role in the architectural design process:

> For feedback, client satisfaction is first. We also give clients a 3D program to explore the building project—like a playstation to walk through, turn layers off, go inside and check it all out. That gives you real feedback at the point you need it. (McKendry-Hunt, personal interview, May 15, 2015)

McKendry-Hunt emphasizes the bespoke approach used by architects:

> I really think that every site, whether it's a house, office building or apartments, the structure should be designed for that site, for that environment, for that brief. It's not something that you can transport to another site. (McKendry-Hunt, personal interview, May 15, 2015)

Once the design of the building is approved by the client, the architect manages the construction process, effectively becoming a superintendent, ensuring compliance approvals are in place, undertaking site inspections, and continuing to manage the design process as the building is erected and takes its place inside an environmental landscape, be it rural or urban. This situation brings us back to the contexts creative practitioners, like architects and others, exist within. As we argued earlier, there is a deep set of interconnections that exist in any creative system. We suggested that nothing occurs in isolation from anything else, especially in regard to the STEEPLE factors we explored in Chap. 6. Creative industry entrepreneurs in the twenty-first century are constrabled (Criticos, 2021), that is, both enabled and constrained at one and the same time, not only by environmental factors but also social, technological, economic, political, ethical, and legal ones.

Buildings can stand for decades or even centuries. Sometimes a number of architects will be involved in one project and most, if not all, architects agree that it is important to protect and acknowledge the original design work of a previous architect. In the same way it applies to other creative professions, copyright applies to architecture. But for architects, one of the rights covered by copyright law, that is, moral rights, needs to be given consideration in order to protect the creative reputation, the symbolic capital, of the original 'author' of the work. The Architectural Code of Conduct in Australia sets out the principles around copyright and the moral rights set up as a part of those rights. This Code of Conduct is important, for example, when refurbishments of large buildings take place, as well as work around heritage architecture. Architects, additionally, have to comply with the building codes of the country where the construction is happening, which is often a legal requirement for some countries. Further, some countries such as Australia invoke standards. There are Australian Standards which ensure that buildings meet safe design standards. Finally, architectural firms need to have professional indemnity insurances in place and these are audited by the Architects Registration Board (McIntyre et al., 2019, pp. 473–474).

The Architects Act protects the profession in Australia. As McKendry-Hunt explains, '[being an architect] is a legally protected title and you can't use it unless you have qualifications and a registration number' (personal interview, May 15, 2015). To practice as an architect requires a lot of expertise, a deep immersion in the domain of architecture, with an experienced sense of more than just designing a building. In Australia there is also an award in place that helps architects cost the value of their designing processes, and McKendry-Hunt admits it can be challenging to be 'paid what you are worth' (personal interview, May 15, 2015). In her boutique practice, operating since 2002, McKendry-Hunt undertakes a diverse volume of work, and her architectural designs include commercial, multi-story, and residential buildings as well as designing and renovating childcare centers, houses, and office fit-outs. Without a form of income, being paid what she is worth, she would find it difficult to practice creatively. She graduated from university in 1990, and it took six years to become a registered architect. She is fully aware that securing professional qualifications as an architect is challenging for females. While nearly 40% of architectural students are female, 'participation in the profession drops sharply after graduation. It continues to drop, apparently due to long hours, relatively low pay and scarce mentoring options pre-registration.

All of these factors also lead to difficulty in accommodating family responsibilities' (McIntyre et al., 2019, p. 483). But McKendry-Hunt persisted and loves the creative work she is now involved in:

> My work as an architect is creative because it is context driven. A building must sit comfortably in its setting as well as being functional and appealing—translating that to a form is creative. In Australia people want identity, character and self-expression—not cookie-cutter designs. (McKendry-Hunt, personal interview, May 15, 2015)

She enjoys the hand-to-eye process of sketching her ideas and admits to 'getting a bit antsy, a bit irritated if I haven't got a design project going. If I've got all my projects in the construction phase (which is stressful with paperwork and contractual things)—I need something else to balance it' (McKendry-Hunt, personal interview, May 15, 2015). For her, the architectural adage 'form follows function' is true:

> I do think that there is a strong form of reasoning that comes from looking at the functional diagrammatic relationship and then looking at the built form of it. From an aesthetic point of view but also allowing the function to drive it. But it is always going to be affected by fashion. Personally, I always try to go for a classic approach. (Personal interview, May 15, 2015)

In summary, these case studies show the enterprising activity that exists in the graphic design, industrial design, fashion, and architectural sectors. They also show the breadth of activities and the contextual dependencies that now exist under the catch-all omni-category of design itself. The one essential that is common to all is the fact that these things represent continual change. This is certainly also the case with the electronic games sector of the creative industries.

References

A. Foong & R. Foong. (2016, March 31). Personal communication [Personal interview].

AACA. (2016). *Industry profile: Architecture in Australia*. Architects Accreditation Council of Australia. Retrieved August 11, 2017, from http://www.aaca.org.au/wpcontent/uploads/Industry-Profile.pdf

Architects of Australia. (2017). Suters architects. *Architects of Australia*. Retrieved September 25, 2017, from http://www.architectsofaustralia.com.au/listings/sutersarchitects-newcastle.htm

Architecture and Design. (2013). *Suters architects and DWP announce collaboration*. Retrieved April 12, 2017, from http://www.architectureanddesign.com.au

Bleby, M. (2017). Architecture firm Suters throws lot in with Bangkok-Based DWP to focus on Asia. *Australian Financial Review*. Retrieved September 25, 2017, from http://www.afr.com/real-estate/architecture-firm-sutersthrows-lot-in-with-bangkokbased-dwp-to-focus-on-asia-20170403-gvcsye

Burrell, D. (2016, April 5). Personal communication [Personal interview].

Criticos, H. (2021). The constrabling effect of internet radio. *Journal of Radio & Audio Media, (online)*. https://doi.org/10.1080/19376529.2021.1937629

Gershon, I., & Deuze, M. (2019). A business of one or nurturing the craft: Who are you? In M. Deuze & M. Prenger (Eds.), *Making media: Production, practices, and professions* (pp. 297–306). Amsterdam University Press.

High Tea with Mrs Woo. (2021, January 1). *High Tea with Mrs Woo – Slow fashion, slow wearing well*. Retrieved December 21, 2021, from https://hightеawithmrswoo.com.au/

Kelly, J., & Jamieson, C. (2020). Practice, discourse and experience: The relationship between design history and architectural history. *Journal of Design History, 33*(1), 1–15. https://doi.org/10.1093/jdh/epz045

Keys, L. (2019, June 27). Personal communication [Personal interview].

Lawler, M. (2017). *About*. Mark Lawler Architects. Retrieved September 17, 2017, from http://marklawlerarchitects.com.au/

Liebenberg, C. (2017, February 22). *5 minutes with Lara Lupish: Façon*. Façon | Australian Fashion Magazine. Retrieved December 21, 2021, from https://www.faconaustralia.com/5minuteswith-lara-lupish/

Lodewijks, P. (2019, June 25). Personal communication [Personal interview].

Lupish, L. (2011, January 1). *Bio*. Lara Lupish. Retrieved December 21, 2021, from http://laralupish.com/bio.html

Lupish, L. (2016, October 27). Personal communication [Personal interview].

Lupish, L. (2019, January 1). *Façon*. Façon: Australian Fashion Magazine. Retrieved December 21, 2022, from https://www.faconaustralia.com/

Mazzarol, T., & Reboud, S. (2020). *Entrepreneurship and innovation: Theory, practice and context*. Springer Singapore.

McIntyre, P., Balnaves, M., Kerrigan, S., Williams, C., & King, E. (2019). *Creativity and cultural production in the Hunter: An applied ethnographic study of applied entrepreneurial systems in the creative industries: Final report, ARC Grant LP130100348*. University of Newcastle.

McKendry Hunt, D. (2015, May 25). Personal communication [Personal interview].

Naiman, L. (2017). *Design thinking as a strategy for innovation*. Creativity at Work. Retrieved December 13, 2021, from www.creativityatwork.com

Nizan, A., Solomon, M., & Duke Cornell, L. (2009). *Launch! Advertising and promotion in real time*. Flatworld Knowledge.
Trembath, J., & Fielding, K. (2020). *Australia's cultural and creative economy: A 21st century guide* (Pre-release extract). A New Approach think tank with lead delivery partner the Australian Academy of the Humanities, Canberra.
Villi, M., & Pickard, R. (2019). Transformation and innovation of media business models. In M. Deuze & M. Prenger (Eds.), *Making media: production, practices, and professions* (pp. 121–132). Amsterdam University Press.
Walsh, J. (2019, 27 June). Personal communication [Personal interview].
Young, A. (2015). Commercial art to graphic design: The rise and decline of commercial art in Australia. *Journal of Design History, 28*(3), 219–234. https://doi.org/10.1093/jdh/epv021

CHAPTER 13

Entrepreneurship in Gaming and IT

This chapter examines, through two case studies, how entrepreneurial and intrapreneurial activity has been affected by the challenges and opportunities facing the gaming and IT sectors of the creative industries. Creative practices, those activities that drive innovation, occur at the convergence of individual agency, the actions of social fields, and the immersive processes of gaining domain knowledge. The first case study we will look at is of the successful free-to-play mobile game *Crossy Road*, its co-founder Matt Hall, and the company Hipster Whale. The second case study is focused on the company Stackla and its co-founder Damien Mahoney. Both Hall and Mahony are entrepreneurs in their fields. The entrepreneur, following Schumpeter's (1934) Mark 1 logic, is seen as the person responsible for innovation, for 'the creation and commercialization of new combinations of (old and new) knowledge' (Elert & Stenkula, 2020, p. 2), while Schumpeter's Mark 2 logic includes the actions of institutional organizations such as those that surround big business structures. This entrepreneurial activity occurs inside and across industries. The related term intrapreneur, coined by Pinchot (1985), refers to '[t]hose who take hands-on responsibility for creating innovation of any kind, within a business' (Pinchot, 1985, p. ix). This distinction between the industry, which operates at the macro level, and the individual businesses operating at a micro level is not only crucial for the purposes of defining entrepreneurial and intrapreneurial activity but it also suggests that industries operate in a

P. McIntyre et al., *Entrepreneurship in the Creative Industries*,
https://doi.org/10.1007/978-3-031-19455-9_13

socio-cultural-economic system, and one of the inputs into this broad industrial system is the individual businesses themselves.

It is worth noting, before we proceed too much further, that the evidence for the size of the games system has garnered some serious critique. For example, David Hesmondhalgh revealed that:

> claims about how games were outstripping other industries were based on dubious data. For example, the sales of hardware (consoles, hand-held devices) were usually included alongside games software. This was like including figures for the sale of DVD players and recorders in the figures for film, or iPods in the figures for music. These figures were then compared to the box office figures for industries such as film or sales figures for music…When sales of games (as opposed to devices such as consoles) were compared with revenues from cinema box office and DVD sales and rentals, it was apparent that the games industry had not yet reached the size of television or even film. (2019, p. 316)

Despite the methodological problem in the way it is measured, it is still the case that the games industry over the past 20 years has experienced a radical shift in its structure. As it has done so it has adopted, or more precisely, adapted a set of older more traditional cultural mores. Traditionally, development was dominated by large, AAA [triple A] companies who would construct games on a fee-for-service basis where individual developers, or teams, were paid to undertake the programing, asset creation, and design of a game. On this fee-for-service basis the intellectual property (IP) resided with the contracting company. More recently this has changed:

> Industrially, a dominant narrative in the industry has been the desire to move from fee-for-service (where the company is a price taker and doesn't control its own destiny) to original IP. Culturally, this aspiration also speaks to many developers' creative impulse and is actually enshrined in the advocacy and the definition of indie [independent] established by the representative body, the Games Developers Association of Australia (GDAA). It is reinforced by normative criteria built into state policy and program funding support. (Banks & Cunningham, 2016, p. 188)

The cultural element in this STEEPLE-based change, that is changes in this case in the operation of financial and legal structures, was tied to the ethos of indie developers. This ethos had roots in a mythology of highly individualized production, supported by what is thought to be greater creative control and autonomy. This cultural element is underpinned by the concept of 'doing what you love', itself a product of remnant Romanticism. This myth, or in Bourdieu's terms the doxa it operates by, the unquestioned assumptions that regulate behavior in this area, has 'helped establish a widespread view in the West that … creativity can only flourish if it is as far away from commerce as possible' (Hesmondhalgh, 2019, p. 97). Independent production companies, seen to be 'free' from the larger corporate structures, can be defined as 'typically small-scale enterprise that concentrates exclusively on original IP and self-publishes on the new digital platforms (Apple App Store, Android, Steam)' (Banks & Cunningham, 2016, pp. 187–189).

However, as the case study of Matt Hall, the company Hipster Whale, and its incredibly successful game *Crossy Road* shows, the cost of creative freedom and autonomy comes with an increase in risk. This is not surprising given that 'measures of risk-taking behavior have been found to correlate significantly with entrepreneurial orientation' (Mazzarol & Reboud, 2020, p. 49). As Hall moved closer to developing his own games with his own business, he had to assume the risk associated with that in order to reap the potential rewards his work offered.

Hall is a prolific programmer and game developer immersing himself in the domain of games, publishing titles on iPhone, iPad, Android, Amazon, PC, Mac, Wii, Xbox, Game Boy Advance, Nintendo DS, and Playstation Portable. In 2011 he increased his level of symbolic capital as the recipient of Film Victoria's Tim Richards award for outstanding achievement in digital media. *Crossy Road* had immediately shot to #1 and generated over a million downloads in its first week; its 'combination of solid gameplay, unobtrusive in-app purchases, and optional in-app ads powered by the Unity engine, has earned $10 million from 50 million downloads' (Tach, 2015). The *Crossy Road* story 'is the rare story of success at the intersection of art, commerce, design and marketing' (Tach, 2015) and, one could add, an intersection with the structures that facilitate government funding (M. Hall, personal interview, August 12, 2019). Further, the success of *Crossy Road*, based on years of professional experience, a significant immersion in the field of games, and concerted skill development within the domain took, as Hall attests, 30 years to become an 'overnight success' (Blayney, 2016).

Crossy Road is a free-to-play, arcade-style game for mobile devices that blends elements of *Frogger* and *Flappy Birds* into an endless runner game. Players earn coins by negotiating roads, highways, rivers, and other obstacles. These coins can then be used to unlock other characters. At the outset, the game contained 50 characters and players aimed at unlocking them all. The character count grew to more than 90 over the years, as specialist or popular culture reference-rich characters were added based on player feedback.

As argued earlier, the cost of creative freedom and autonomy is an increase in risk as one assumes the financial liabilities and profits of the entrepreneurial endeavor. A strategy for mitigating that risk is to have multiple projects in development at the same time and to carefully commit resources to those projects. Initially, Matt Hall and Andy Sum decided to commit just six weeks of their time, a valuable resource for an entrepreneur, to the game development. Both Hall and Sum 'had other projects going on at the time and we didn't want to distract ourselves from that. Yeah, just six weeks' (Hall & Sum, 2015, 5:49).

Limiting the production time frame was fundamentally a risk management strategy:

> Because of the short time frame, we were happy to take big risks because if we failed, that meant that we would only waste a fraction of our lives and not, you know, years. So, this appetite for risk meant that we could experiment in all areas of the game. And this is really important because, you know... since we didn't care that we, if we, failed, we had the opportunity to try new free-to-play concepts and make a game that we enjoyed. (Hall & Sum, 2015, 5:49)

The free-to-play segment of the games industry had grown dramatically and was supported by indie developers distributing their work through a range of platforms such as Apple App Store. The difficulty faced by game developers in this market is how to earn an income from their IP. 'We actually didn't know how we wanted to monetize the game...we wanted to make it free, like that was really important' (Hall & Sum, 2015, 9:32). Matt Hall's intrapreneurial spirit and understanding of the industry came to the fore: 'We wanted to make a phenomenon. And you're not going to make a paid game a phenomenon anymore. And we also wanted players to play over a long period of time, which is sort of the antithesis of a throw-away arcade title' (Hall & Sum, 2015, 9:47). The ethos of the risk-taking indie producer also played a role, as Matt Hall expressed the main concern of game developers who adhere to the doxa they assume to be true: 'if we just make a game that's really popular and makes no money, we'll still be happy' (Hall & Sum, 2015, 10:10).

The story of *Crossy Road* is one of balancing creative innovation in the craft of game design and the intrapreneurial business activities necessary to optimize return on invested time. The game development and monetization of *Crossy Road* were intimately related; however, this is a relationship that is not solely based on business decisions designed to generate revenue at the cost of ethical or social considerations. One strategy for monetizing a free-to-play game is to encourage players to buy in-game coins or characters with real-world coins. Another strategy is to position interstitial advertising, that is, a full-screen ad that the player has no option to skip, between levels in the game. Although both of these strategies could have made for increased revenue, they were both rejected within the game design.

> There were two absolutes for *Crossy Road*. It was going to be free-to-play and we're going to have rewarded video. So, we got about four to six weeks into the game, and we hadn't talked about monetization at all. And. For me, I don't really like to buy consumables, I don't like to buy coins in-game. And this was a game that my daughter was really enjoying, and I would never buy coin packs for her because it creates a false perception of value. That's just a parent. That's just a parent thing. Other people wouldn't necessarily feel the same, but I thought maybe some people would feel the same. So that's something I wanted to try, and we sort of both came up with that idea, really…you know, they stay competitive because you can't pay to win. (Hall & Sum, 2015, 20:47)

In a similar vein, Matt Hall decided against investing in user acquisition (UA). UA is a suite of marketing tools that promote a game or app through platforms and social media channels. A UA campaign can be an expensive strategy to implement, as Matt Hall argues: 'Not many people have the funds to start throwing $60,000 a day to see a chart place similar to what we have. You mean you can get a bank loan for that?' (Hall & Sum, 2015, 43:00). The need to craft the game so that it makes enough money per user so you can afford to advertise the game places great pressure on the game design process. Advertising also affects the profitability of the game: 'Money in, minus money out, is your profit. It's not just scary, but it's really enormously restrictive on game design where… every decision you make has to…maximize your revenue' (Hall & Sum, 2015, 13:34). Matt Hall's suite of entrepreneurial skills include a deep understanding of how finance and monetization work in the industry, and how different strategies can be employed in free-to-play games. This information he gathered by attending conferences and engaging with his peers: 'So, talks with revenue, [were] some of the most valuable ones I heard when I first started going to conferences' (Hall & Sum, 2015, 2:55).

Hall describes the games business as being made up of programmers, games producers, and a marketing team, and so 'one of the biggest things I was most looking forward to when I went independent, was to completely peel back the curtain and learn: what is marketing? And I've considered that for the longest time to be my most valuable skill' (M. Hall, personal interview, August 12, 2019). Hall believes the relationship between design and marketing is critical, and this means it's essential to have the right marketing image to attract the right player through the app store (M. Hall, personal interview, August 12, 2019).

Mounting a strategy for monetizing is crucial and the games industry has had a variety of income modes. As Banks and Cunningham explain, 'along with licensed IP, there are five distinct variations on the exploitation of original IP: subscription, premium payment, free-to-play with in-game monetization, advertising supported, and pay-to-play' (2016, p. 191). However, funding the development phase to create the project in the first place presents a greater risk and requires a different set of tactics:

> The funding for games development takes a variety of forms, depending on the availability and the scale of the project. Briefly, these sources include government funding, in the form of loans or grants with funds available not just for development costs but also for travel or to engage marketing expertise; crowdfunding through platforms like Kickstarter; the traditional publisher model, where the developer is engaged to produce content at a set fee and with set milestones for delivery, essentially work-for-hire; variations on the work-for-hire approach that may involve undertaking projects such as game installations, serious games, or nongaming apps; and securing donations, where donations are received against the development costs. (Banks & Cunningham, 2016, pp. 190–191)

Hall self-funded that initial period, 'while working on the game from [his parents] kitchen table. Although I did at one point apply for Newstart but that simply didn't feel like entrepreneurship at all' (M. Hall, personal interview, August 12, 2019). It took a year for Hall to release his first game. Hall had a series of successes, with at least three games, one of which was *Doodle Find*, before his major success with *Crossy Road*. During this time, he worked out how to manipulate the advertising banners in the games and decided to use his ads to support other Australian games developers. *Doodle Find* was really successful in the games charts and it was a moderate financial success, and Hall was then able to apply what he had learnt to *Crossy Road*, which was 'extremely huge with regard to number of downloads, I think we're at 250 million now. And, of course, that was a big financial success too' (M. Hall, personal interview, August 12, 2019).

Rejecting traditional strategies for generating revenue such as in-game purchases and interstitial advertising and deciding not to engage in UA were risky decisions. However, Hall believed it was possible to monetize the game using other strategies:

> I knew it was possible to make a game that could get up to the charts and be top grossing without having that UA spend. I kept that idea in my head for years and I always wanted to execute on it…We knew we had to get working perfectly [on] retention, virality and re-engagement. (Hall & Sum, 2015, 14:23)

In this case, retention means keeping the player engaged for as long as possible and having them come back tomorrow to play again. The endless runner structure of *Crossy Road* and the ability to unlock new characters elements of the game design supported this ambition. 'Virality is having players share the game with their friends for all number of reasons' (Hall & Sum, 2015, 14:51). Built into the game interface were opportunities to screen capture and post those images to social media platforms. In effect, the players were doing that advertising for them. *Crossy Road* was built in a manner that allowed for new characters and upgrades to be added. This supported the ambition of re-engagement. The promise of new characters, even the existence of secret characters, was disseminated through social channels and drew current players back to the game and attracted new players.

These entrepreneurial strategies worked exceptionally well: 'We have spent no money on user acquisition at all. We are 100% organic traffic. We were the number one free game on the App Store in 39 countries and the number one app overall in 23 countries' (Hall & Sum, 2015, 37:20).

His strategy has paid off over the longer term. However, the success of the strategy was built on Hall's willingness to engage with risk. In 2000, Hall was retrenched from his job and took the opportunity to 'build a portfolio' for the games industry, which led to him getting a job at Tantalus Interactive, who were official Nintendo games developers. He was employed there for seven years (M. Hall, personal interview, August 12, 2019). Following that, the Steam and Xbox Live Arcade was released and 'there were opportunities to be a bedroom coder again' (M. Hall, personal interview, August 12, 2019), so Hall and his family decided it was a perfect time 'to start over', returning to his parent's farm near Ballarat to work and raise their family (M. Hall, personal interview, August 12, 2019).

Kerrigan et al. state that the 'Victorian Government has been particularly proactive with games development' (2020, p. 15). Film Victoria also had a number of funding programs that Hall benefited from. Hall says those funding programs have improved based on gamers' feedback, for example, there are smaller grants, applicants need to submit a prototype, and there have been adjustments to accommodate mobile games (M. Hall, personal interview, August 12, 2019). Hall asserts that 'it does help if you go with these funding rounds and.... I've heard of other people even moving to Victoria to make use of the program' (M. Hall, personal interview, August 12, 2019). Hall passes comment on other state funding schemes, saying that 'Queensland's doing pretty well in terms of state funding, but NSW has poor state funding. Adelaide has suddenly realized, and is improving things. I don't think I know a single developer in Western Australia, maybe one, maybe two' (M. Hall, personal interview, August 12, 2019). Hall says that he has had a bit of local contact with Federation University: 'they are putting on Get Into Games each year in Ballarat where they encourage children to apply to Federation University to do games' (M. Hall, personal interview, August 12, 2019). Hall explains his games are available to the global community: '[we] made a big effort to make sure our games are sold everywhere', with the US market returning 40% of revenue. 'In Australia, I think it's something between 3% and 4% of our financial revenue. Like, there was just no way at all that a game is feasible to be targeted towards Australians. It's not possible...But it is quite difficult to sell and market a game into China. Like, that's not trivial. That money is not easy to access, neither culturally [nor because of] regulatory barriers...particularly the last few years' (M. Hall, personal interview, August 12, 2019).

The process of peeling back the curtain on marketing led Hall to an understanding of the importance of metrics and social analytics. Much of this work is undertaken as part of a User Acquisition strategy, often undertaken by a contracted third-party company. Examining download and player trends not only helped track the success of *Crossy Road*, it also informed updates to the game itself. Hall's understanding of the relationship between game design and marketing allowed him to manage risk and distribute resources to the project.

It is a little surprising that the company Hipster Whale only came into existence just weeks before the official release of *Crossy Road* (Hall & Sum, 2015, 22:41). Hall and Sum's focus had been on the development of the game, including the design, game play, reward structures, and interface interaction. As noted earlier, the marketing and monetizing elements were integrated into the game development. However, all of this work and commitment were undertaken due to Hall and Sum's shared ambition, the desire to make a phenomenon, rather than under the formal contractual constraints of a company structure. Only when it became a necessary component to support their creative activities did Hall and Sum develop the financial and structural entity called Hipster Whale. Before Hipster Whale existed, Hall was operating as an entrepreneur working across the games industry, drawing on a diverse skill set in game design, interface design, and his ethical stance on free-to-play games. Inside Hipster Whale his position could be defined as more intrapreneurial, although as the owner and CEO he remains entrepreneurial.

Elert and Stenkula note that '[m]ost intrapreneurship research assumes that the phenomenon is beneficial' (2020, p. 11), that is, the intrapreneur's activities will be advantageFsous for the company and that these activities will also align with societal values. However, the obverse situation is just as possible. It is of note that the case study of Matt Hall illustrates how intrapreneurial activity, guided by social and ethical concerns, can be reconciled with the needs to generate revenue.

Considerable research has been undertaken into the precarious nature of work in the creative and media industries (cf. Banks & Cunningham, 2016; Bulut, 2020; Curtin & Sanson, 2016; Deuze & Prenger, 2019; O'Donnell, 2019). Entrepreneurial and intrapreneurial activities are, by their nature, risky and precarious. Engaging in these activities in an industry recognized for its precarity appears counter-intuitive. Why would people purposefully engage in these activities that double down on risk? Part of the answer may be that in the creative industries practitioners love what they do. However, as Bulut argues, love of a craft and practice is a two-edged sword:

> [D]oing what one loves is probably one of the best things that can happen to anybody because jobs currently are not only scarce but also increasingly standardized, meaningless, and administrative. Yet, at the same time, doing what one loves can be a mixed blessing; joyful as it is, love can be precarious and alienating. In fact, leading to illusions, love does hurt in the game industry. (Bulut, 2020, p. 382)

The story of Damien Mahoney and his company Stackla mirrors many of the entrepreneurial elements of Matt Hall's journey.

Stackla is a visual content marketing platform, working with big businesses who have big customer bases who post about their products or services or experiences on social media: 'What our software does is collect customer-generated content, put it into a library that our customers can sift through and find really cool pieces of content, customer stories, and then use that content in their own marketing activity' (Mahoney in Spencer, 2021). The clients, Ford for example, reach out to content producers to seek permission to use their content: 'They're [the content producer] pretty excited that somebody reached out to them, particularly the brand that they're passionate about, and they're a customer of, to utilize that content. I would say 95% of requests are fulfilled by the customer' (Spencer, 2021).

Damien Mahony had a range of careers before launching Stackla. After completing his BA (CS) in 1993, he was the first editor of the AFL's official website, a school teacher, AFL commentator, worked for TripleM, ABC, 2GB and ninemsn, and was a digital consultant for the NRL. Mahoney then started his own agency and was providing digital strategy for the NRL when he and his partner Peter Cassidy came up with the idea that would change their lives:

> Peter Cassidy is my co-founder. We actually started working together at the McCrory Radio Network, where we worked together on a number of digital products there. We continued [our] working association when I moved to the NRL, he was working with Telstra, the digital rights holder for the NRL. And we came together post–those roles to form an agency. That was called Pillar Sports, so we started that. It was probably through Peter's product vision around this concept that we had around user-generated content that enabled us to get the company off the ground. (Spencer, 2021)

Mahoney recalled that in the years 2011/2012 Facebook was already massive, Twitter was quite prominent, and Instagram had just been bought by Facebook: 'It was this really sort of interesting trend that was occurring' (Spencer, 2021). At the same time smartphone usage was expanding rapidly (Moses, 2011). This combination of technologies presented novel opportunities for collecting, tagging, and collating user generated content. This in turn had presented new opportunities for marketing and promotion:

> So it was this revolution in content creation, we thought, there's got to be a great way…for our customers, which at the time, were sporting clubs, to be able to tap into this rich source of content. And it was authentic, it was created by their fans…And it was this constant flow of content, it wasn't just a one-off pieces of content you might create write one news article a day, there'd be 1000s of photos or videos taken every day by people who were associated with that brand or that club. (Spencer, 2021)

The content sourced from Stackla complemented the promotional material that the sporting clubs were producing and publishing. Working closely with sports and broadcasters, the pair soon identified a central challenge facing their clients: content was expensive to create, web audiences were being cannibalized by social networks, and nobody quite knew how to derive value from social engagement. The idea for Stackla was simple. They would save clients from spending huge sums on boring content. Instead, they would allow them to tap into and showcase the wealth of amazing stuff their fans were sharing online:

> '[O]ne of the cool I guess efficiencies of the platform is that you can identify the content creator and send them a bespoke message. And then they'll generally respond. And that's all logged in our platform. And it's sort of simple, a simplified workflow that our customers use' (Spencer, 2021).

This component of the program that clearly tagged the content producer to their aggregated posts, and allowed the client company to seek usage permission from the content producer, would prove to be a crucial company saving facility.

Due to Damien Mahony's background in sport and sports media Stackla initially drew on his existing networks, his social capital in the field, and focused on sporting clubs. Stackla worked with SBS on its coverage of the Tour de France. These were very high-profile clients that added greatly to Stackla's symbolic capital, generating credibility and marketability. Mahoney stated,

> I think that being able to hold up SBS as a logo and the Tour de France, and quickly following that we worked on the World Cup as well. I think that one of the great strengths of the company from day one was our ability just to hold up a customer portfolio of just household logos…we still work with the International Olympic Committee, we work with World Rugby, we work with ICC and a host of other sporting organizations throughout the world. It makes us extremely proud that we've worked with all those organizations. (Spencer, 2021)

The growth of the company drew the attention of venture capitalists, and in late 2014 they realized that it was the venture capital that allowed them to invest quite heavily, 'and we really added a lot of team members. We opened up our US and UK offices. The monthly operational costs of the business tripled pretty quickly' (Spencer, 2021). The risks were, at times, palpable:

> I think some of the most stressful times that we had was where then not only my livelihood and my family's livelihood was at stake, but that of our workers as well. There was a couple of times like that where cash became tight and we had to really work hard to rectify the situation, which luckily we did. Yeah, I think that number one, identifying that, doing something about it and then learning from it and making sure that it doesn't happen again is important. (Spencer, 2021)

A major change in focus also occurred at this time. Stackla went from having a sport and agency focus to concentrating on travel. As Mahony explained, 'so you think about travel, and what people do when they're on holidays, they take photos, and they put those photos on a social network, it seems to have become almost like an intrinsic part of anybody's travel experience' (Spencer, 2021). Employing a range of data mining and analytics tools, Stackla identified travel as a key lifestyle activity that people were passionate to share on social media and this opened the door to engagement with a broader range of industries and possibilities.

> The White House has tapped Stackla to power the Better Make Room campaign, championed by First Lady Michelle Obama as part of her Reach Higher initiative. Stackla's technology is being used to aggregate social content from participants on the homepage of bettermakeroom.org and power the campaign's digital billboards in Times Square. (Stackla, 2016, online)

However, with their attention focused on expanding, two STEEPLE-focused events occurred that had dire consequences for the company.

> In July 2019, Facebook were fined five billion dollars for privacy violations. Cambridge Analytica, a British consulting firm, harvested the data of up to eighty-seven million Facebook profiles, and used the data, without permission, to help the twenty sixteen presidential campaigns of Ted Cruz and Donald Trump. In wake of the scandal, Facebook banned thousands of apps that were collecting content from Facebook and Instagram, including Stackla. (Spencer, 2021)

It took a legal battle and six weeks before Stackla's access was reinstated. Stackla's software provided their clients with the ability to seek permission for use from the people who posted material. Because of this, Stackla could correctly prove that they were not simply skimming content from social media sites:

> But during that time it was pretty tough going for us. We had to let half of our team go. We weren't too sure when we were going to be put back on and it was such a critical component of how our product functioned. So not knowing that and having a finite cash resource led us to make that decision, and it was the right decision to make despite the difficulty of it. Having just let 30 people go in one day was an incredibly tough thing. (Spencer, 2021)

Although investor confidence was quickly restored, it was a time of major restructuring for the company:

> I think that we sustained a lot of damage from that period, and it was ongoing. The wounds that we suffered continued to bleed for probably six months after, and almost to the day, six months after COVID hit. That was the next severe body-blow that we sustained as a business. We've got a huge customer base in the travel sector, so almost all of our customers were shut down, unable to operate. (Spencer, 2021)

These two major body-blows to the company were sustained due, according to Mahoney, to the resilience of the team and qualities of their staff. He argues that entrepreneurs should 'never get too comfortable and never think that your business is bulletproof. Yeah, this was a great lesson or a great example of you can be totally sideswiped and not see it coming' (Spencer, 2021). Resilience is a key feature in the story of Stackla, that is, 'the capacity of a system, enterprise, or a person to maintain its core purpose and integrity in the face of dramatically changed circumstances' (Zolli & Healy, 2012, p. 165). As Mahoney notes, 'I think the last two years have really underpinned the importance of being able to get up and go again' (Spencer, 2021).

In the early days Mahoney suggests that he was somewhat overconfident and naïve. However, these attributes appear to be necessary ingredients for start-ups and entrepreneurial activity. In hindsight, reflecting on what he could have done differently, Mahoney suggests he could have been 'more conservative in forecasting our success. We were very bullish and we certainly needed to be a bit more conservative. And that only comes through learning' (Spencer, 2021). One of the key lessons he learnt was in outsourcing the development:

> In hindsight I'm fairly comfortable with the path we took outsourcing the development of Stackla. What we were trying to build had a certain level of complexity and therefore we needed experienced engineers to set us on the right path. While we have changed much of what they initially built, they delivered us a finished product that enabled us to test the market and validate our idea. Yes, it was more expensive than doing it in-house, but they had a brief to deliver to their client (us) and therefore were compelled to do just that. So we had a level of security in the quality of work they were delivering us. Once we knew Stackla had real legs, we began hiring our own tech team. (Founders Grid, 2014, online)

They also faced challenges in launching their platform:

> The cost of product development was a big concern, but we were lucky our agency business was profitable and making good returns, which enabled us to fund it. Not many start-ups have this source of funding, but if you can run a reasonably successful service-based business on the side, it's a good way to get up and running without 'selling-out' spending time courting investors. Additionally, not having anyone in the business with strong technical skills meant we were at the mercy of our outsourced dev partner. The solution to this was hiring a CTO, and we sought out the best we could find for the money that we had (plus some more), resulting in one of the best decisions we've made. A tech business needs tech expertise. (Founders Grid, 2014, online)

One of the key lessons that Mahoney advocates is investing in people:

> We just really, highly value people who [have ingenuity], who can make decisions for themselves and bring something to the table that we don't know. I think a lot of times when employees come into a business, they're waiting to be told what to do. We try and hire people that will tell us what to do. 'You're doing this wrong. This could be better.' We really look out for people who bring special expertise and experience to our company. And I think that you live and die by everybody you hire. (Spencer, 2021)

Interestingly, the attributes that Mahoney describes are those of an intrapreneur. As noted earlier, entrepreneurial and intrapreneurial activities are, by their nature, risky and precarious. Mahoney seeks out people who are prepared, just as he was, to engage in the development of the company and share in its risk-taking ethos:

> The career path Mahoney has found himself in is a bit like a roller coaster. Except it never really ends, unless you crash. 'The life of an entrepreneur is juxtaposed with elation and terror all within the course of a week,' he says. 'Historically I have played things fairly conservatively, but a series of events where I took risks and made critical decisions have led me into the tech entrepreneurial world, not necessarily by design either.' (Rigney, 2015, online)

In 2021, Stackla was acquired by Finnish company Nosto Solutions: 'Mahoney said the acquisition was a big moment after nine years of work. He added he is looking forward to taking less of a leading role thanks to this exit, while still working hard' (Gillezeau, 2021).

The two case studies presented in this chapter, both highlighting the work of successful technopreneurs, share several attributes: the individual agent in the system who was responsible for many of the active decisions being made managed to parley their existing industry knowledge into new ventures. They learnt to read the field very well. They realized the games and IT industries are, like many of the creative industries, highly precarious, and, while both stories have happy, successful endings, these creative agents had learnt to be resilient as they took a number of necessary risks. They also learnt to engage themselves with the problems they faced, immersing themselves in what they needed to know from the domains of knowledge they encountered. This reading of the case studies supports a generally positive view of the role of entrepreneurship and intrapreneurship in the media industries:

> The rise of entrepreneurship, framed as an individual solution to systemic problems, is clearly visible within media industries. It is a dominant frame in contemporary policy and management discourse. One's ability to take risks, find new business opportunities, and being a successful self-promoter tends to be heralded as an appropriate response to a contingent and altogether precarious industry context. (Deuze & Prenger, 2019, pp. 21–22)

In both the cases examined in this chapter, much of the entrepreneurial and intrapreneurial activity was predicated on the need to minimize risk. This is not to say that Hall or Mahony were or are risk-averse; if anything they exhibit a hunger for risk. However, as their stories demonstrate, 'the ability of members from certain communities to bounce back from adversity is also aided by high-functioning social networks' (Zolli & Healy, 2012, p. 169). Each could access and exploit the contacts they had generated in their early careers, and both also interacted with much larger structures than themselves as they negotiated government and corporate funding, ensured the legal constraints they faced became advantageous enablers for their work, and relied on collaborators, that is, those with intrapreneurial and entrepreneurial skills, as they built the necessary capital—financial, social, cultural, and symbolic—to aid them in their ambitious quest for success. This not only reinforces the fact they were working inside a potentially profitable creative system but also the fact that 'even the hardiest individual cannot go it alone—our resilience is rooted in that of the groups and communities in which we live and work' (Zolli & Healy, 2012, p. 169).

References

Banks, J., & Cunningham, S. (2016). Games production in Australia: Adapting to precariousness. In M. Curtin & K. Sanson (Eds.), *Precarious creativity: Global media, local labor* (pp. 186–199). University of California Press.

Blayney, M. (2016). *Mobile gamer behind Crossy Road explains why overnight success took him 30 years*. In the Black. https://www.intheblack.com/articles/2016/06/01/mobile-gamer-explains-why-overnight-success-took-30-years

Bulut, E. (2020). *A precarious game: The illusion of dream jobs in the video game industry*. Cornell University Press.

Curtin, M., & Sanson, K. (Eds.). (2016). *Precarious creativity: Global media, local labor*. University of California Press.

Deuze, M., & Prenger, M. (Eds.). (2019). *Making media: Production, practices, and professions*. Amsterdam University Press.

Elert, N., & Stenkula, M. (2020). Intrapreneurship: Productive and non-productive. *Entrepreneurship Theory and Practice*, (October), 1–17. https://doi.org//10.1177/1042258720964181

Founders Grid. (2014). *Founders grid: Startups, business, tech & design*. Retrieved May 22, 2016, from https://foundersgrid.com/social-media-curation/

Gillezeau, N. (2021). Australian social marketing start-up Stackla snapped up by rival. *The Australian Financial Review*. https://www.afr.com/technology/australian-social-marketing-start-up-stackla-snapped-up-by-rival-20210602-p57xfu

Hall, M. (2019, August 12). Personal communication [Personal interview].

Hall, M., & Sum, A. (2015). *Crossy Road: A whale of a time* [video]. Game Developers Conference 2015. https://www.gdcvault.com/play/1021897/

Hesmondhalgh, D. (2019). *The cultural industries* (4th ed.).

Kerrigan, S., McIntyre, P., & McCutcheon, M. (2020). *Australian cultural and creative activity: A population and hotspot analysis: Ballarat*. Digital Media Research Centre.

Mazzarol, T., & Reboud, S. (2020). *Entrepreneurship and innovation: Theory, practice and context* (4th ed.). Springer.

Moses, A. (2011, September 8). Australia's white hot smartphone revolution. *The Sydney Morning Herald*. https://www.smh.com.au/technology/australias-white-hot-smartphone-revolution-20110908-1jz3k.html

O'Donnell, C. (2019). Reflections on the shifts and swerves of the global games industry. In M. Deuze & M. Prenger (Eds.), *Making media: Production, practices, and professions* (pp. 427–438). Amsterdam University Press.

Pinchot, G. (1985). *Intrapreneuring: Why you don't have to leave the corporation to become an entrepreneur*. Harper & Row.

Rigney, S. (2015, November 16). Newcastle-born Stackla cofounder Damien Mahoney meets First Lady Michelle Obama. *Newcastle Herald*. Retrieved May 22, 2016, from http://www.theherald.com.au/story/3521605/from-warners-bay-bulldog-to-the-white-house/

Schumpeter, J. A. (1934). *The theory of economic development: An inquiry into profits, capital, credit, interest and the business cycle*. Massachusetts Harvard University Press.

Spencer, A. (host). (2021, May 25). Damien Mahoney from Stackla (Episode 6) [Audio podcast episode]. In *Welcome to day one*. W2D1 Media. https://day-one.w2d1.media/stackla/

Stackla. (2016). Stackla Website. Retrieved May 22, 2016, from https://stackla.com/

Tach, D. (2015). *They wanted to make a video game phenomenon. They made $10 million. The story of Crossy Road*. Polygon. Retrieved April 19, 2022, from https://www.polygon.com/2015/3/3/8142247/crossy-road-earnings-10-million-gdc-2015

Zolli, A., & Healy, A. (2012). *Resilience*. Headline Publishing.

CHAPTER 14

Conclusions and Caveats of Entrepreneurship in the Creative Industries

We can see from the preceding chapters, and the case studies embedded in them, that each of the creative agents we highlighted in those stories has been entrepreneurial in some way or another as they have attempted to gain an income in the creative industries they work within. They have certainly been innovative and creative in their approaches to producing novel ways of making money, which has afforded them the possibility of producing the creative work they do. As we saw, they were often highly motivated by what they were doing and willing to take risks, sometimes enormous ones, in pursuing their goals. For example, Alexandra Joy's career trajectory in PR and communications reflects her proactive and highly motivated entrepreneurial spirit. Jaye Forde, after a successful career in broadcast journalism, made the entrepreneurial decision to start her own public relations consultancy and then took another large risk throwing herself into writing novels. Her contract with Random House came just in time. While we have concentrated, by and large, on relatively successful careers in order to illustrate what is possible in adopting an entrepreneurial mode of being, this is not to say that many of these creative agents have found this road an easy one. Failure is part and parcel of risk-taking. If that is true, becoming resilient is a prime outcome of all entrepreneurial activity. At the same time, the entrepreneurial activity we have illustrated here has never been the exclusive outgrowth of these decision-making agent's actions alone. There are many other causal factors we must account for as we determine why we are faced with engaging in

P. McIntyre et al., *Entrepreneurship in the Creative Industries*,
https://doi.org/10.1007/978-3-031-19455-9_14

entrepreneurialism, and then pragmatically finding our way through these structures.

Each of the case studies we presented saw individuals interacting with and using the structures they encountered and were embedded in as they pursued their creative and innovative activity. They took those structures, be they social, technological, economic, environmental, legal, or ethical, into account or were forced to take those into account, as they pursued their creative and innovative practices. Many of these were out of their control. Legislation like the Berne Convention and the Australian Copyright Act which complies with it, or economic events like the Global Financial Crisis of 2008, or the disruptive forces unleashed by technological change, or indeed the increasing dominance of neoliberalism in the political world, all played their part in the decisions that were being made. These entrepreneurs had to work with them, rather than against them, whether they liked it or not. Rosemarie Milsom's end to her print journalism career was not of her own making, but her very successful Directorship of the Newcastle Writer Festival was, illustrating that there are also many things that can be controlled. In recognizing what we can control, it might help to approach entrepreneurship as a game, even though there are many who are seriously involved in struggling with the precarious nature of work in the creative industries.

In this game we can see there are many conventions, rules, and mores to be negotiated as we undertake the necessary step toward gaining a livable income. The game is situated within a field and, increasingly, across a number of fields, as a number of our case studies illustrated. The state of flux and dynamism seen across the omni-category of design and what it is constituted by is a good example. Agencies no longer simply work in design *per se*, but across advertising, fashion and graphic design, architecture, and PR to name but a few. Apart from these increasingly interrelated fields, the other immediate structure players with an entrepreneurial orientation, like Sean Ison, must immerse themselves in is that of the domain of knowledge pertinent to the field they are in. Ison's skill set moved from radio to music to IT. Regardless of the fields they work with, our case examples all used domain knowledge to a greater or lesser degree. The skill sets they possess consist of the formal and informal knowledge, the conventions, codes of practice, and techniques the field identifies itself with. Entrepreneurs who run an IT-based company—we are thinking of Damien Mahony and his company Stackla here—need to know about technology or be able to draw on the skills of someone who does, since fields, socially organized arenas of contestation and cooperation, are built around specific types of domain knowledge. Each member of the field must recognize this, to a certain extent, as they engage in a degree of strategic and tactical maneuvering in the field in order to better their position in relation to others. Individuals, groups, organizations, institutions, and corporations are all choice-making entities, that is, agents in the game who deploy the resources they have in their possession as they negotiate their way through this game. It is risky business. Possible success and imminent failure are constant bedfellows—each successful game developed and released by Matt Hall through his company Hipster Whale, for example, could be his last. As each of these agents gains more experience in the game—Steven Pickett and his movement from recording studio, to booking agency, marketing company, and a franchised online platform using podcasting and internet radio is a good example—they also learn to be adaptable and resilient, strategizing their moves—derived from their habitus, their inculcated predispositions to make certain choices—in a way that is calculated to help achieve success. In this process, which is often initially reliant on a gift economy and the levels of reciprocity that exist there, forms of social, cultural, symbolic, or financial capital, that is, contacts, skills, experience, or cash, are accumulated and put into play to improve the agent's position in the field. Jamie Lewis drew on his social capital, his extensive networks, and the good will he held there, to make his first feature film. The awards, the symbolic capital, won by Morgan Evans in the field of country music became the impetus he needed to propel himself into the Nashville songwriting arena. The same argument could be applied to Vanessa Alexander and her growing social and cultural capital as her career developed in writing for television and streaming services. All of this means that the structures of the game, the structures of the field, and the broader set of sociocultural structures that form the arena of play are interlocked with each agent's innovative and creative actions.

There is also the field and domain of entrepreneurship, itself intersecting and overlapping with the fields and domains of the creative industries sectors we outlined above, be it writing, publishing and journalism, radio and the music industry, film and screen, advertising and public relations, design, fashion and architecture, or gaming and IT. Each sector displays a level of complexity across the micro, meso, and macro scales they all operate across (Comunian, 2019) but, to add to this complexity, we also assert that entrepreneurship requires its own set of knowledges and social interactions. For us the domain of knowledge of entrepreneurship consists of the fundamentals of operating a business and it includes a foundational understanding of business plans; carrying out SWOT and STEEPLE analysis of the business environment around you; gaining various forms of finance, ranging from the positives and negatives of personal loans through to crowdfunding and accessing venture capital; identifying a set of possible business models that suit and amplify the value being innovatively created; setting out an elementary understanding of intellectual property and its importance within the creative industries; coming to grips with ownership structures; basic bookkeeping, especially how to calculate an hourly rate for yourself; and treating yourself as your most valuable human resource so you can sustain the energy levels and concentration required for a complex game like this.

Knowing the field of entrepreneurship is just as important. Instead of just focusing on the supposed individual traits of entrepreneurs, as important as the individual creative agent may be, we argued in this book that the structures and actions of the field are just as important as knowing how to make a film, music recording, television, podcast, or piece of software. This section of our book demonstrated just how necessary, but not sufficient, the social and cultural contexts creative industries entrepreneurs work within. The important point we wanted to emphasize, again, is that these structures both enable and constrain an individual's journey into and within entrepreneurialism. We set out the term constrabling, originally coined by Harry Criticos (2021), to bring the complementary pair of constraining and enabling activity together into one complex action. We used it to show how individual agents take care of business by deploying social, cultural, symbolic, and financial capital in a creative world that is increasingly focused on entrepreneurial practices. We not only discussed individual skill sets and their relation to the structures creative and innovative agents embody, briefly set out again above, but began to scale this outward to the reciprocal actions of the gift economy, the effects of clustering together with like-minded operators to leverage the synergies this produces, and also the ongoing entrepreneurial activity of the state as it contributes to the evolving success of innovative businesses like Apple and many others (Janeway, 2012; Mazzucato, 2014). The importance of these larger institutional structures is something usually played down, at best, and denied, at worst, by neoliberal ideology. It was also something economists like Schumpeter picked up on as they continued to explore what was going on in this entrepreneurial endeavor. His Mark I and Mark II thinking is an able demonstration of this situation.

Yes, Schumpeter (1994 [1942]) had argued innovative change comes from entrepreneurs, who he initially saw as wild-spirited individuals or *unternehmergeist*. This Mark I view may have been a factor of an implicit agreement with a culturally embedded and widespread Romantic understanding of the way creativity and innovation were thought to emerge. But, once he began to gather more evidence, Schumpeter Mark II eventually realized that meta-structural entities like big business organizations, institutions, and corporations may be the primary drivers of innovation, given their ready access to the necessary capital to finance these entrepreneurial endeavors. He saw even larger structural factors at work in the long-term economic cycles identified by Kondraitev, which, in a complementary fashion (Kelso & Engstrøm, 2006), both drove and were driven by innovation.

We argued that these complementary interactions, where 'two opposing tendencies are complementary and do coexist at the same time' (Kelso, 2020, p. 84), can be seen across a wide spectrum of ideas. For example, technology is often seen as 'a thing directing our lives' (Arthur, 2009, p. 214) or 'a thing blessedly serving our lives' (Arthur, 2009, p. 214). But instead of seeing these complementary pairs as just that, complementary and both 'simultaneously valid' (Arthur, 2009, p. 214), there is a widely held tendency to see them instead as oppositions, either/or dichotomies, leading us to treat them as though they are mutually exclusive. These opposing tendencies have also been embedded in the world events that led to the invocation of entrepreneurialism as the way forward for many industries. We pointed earlier to the oppositions that drove the Cold War—capitalism versus communism, the free market versus planned economies, individual freedoms versus the collective spirit—and the bald assertion that one was faced with a simple, and what we see as a naive, choice between one set or the other. We explored this before we tracked down what we argue is one of the central dichotomies that are not, in fact, oppositional, but are indeed complementary. This we see as the false dichotomy set up between agency and structure, agency being the ability to make our own decisive choices and structures being those things thought to determine our actions. From this latter perspective, most surface events, daily subjective actions taken by individuals, can be understood by looking directly at the underlying supposedly objective structures that are believed to be the foundation of all biology, human psyches, languages, societies, and cultures. With these ideas on board, we then tracked our way down two paths, one agent centered and the other structuralist, before attempting to join them together in a complementary fashion as a way of creating a theoretical framework to hang our own thinking about entrepreneurship in the creative industries on.

The structuralist path we chose to initially track down was via the thinking of Karl Marx (2007 [1867]) and those who followed him. In setting his ideas out we were keen, like David Hesmondhalgh, to avoid the simple idea that, 'economic change "happens to" politics and production organizations and this then brings about changes in the cultural industries and thereafter in cultural life more generally, moving upwards from the economic "base" to the building or superstructure' (2019, p. 124) and from there to individual agents. We think it is far more complex than that. This is why we then tracked our way down a second path of thinking, the thinking that valorized individual agency. The path we chose here was that of phenomenology, given the phenomenologists were trying to encompass and account for an agent-centered, less deterministically focused understanding of subjective human experience, the kind that can be found in creative action. As we suggested, Edmund Husserl (1962[1913]) set the framework for this approach. He argued that an examination of the content of consciousness would allow us to arrive at the essential and subjective experience encountered by individual agents. This latter tracking was important to do, as neoliberalism rested its case within this idea and used it as its major justification. The neoliberals idealized free will and free choice (Harvey, 2005) but unfortunately the pragmatics of the neoliberal program came to dominate it—we will return to that in just one moment—as they, in particular Herbert Giersch, ignored Schumpeter's commitment to macroeconomic innovation but wholeheartedly embraced Schumpeter's Mark I concept of wild-spirited entrepreneurship and the economic dynamism individuals were thought to introduce to an economy (Plehwe & Mills, 2012, online). The idea of the primacy of the individual human as a free, rational, self-determining being was, then, an important theoretical precursor to neoliberalism, with its emphasis on individual agency over the collectivist structures it found itself in opposition to. However, if agency is not at the center of innovation, as the neoliberals believed it was, nor is structure alone the determiner of creative action, is it possible to look beyond seeing both of these as oppositional and, instead, combine both approaches in a complementary way? Pierre Bourdieu (1977, 1993, 1996) certainly thought it was possible to do so. He argued against:

> conceptualising human action as a direct, unmediated response to external factors, whether they be identified as micro-structures of interactions or macro-level cultural, social, or economic factors. Nor does Bourdieu see

> action as the simple outgrowth from internal factors, such as conscious intentions and calculations, as posited by voluntarists and rational-actor models of human action. For Bourdieu, explanations that highlight either the macro or the micro dimension to the exclusion of the other simply perpetuate the classic subjective/objective antimony. Bourdieu wants to transcend this dichotomy by conceptualizing action so that micro and macro, voluntarist and determinist dimensions of human activity are integrated into a single conceptual movement rather than isolated as mutually exclusive forms of explanation. (Swartz, 1997, p. 9)

Schirato and Yell, summarizing his position, stated that 'Bourdieu, reading across both approaches simultaneously, insists that practice is always informed by a sense of agency (the ability to understand and control our own actions), but that the possibilities of agency must be understood in terms of cultural trajectories, literacies and dispositions' (1996, p. 148). In this case we can see that he proposed a 'structural theory of practice that connects action to culture, structure and power' (Swartz, 1997, p. 9). It is a theory that 'undergirds his key concept, habitus, which, along with cultural capital, has become one of his conceptual trademarks' (Swartz, 1997, p. 9). This habitus gives practitioners 'a "feel for the game", a "practical sense" (sens pratique) that inclines agents to act and react in specific situations in a manner that is not always calculated and that is not simply a question of conscious obedience to rules' (Johnson in Bourdieu, 1993, p. 5). Instead, it is 'a set of dispositions which generates practices and perceptions' (Swartz, 1997, p. 9).

Given that we have argued here, and elsewhere (e.g. McIntyre, 2012, 2021), that there are many similarities to be found between Bourdieu's ideas on cultural production and Csikszentmihalyi's (1988, 1997, 1999) work on the systems of creative practice, in that both locate choice-making innovative agents within sociocultural structures, we assert it is the interplay between structure and agency that makes that creative practice possible (Kerrigan, 2013). It bears repeating that the creative and innovative system that entrepreneurial behavior emerges from and that we have detailed in this book

> consists of three interlocking and interactive subsystems. These include a structured knowledge system manifest in all the collected works pertinent to that symbol system. This is called a domain. It also consists of a field, that is, a structured social organisation that operates using domain knowledge in a process of coopetition. This field is populated by all those who can act upon

> and effect the symbol system, that is those with varying expertise including other produsers, gatekeepers, cultural intermediaries and audiences. The third subsystem we will call an agent. This agent is an active choice making entity which may be scaled outward from individuals to dyads, groups and other collective entities such as institutions who make 'changes to the stored information that pre-exists them' (Csikszentmihalyi, 1988, p. 329). These agents necessarily have a unique but shared background and bring their distinctive characteristics to bear on the entire system. (McIntyre, 2021, p. 9)

Each of these necessary but not sufficient elements, the domain, the field, and the agent, enables novel and valued products and processes to come into being as they emerge from the non-linear interactions of all three. It is this system, operating at the macro scale, that has also led, in many ways, to the emergence of digitization, globalization, and neoliberalism.

Neoliberalism's pragmatic agenda, given cover by its utopian ideals centered on individual freedom, worked instead to protect the freedoms of businesses, making the assumption that if businesses do well all societies will benefit. This pragmatic neoliberal program has sought and largely succeeded in privatizing many industries—education, public services, the media, manufacturing, transportation, finance, construction, the military—and won important concessions from nation states including market de-regulation, which some see as a form of re-regulation (Chan, 2021). It has brought about the abolition of many trade barriers, except where it interferes with nationally important industries like agriculture. It has persuaded governments to push for a supposed flat tax system that in reality favors the wealthy and increases inequality, where 'the richest 1 percent of the world's population owns about 40 percent of the world's assets, while the bottom half owns no more than 1 percent' (Thussu, 2019, p. 267). It has engaged in 'freeing' the labor market through abolishing the collective right to strike and introducing 'flexibility' in the form of lopsided enterprise bargaining, and, most importantly for us, the pragmatic program of neoliberalism has seen the promotion of an entrepreneurial spirit centered on creative action, in order to innovate *ad infinitum* while operating on the assumption that this process was and has always been a general good (Godin, 2015). Entrepreneurship and innovation are needed, so it is argued from this ideological position, to move an economy forward in an unending process of growth. As the system evolves, which it will do one way or the other, it will lead to other manifestations of political, technological, legal, and social ways of organizing ourselves in relation to our cultural output. But, until it does, the way we gain an income has to take account of these current factors.

As we said in the very beginning, working in the creative industries is certainly glamorous and it is lots of fun, but it's not currently easy. As forms of work mutate and become increasingly outsourced, casualized, short-term contracted, and occasionally manifest as full-time employment, the creative industries and those who are creative practitioners within them must embrace the pragmatics of being entrepreneurial in order to gain an income of some sort. Until the political and ideological winds change again, of course. Even then, we will need to remain engaged with the structures that we are embedded in, and continue to take risks, be resilient, and above all, motivated as creative agents, to keep creating novel and valued products in as many innovative ways as we can think of.

References

Arthur, B. (2009). *The nature of technology: What it is and how it evolves.* Free Press.

Bourdieu, P. (1977). *Outline of a theory of practice.* Cambridge University Press.

Bourdieu, P. (1993). *Field of cultural production.* Columbia University Press.

Bourdieu, P. (1996). *The rules of art: Genesis and structure of the literary field.* Polity Press.

Chan, G. (2021). *Why you should give a f*ck about farming (because you eat).* Vintage Books.

Comunian, R. (2019). Complexity thinking as a coordinating theoretical framework for creative industries research. In S. Cunningham & T. Flew (Eds.), *A research agenda for creative industries* (pp. 39–57). Elgar.

Criticos, H. (2021). The constrabling effect of internet radio. *Journal of Radio & Audio Media*, (online), 1–12. https://doi.org/10.1080/19376529.2021.1937629

Csikszentmihalyi, M. (1988). Society, culture, and person: A systems view of creativity. In R. Sternberg (Ed.), *The Nature of creativity: Contemporary psychological perspectives* (pp. 325–329). Cambridge University Press.

Csikszentmihalyi, M. (1997). *Creativity: Flow and the psychology of discovery and invention.* Harper Collins.

Csikszentmihalyi, M. (1999). Implications of a systems perspective for the study of creativity. In R. Sternberg (Ed.), *Handbook of creativity* (pp. 313–335). Cambridge University Press.

Godin, B. (2015). *Innovation contested: The idea of innovation over the centuries.* Routledge.

Harvey, D. (2005). *A brief history of neoliberalism*. Oxford University Press.
Hesmondhalgh, D. (2019). *The cultural industries* (4th ed.). Sage.
Husserl, E. (1962 [1913]). *Ideas: General introduction to pure phenomenology* (B. Gibson, Trans.). Macmillan.
Janeway, W. (2012). *Doing capitalism in the innovation economy*. Cambridge University Press.
Kelso, S. (2020). The complementary nature of coordination dynamics: Toward a science of the in-between. In R. McDaniel Jr. & D. Driebe (Eds.), *Uncertainty and surprise in complex systems* (pp. 77–85). Springer.
Kelso, S., & Engstrøm, D. (2006). *The complementary nature*. MIT Press.
Kerrigan, S. (2013). Accommodating creative documentary practice within a revised systems model of creativity. *Journal of Media Practice, 14*(2), 111–127. https://doi.org/10.1386/jmpr.14.2.111_1
Marx, K. (2007 [1867]). *Capital: A critique of political economy: The process of capital production* (Vol. 1). Cosimo Classic.
Mazzucato, M. (2014). *The entrepreneurial state: Debunking public vs. private sector myths*. Anthem Press.
McIntyre, P. (2012). *Creativity and cultural production: Issues for media practice*. Palgrave Macmillan.
McIntyre, P. (2021). Songwriting practice and production: The past, present and future. *The Songwriting Studies Journal, 1*, 5–26.
Plehwe, D., & Mills, T. (2012). Defending capitalism: The rise of the neoliberal thought collective (part 2). *New Left Project*. Retrieved February 6, 2016, from http://www.newleftproject.org/index.php/site/article_comments/defending_capitalism_the_rise_of_the_neoliberal_thought_collective_part_2
Schirato, T., & Yell, S. (1996). *Communication and cultural literacy: An introduction*. Allen & Unwin.
Schumpeter, J. (1994 [1942]). *Capitalism, socialism and democracy*. Routledge.
Swartz, D. (1997). *Culture and power: The sociology of Pierre Bourdieu*. University of Chicago Press.
Thussu, D. (2019). *International communication: Continuity and change*. Bloomsbury Academic.

Index

P. McIntyre et al., *Entrepreneurship in the Creative Industries*,
https://doi.org/10.1007/978-3-031-19455-9

J

Kolibri 360 GmbH
Ferdinand-Jühlke-Straße 7
99095 Erfurt, Deutschland
produktsicherheit@kolibri360.de